The Other Jews

THE OTHER JEWS

The Sephardim Today

DANIEL J. ELAZAR

Basic Books, Inc., Publishers

NEW YORK

Library of Congress Cataloging-in-Publication Data

Elazar, Daniel Judah.
The other Jews: the Sephardim today/Daniel J. Elazar.
p. cm.
Bibliography: p. 214
Includes index.
ISBN 0-465-05365-3
1. Sephardim—History—20th century. 2. Sephardim—Israel—History. 3. Israel—Ethnic relations. I. Title.
DS134.E4 1988
909'.04924—dc19 88-47689
CIP

Printed in the United States of America
Designed by Vincent Torre
89 90 91 92 RRD 9 8 7 6 5 4 3 2 1

This book is dedicated to the memory
of my Uncle Isaac Elhasid,
and to the continued good health
of my Aunt Rachel.

CONTENTS

A NOTE OF ACKNOWLEDGMENT

THE OTHER JEWS emerged out of the efforts of one political scientist who is also a Sephardi to understand what is happening in present-day Israel as a result of the demographic changes within its Jewish population, and how those events influence Israeli politics and the rest of the Jewish world. In seeking understanding, I found myself exploring in four directions. First, and most important, I studied Israel's new Sephardic majority, its interests and aspirations, its struggle for a place in the Israeli sun, the nuances of division within its ranks, and the response of the Ashkenazim to the whole process. Second, in order to understand better what might occur in the future, it was necessary to pursue the question of whether there is a special character to Sephardic Zionism, and, if so, in what manner it is manifested. Third, I had to understand better in what ways, if any, beyond surface manifestations, Sephardim and Ashkenazim differ within the context of their common Jewishness, which has proved to be by far the strongest element in the lives of both groups despite a millennium of either more or less separation. I also needed to understand whether those differences were merely products of bygone circumstances or were of lasting significance to Jewish civilization. And fourth, through research into Jewish communities in the diaspora, I was led to examine the present state of Sephardim outside of Israel. This book reflects all four lines of investigation.

At certain critical points in the research process, invitations to present papers on each of these four issues encouraged me to compile my thoughts in a systematic and analytic form. I was asked by Peter Grose and the New York Council on Foreign Relations to present a paper on Israel's new majority. The Israeli President's Study Circle on Diaspora Jewry invited me, at the request of President Yitzhak Navon, to talk on the Sephardic vision of Zionism. A keynote speech, requested by Professor Shlomo Deshen, organizer of a summer seminar on the Sephardim in Israel for the Kotlar Institute for Judaism and Contemporary Thought, gave me the chance to explore Sephardic culture as the classical dimension of Jewish life and Ashkenazic culture as the romantic. And, fourth, when the Council of Jewish Federations incorporated a regular session on Sephardic Jewry in its annual general assembly, I was asked by Ted Comet to speak on the condition of Sephardic Jewry in the world outside of Israel. I am grateful to these four institutions, and the individuals who invited me, for the opportunity of bringing my thoughts together to the point where I could see a book emerging.

I also like to think that my own family background and experience helped me to understand the issues addressed in this book. My immediate family members are descendants of exiles from Spain, more specifically the kingdom of Aragon, who settled in the Ottoman Empire at the end of the fifteenth century, concentrating in Salonika (the Jerusalem of the Balkans), Gallipoli, and Izmir. Members of the Abulafia branch of our family became pioneers in Eretz Israel, some reputedly among the seven families that arrived immediately after the expulsion in 1492. My immediate forefathers settled in Jerusalem in the nineteenth century. By a quirk of fate, I was born in Minneapolis, Minnesota, and spent the first thirty years of my life in the American Midwest and West, far from other Sephardim, before returning to Jerusalem.

Meanwhile, another branch of the Elazar family fled from Spain to Portugal, and there was forcibly converted to Christianity in 1497. After living as Marranos for over 250 years, and in the wake of the great Lisbon earthquake of 1755, they fled to Newport, Rhode Island. There they lived until the American Revolution, during which they moved to Charleston, South Carolina, briefly flourishing before they disappeared early in the nineteenth century.

At the end of the nineteenth century, other members of the Elazar and Abulafia families followed the paths of the Sephardic diaspora to Paris, New York, and Buenos Aires, where they became linked with other great Sephardic families, such as the Yohais, the Kattans, and the Chicorels, just as the family in Israel became linked to the Baruhielis, the Tocatlis, and the Elhasids. By now there is hardly a country or region-of-origin community in Israel with which my family has not established connections by marriage—Persians and Moroccans, Iraqis and Bukharans, not to speak of Bessarabians and Litvaks. At the same time, I find myself living in Jerusalem only doors away from families who have been our neighbors for generations—the Eliachars (in Jerusalem since 1485, seven years before the expulsion of the Jews from Spain), the Valeros, the Kimchis, the Sitons, the Elhananis, the Angels, the Russos, and so many more. At the very least we meet for prayer at the Yisa Bracha synagogue, the home of the *Rishon Le-Zion*, the Sephardic chief rabbi of Israel, and the leading congregation of the old Sephardic families of Jerusalem.

In 1972, I was fortunate enough to be asked to serve as the first president of the reconstituted American Sephardi Federation (ASF) and, along with such stalwarts as Mati Ronen, Haim Eliachar, Lilliane Winn Shalom, Steven Shalom, Rabbi Jacob Ott, Rabbi Arnold Marans, Rabbi Louis Gerstein, Edgar Nathan, and my aunt Rachel Elhasid, succeeded in organizing the ASF from coast to coast. In that capacity, I was able to visit every major Sephardic community in the United States and to meet people from all of them.

Since settling in Jerusalem, my activities in the Sephardic community have included several efforts to organize young Sephardim to advance within the system. This has included developing the Institute for Local Government at Bar-Ilan University, assisting Eli Gabbai and others in the development of a forum for young religious Sephardim active in politics, participating in various leadership development programs, and serving the Sephardic Educational Center established by Dr. Jose Nessim in Jerusalem and now headed by Edward Cohen. At our own Jerusalem Center for Public Affairs, we organized a Sephardic Forum. Hence, this book should reflect some understandings that can be gained only through activism, as well as those gained in more conventional scholarly ways. I am grateful for all of those who have helped me to gain that understanding.

My principal introduction to the Sephardic heritage came through my father, Albert Elazar, and my uncle Yaakov Elazar, who have told me their stories of late Ottoman Jerusalem and Eretz Israel since my childhood, making vivid to me the last generations of the old order when the Sephardic diaspora still lived within the framework established in the years immediately following 1492. They also explained what happened during the transition after the British conquest of Eretz Israel in 1917, when power passed to the Ashkenazic Zionists and the Sephardic leadership found itself excluded after a domination of four hundred years. During the 1920s, my father served as a Zionist emissary in Salonika, so he was also able to give me a sense of that special community in its last years before the Holocaust destroyed it forever.

No book that I write can come into existence without the myriad of services rendered by the staff of the Jerusalem Center for Public Affairs, especially the contributions of my research assistants, Alysa Dortort,

Naomi Linder, and Shai Franklin. The secretarial and typing staff of the JCPA was unfailingly helpful. The JCPA's activities in the Sephardic world were aided by Sara Mayer and Tzippora Stein. As always, I could count on Mary Duffy of the Center for the Study of Federalism at Temple University, who handled details relating to the book in the United States. My thanks to them all.

Special thanks are also due the Lucius N. Littauer Foundation and William R. Frost, its president, for their generous support that enabled me to prepare the manuscript for publication.

DANIEL J. ELAZAR
Jerusalem
August 1987/Av 5747

The Other Jews

Introduction

The Old Establishment and Its New Myth

IT IS a Friday night—Sabbath eve—in Jerusalem, July 1987. An extended family with guests is sitting around the table for Sabbath dinner, and the talk turns to the trial of John Demjanjuk, who was accused (and later convicted) of being "Ivan the Terrible," one of the scourges of the Sobibor concentration camp in World War II. Since the hosts are a mixed couple—he, Sephardi, and she, Ashkenazi—it is not surprising that the company is also mixed: by happenstance, six Sephardim and six Ashkenazim, including people born in Israel, Iraq, Russia, Lithuania, England, and at least two American states. The conversation focuses around one in the company who cannot see any reason for Israel to be spending so much time and money on this trial so many years after the war. Some suggest that the Sephardim, particularly those from Africa and Asia, do not feel the Holocaust in the same way as the Ashkenazim, who suffered directly or through their families. There is general agreement with one exception, the host, whose view that there is no appreciable difference on the subject between Ashkenazim and Sephardim is dismissed as overoptimistic.

Who, then, was least concerned about the trial of John Demjanjuk? Curiously enough, it was one of the Ashkenazim, an older woman, American-born, who had lost family in the Holocaust. On the other hand, the guest of Iraqi birth was one of the most vehement in supporting the necessity of the trial. Yet it is true that many Sephardim are distanced from the Holocaust, partly by the generation gap—there are many more younger Sephardim because of birthrate differences—and partly because they do not have personal or family experiences to draw on. As the host pointed out, however, studies show that among those who have been exposed to teaching about the Holocaust, there are no visible differences between the two groups.

The complexity of the relationship among Sephardim, Ashkenazim, Israel, and contemporary Jewish history is paralleled by, indeed reflected in, the complexities of contemporary Israeli politics. Israeli politics in the 1980s is a politics of deadlock. In 1977, Menachem Begin's Likud bloc succeeded in breaking what had been a Labor monopoly on political power with the help of a huge Sephardic vote, exceeding two-thirds of the Sephardic population, as well as the votes of younger Ashkenazim. Likud proved it could win, but it did not do as well in demonstrating that it could govern, so that four years later, in the 1981 elections, a resurgent Labor party came close to toppling the new governing coalition. Still, Begin triumphed once again with the overwhelming support of the Sephardim, only to have a disastrous second term. Even so, with both the failure of Begin's Lebanon policy and an economic policy that brought the country close to the brink of catastrophe, the sharp divisions between Ashkenazim and Sephardim led to a repeat in the 1984 elections of the earlier political deadlock, only worse, forcing both of the major parties to join in a National Unity government. That government, which provided for Labor party leader Shimon Peres to become prime minister for the first two years and Likud leader Yitzhak Shamir to take over for the last two, soon came to resemble Neil Simon's "odd couple." Like the odd couple, the National Unity coalition held together because neither party had any other place to go. Over two-thirds of the Sephardim still voted for the Likud bloc and over two-thirds of the Ashkenazim voted for Labor in 1984, and all signs were that this polarization would continue. And it has. Thus, the future of Israeli politics may very well hinge on the relationship between the two major Jewish groups within the country.

The Myth of the Sephardim

One of the principal changes in Israel during the early 1980s was the emergence of its Sephardic majority as an influence on the shape of Israeli politics, domestic and foreign. This change was first noticed when the Likud came to prominence in Israel's 1981 elections, which led in turn to a growing recognition that Menachem Begin's 1977 electoral victory was not a fluke but possibly the beginning of a new political era, one dominated by the Likud and its political camp. The "discovery" of the Sephardim was further stimulated by the international attempt to understand Israel's incursion into Lebanon during the summer of 1982, and it was increasingly fueled by a spate of articles in the international press, mostly but not exclusively written by prominent Israelis, lamenting changes taking place on the Israeli political scene as a result of the rise of the Sephardim.

The fact is that today a real and growing majority of Israel's Jews are not only native to the geocultural region conventionally known as the Middle East or the Islamic world, but are also from families that have been in that region from time immemorial, with as much right to be there as any other of the region's inhabitants. This has very real implications for the Israeli-Arab conflict. By any measure, Israel cannot be considered a "settler state"—if it ever actually was one. Rather, it is a product of an interregional exchange of population.

Unfortunately, the process of discovering that Israel now has a Sephardic majority has been accompanied by many false myths about it, propagated in great measure by intellectuals of the Labor camp, many of them Labor party activists, members of the old establishment who are fearful of losing their hegemony in Israeli society. Those myths were able to take root because of widespread ignorance about the Sephardic Jews in general, and those of Israel in particular.

No better illustration of such myths can be found than in two articles by leading Israeli intellectuals: one by Amos Oz, "Has Israel Altered Its Vision?" which appeared in *The New York Times Magazine*, July 11, 1982, at the height of the Israeli siege of Beirut, and one by Shlomo Avineri, "The Beirut Massacres and the Two Political Cultures of Israel," which appeared in the *International Herald Tribune*, October 14, 1982. Both Oz, a well-known Israeli novelist, kibbutz member, and left-wing intellectual, and Avineri, a prominent political scientist and former director-general of the Ministry of Foreign Affairs under the previous Labor government, provided American and, indeed, world audiences with stereotyped generalizations, which, if written about a minority group in the United States, would probably not have gotten past the newspapers' editors, who at the very least would have buried them for fear of being charged with group defamation. Since the common approach of the two articles and the subtle differences between them establish both the mainstream and the parameters of the new myth about Israel's Sephardim, which is now beginning to influence American opinion about the Jewish state, it is worthwhile examining them in some depth.

Oz begins by suggesting that Israel is divided between those who oppose the Likud government's policies and favor a negotiated "peace now"—"the better-educated young"—and the rest of the country, which he stops just short of referring to as the "great unwashed." He identifies the "peace now" movement with "some elements of the Labor Party opposition" and leaves no doubt as to the virtue of those elements. Going beyond that, Oz traces their dispute with the Likud government to the very beginnings of the history of modern Zionism, portraying Israel's "doves" (his term) as enlightened and rational and Israel's "hawks," namely, the Likud government and its supporters, as superstitious, mystical, and medieval.

Oz then gives his version of the Zionist founding of the state as growing out of Russian socialism, painting a nostalgic picture of a never-never land to which idealists came without prejudices or interests other than their shared ideology and common commitment to improving the Jewish situation and humanity as a whole. There they began to build an ideal state, without any conflict, pettiness, or corruption of the kind that usually plagues mortals, even good people with good intentions. He handles their penchant for ideological dogmatism by writing: "The world is full of dogmatic movements pretending to be pragmatic; observing these founders of kibbutzim in Israel, I tend to believe that they have been a pragmatic lot pretending, because of some emotional urge, to be dogmatic." Oz concludes his idyll by describing the "underground army, the Hagana," which "operated more like a youth movement than a conventional military force, relying on persuasion, voting and consensus rather than on orders."

Nothing is taken away from the truly noble achievements of the Zionist pioneers by rejecting Oz's Parson Weems version of Israel's founding. In reality, those pioneers were tough, ideologically committed, contentious human beings, who, convinced that they were right, were often intolerant. Perhaps they succeeded against all odds precisely because of those characteristics.

Oz himself does add something of a footnote to modify what even he perceives as an overly idyllic description, but he modifies the modification by indicating that if there were "quasi-Bolshevik methods used by the leadership to manipulate public opinion," it was because the Socialists of the Labor movement were engaged in a ruthless struggle against their "right-wing, chauvinist, religious and conservative opponents within the Jewish community in Palestine." Sound familiar? There they are—the same old "bad guys" as we have in power today but whom the "real pioneers" managed to keep under control.

Oz concludes: "In short, Israel could have become an exemplary state, an open, argumentative, involved society of unique moral standards and future-oriented outlook, a small-scale laboratory for democratic socialists, or—as the oldtimers like to put it, 'a light unto the nations.' " All this came tumbling down, says Oz, because of the "mass immigration of Holocaust survivors, Middle Eastern Jews and non-Socialist and even anti-Socialist Zionists." Oz describes how prewar and postwar Holocaust refugees brought with them a desire for "bourgeois coziness and stability," which was bad enough, but then came those "horrible" Middle Eastern Jews, "conservative, Puritan, observant, extremely hierarchical and family-oriented, and, to some extent, chauvinistic, militaristic and xenophobic."

So there we have it. For Oz—and many others who agree with him—the virtue of the Socialist pioneers was their downfall. In trying to save other Jews, they let in what Oz seems to regard as riffraff—including, apparently, upper-middle-class German Jewish refugees from Hitler and Jews from Atlas Mountain caves who had spent their days learning to be "chauvinistic, militaristic and xenophobic."

Shlomo Avineri is much less strident and ideological than kibbutznik Oz. Nevertheless, Avineri repeats most of Oz's view, but in a more sophisticated way.

Avineri is basically a Social Democrat, a "liberal" in American terms. To the extent that he still espouses socialism, it is a very bourgeois socialism indeed. Yet, he suggests that the difference between Labor Zionism—the same Labor Zionism that attracts Oz—and the Zionism of the Likud is not just political or even ideological, but also cultural. To Avineri, Menachem Begin represents a different culture.

Avineri goes on to suggest that Begin, the representative of a more militaristic, less humanistic culture, was virtually alone until recently. He writes that

> the elections of 1977 that brought Mr. Begin to power were a change from one political culture to another. They showed a shift in the composition of the electorate. With a shift in the number of Sephardi voters (Jews from Middle Eastern countries), a larger sector of the Israeli population was made up of people from highly traditional societies, much more ethnocentric than the more secularized and liberal European Jews who had dominated Israel's politics for decades. Most of Likud's voters came from the Middle East, while most Labor voters were European Jews or their descendants.

Says Avineri on the Beirut massacre:

> The national outcry released a terrible feeling of guilt, yet the demonstrations were mainly limited to that half of Israel's Jewish population that is of European background, liberal, middle-class and well-educated. There is doubt whether what happened really cut into the hard core of Mr. Begin's support among those Israelis who like his tough style, his "goyim-baiting" language and his ethnocentricity.

Except for the fact that Avineri emphasizes that Labor voters are European and middle class and Oz feels that being middle class is in itself a betrayal, the two of them present the issue in much the same way—the enlightened Europeans versus the Sephardim, who are at the very least "ethnocentric" and "tradition-bound" and at worst "chauvinistic, militaristic and xenophobic." This is a thoroughly self-serving myth that these two men, and indeed the establishment they represent, have created for themselves. Perhaps it makes them feel better as they contemplate their tragic fate, namely, a future in opposition, arising not because they were somehow deficient when they were in power or because they are today somehow inadequate to the needs of the times, but because they are being overwhelmed by the "barbarians."

Although this myth concerning the Sephardim has been expanded and deepened to explain the decline and fall of Israel's old establishment, it rests on foundations laid down by that establishment a generation ago, at the time of the mass *aliyah* (immigration) of Jews from Islamic countries (1948–51). Take, for example, a statement by a leading Israeli social scientist and government spokesman (Ashkenazi) in a brochure designed by the United Jewish Appeal for wide distribution to Jews and non-Jews in the United States in the late 1950s:

> During recent years, we have had a large influx of Jews from the Near East and Africa . . . most of the people who come to Israel from these countries have

> darker skin . . . many of the countries from which they come are underdeveloped. Some of these darker-skinned Jews lived in the Casbah in Casablanca in ghettoes under the most miserable conditions, deprived of all opportunities for education or a decent life. And if you think their lot was bad, put yourself for a moment in the place of some of our Jewish brethren who come from the Atlas Mountains, N. Africa, where they lived in caves!
>
> . . . the lighter-skinned Jews who came from Eastern Europe include professionals, tradesmen, and those who have been exposed to the sciences, the arts, and the professions. I would say that the average Jew who comes from these countries has a minimum of a high school education. So, when you put these relatively cultured, advanced Jews into the melting pot with the Jews from Africa, some of whom have no primary education, you get a great discrepancy. This is a socially unhealthy situation.

The original myth of the backwardness of the Sephardim was fueled by the necessity to raise large sums of money abroad to help integrate the newcomers in Israel. It was useful at the time to focus on the truly backward Jews, those from the Atlas Mountains or the primitive villages of Southern Arabia or the tribal societies of Central Asia, and to use them to exemplify Israel's need for massive support in order to "civilize" these new immigrants. In the process, hundreds of thousands of North African Jews, whose families had learned French long before their counterparts in Poland had learned Polish, and *olim* (immigrants) from sophisticated Iraqi and Egyptian Jewish communities—not to speak of the Judesmo-speaking Jews of the Balkans who were as involved in European culture as any Jews in the world—were lumped together with the most unsophisticated cave dwellers. In essence, everyone outside the Yiddish-speaking world of the Israeli establishment was labeled backward. In actual fact, of the 650,000 Jews who came from Islamic lands, no more than 20,000 were cave dwellers or the like.

The Myth Issue Today

Had the original myth been allowed to die a natural death after the period of the mass immigration, it would today be forgotten, or left for historians to consider as a tragicomic example of how Israel's founders tried to cope with Jews of a kind they had hardly ever encountered before. Instead, the myth has been revived in a new elaboration and is being sold wholesale to the rest of the world, especially to Israel's allies in the West, and, as such, it is coloring their view of Israel's present and future. Hence, this myth must be carefully examined, exposed for what it is, and replaced with an accurate picture of the Sephardim and their critical role in shaping the new dynamics of Israeli politics.

Since the heyday of the Ashkenazim's intellectual attack on the Sephardim at the end of that long Lebanese summer, the issue seems to have cooled off, but that cooling is a false perception based on the reduced amount of time and space devoted to it in the news. The Labor party lessened its Sephardi-baiting to a minimum in the 1984 election campaign (although its patronizing attitude was clearly displayed when it tried to treat the issue humorously by using a well-known Israeli comedy group in television campaign advertisements that portrayed the presumably ordinary Sephardic voters as people with thick Moroccan, Yemenite, or Iraqi accents—a device that backfired). To their credit, some of the most public critics made an effort to reconsider their own positions and, indeed, withdrew from their extreme formulations. Amos Oz, for example, went to Bet Shemesh, a more or less typical development town with a large Sephardic population, sat in a café in the town square to talk with the local residents, and came away with a far better impression of their intelligence, Jewishness, and Israeliness than was reflected in his earlier writings. He later recounted that experience honestly in a widely circulated article that appeared in the Hebrew press and then in his book *In the Land of Israel*. Shlomo Avineri, who had never been quite as extreme as Oz, more or less acknowledged that in the heat of the Lebanon campaign he had overstated his case. The issue of the Sephardim also seemed to fade because other issues came to occupy the public mind. The divided Israelis were reunited by their common desire to get out of Lebanon and by their common effort to cope with the growing economic crisis. Besides, a new division had hit the headlines, one between Orthodox and non-Orthodox Jews and their struggle for control over state resources and public policy.

During this time, the Sephardim continued to advance as individuals on all fronts, as manifested both symbolically and practically by the elevation in 1983 of Moshe Levy, of Iraqi background, to chief of staff of the Israeli Defense Forces. He was the second Sephardi (Yugoslavian-born David Elazar was the first), and the first from the Afro-Asian Sephardic communities, to achieve that position. A similar advance was marked by the 1984 election of Yisrael Kessar, of Yemenite origin, as general secretary—the top position—of the Histadrut, the very inner sanctum of the old establishment.

Nevertheless, it would be a mistake to assume that the issue of the Sephardic myth does not remain a real one. The myths about civilized Western Ashkenazim and barbaric Eastern Sephardim are repeated routinely in the press and from the platform—more in sorrow than in anger—by Israeli Ashkenazim and others influenced by them. Moreover, even as the political and economic gaps between the two groups decline, the social gap remains great, and the cultural gap even greater.

In March 1985, I encountered a typical manifestation of the underside of that reality. At a conference on peace in the Middle East, held in Europe, the Israeli delegation consisted principally of senior members of the Israeli establishment, almost all from the so-called generation of '48, that is to say, those who fought in Israel's War of Independence. A number of them were members of the Knesset, and all of them were associated with the most dovish elements of the Israeli political spectrum. Also in attendance was a professor of Sephardic background, a noted dove in almost exactly the same way as his Ashkenazic colleagues. To his great frustration, however, he was ignored and excluded from their company throughout the meeting, to the point where his own already strong feelings of alienation were substantially reinforced, putting him in a great dilemma and pushing him toward the Likud, despite his views on the peace process.

It was clear to outside observers at the peace conference that the old establishment members simply were not prepared to accept someone in their midst who was obviously Sephardi, no matter what the person's social status, intellectual capacity, or political views. It was easier for one particular establishment member to befriend an American Ashkenazic woman, who had settled in Samaria and represented the Gush Emunim point of view of holding onto all the territories occupied in 1967 even at the expense of formal peace, than to deal with the two Sephardim who were present. (As an outsider, she understood what was happening. As she put it: "Those people are suffering from overwhelming nostalgia for the old Israel of their childhood and youth. That is why they are prepared to surrender the territories. Deep in their hearts, they believe that if Israel first gives back the territories, then the Arabs will disappear and after them the Sephardim. Thus the old Israel will be restored.") It is no wonder, then, that at the American Jewish Congress dialogue on Ashkenazim and Sephardim in Jerusalem in July 1985, those of the Sephardim present who represented the radical left announced publicly that they would still vote Likud because they could not vote for any of the existing left-wing parties that are so extremely Ashkenazified and whose leaders display all the usual Ashkenazic prejudices.

It is at this level of cultural antagonism that the issue is being joined, and upon it will rest the future of Israeli society.

Chapter 1

Sephardim and Ashkenazim: Myth and Reality

IN 1978, Yitzhak Navon was sworn in as president of the State of Israel—the first Sephardi to hold that office. The Jerusalem-born president symbolized the contemporary Sephardic world. His paternal ancestors had emigrated from Turkey at the end of the seventeenth century, when Jerusalem was still part of the Ottoman Empire. Before that, they had been among the exiles from Spain at the time of the expulsion in 1492.

A rabbinical family, the Navons were among the Sephardic notables who served Jerusalem's Jewish community for two centuries before the beginnings of Zionism. Over the years, they were active in public affairs, becoming rabbinical court judges, members of the Jewish community council, and emissaries to the Jewish communities of Constantinople and Gibraltar, as well as to communities in Greece, Morocco, and other parts of North Africa. At least one Navon served as *Rishon Le-Zion*, the chief rabbi and head of the Jewish community in Eretz Israel (literally, land of Israel).

Navon's maternal grandfather moved to Jerusalem from Morocco in the midnineteenth century. Navon often tells the story of how his grandfather's dream one night prompted the move in anticipation of the restoration of the Holy Land to the Jews, and how his mother had walked from Morocco to Jerusalem. Navon's uncle, Joseph Navon Bey, built the first railroad in Eretz Israel in 1890, connecting Jerusalem and Jaffa. Even earlier, Joseph Bey had helped the first two Zionist colonies, Petah Tikvah and Rishon Le-Zion, to secure title to their lands, and he was involved in the construction of several neighborhoods in Jerusalem.

Yitzhak Navon, born in 1921, was raised in a family that spoke Hebrew, Judeo-Spanish (Judesmo or Ladino), Arabic, and French. He graduated from Jerusalem's Hebrew University and entered the teaching profession, was active in the Arab department of the Haganah, and then joined the Israeli Foreign Service, being posted in Argentina and Uruguay before becoming political secretary to Foreign Minister Moshe Sharett. For eleven years (1952–63), Navon was the head of Prime Minister David Ben-Gurion's office. He moved on to become director of the Cultural Division of the Ministry of Education and Culture, joined the Rafi party with Ben-Gurion, and was elected to the Knesset (the Israeli legislature) in 1965, becoming one of the deputy speakers. In 1972, he was elected chairman of the Zionist General Council.

A cultured intellectual, Navon is vitally interested in literature and art, and is the author of two successful musicals based on Sephardic folklore, *Romancero Sephardi* (*Sephardic Ballads*) in 1968 and *Bustan Sephardi* (*The Sephardic Garden*) in 1970. Raised in a religiously traditional family, he became an accomplished *hazzan* (cantor) and one of the best exemplars of the Sephardic liturgical tradition in contemporary Israel. While president of Israel, he continued his traditional Sephardic ways, frequently leading services, especially at Yisa Bracha, the main synagogue of the old Sephardic *yishuv* (settled population) in Jerusalem. Navon also has a fine command of Yiddish. Both personally and through his family history, Navon expresses the multidimensionality of today's Sephardic world.

One People, Two Worlds

The term *Sephardi*, as it is used today, describes that branch of the Jewish people whose roots are in the lands of the Mediterranean and western Asia, including their eastern and western diasporas. In the strictest sense, the term designates only those Jews whose ancestors lived on the Iberian Peninsula, most particularly those whom the Sephardim themselves refer to as Spaniolim, who preserved Spanish ways and the Judeo-Spanish language after their exile from the peninsula at the end of the fifteenth century until the dissolution of Old World Jewry in the twentieth century. That strict definition, however, can be misleading on two points. For one, the biblical term *Sepharad* was applied to Iberia relatively late in Jewish history. The term first appears in the biblical book of Obadiah (chapter 20). Some believe it referred to the city of Sardis in Asia Minor. *Sepharad* is first applied to Spain in the *Targum Jonathan* (a first-century Aramaic translation of the prophetic books of the Bible), where it is translated "Ispamia" or "Spamia." Its application to the Iberian Peninsula was fixed by the end of the eighth century.

Regarding the second point, the geographical distinction gets at only part of the uniqueness of the Sephardim as a group. For Jews, what is most important as a distinguishing characteristic is not the specific culture acquired in any particular country of exile by any particular Jewish population, but the broader issues of *halakhah* and *mishpat* (Jewish law), community organization, and common cultural patterns from food to synagogue rituals. In these respects, the Sephardic world is one, from the Atlantic to the Indian oceans, significantly influenced by its location within Islamic civilization.

The classic Sephardim of Spain were mainly descended from Jews who reached the Iberian Peninsula from other countries of the Mediterranean world after the Muslim conquest of 711 C.E. This Jewish community in Spain was at first shaped by Babylonian Jewry, but in the eleventh century it assumed leadership of the Jewish world. At the time, the Iberian Peninsula was effectively divided between Christians and Muslims, with virtually all the Jews living under Islamic rule. In the thirteenth century, the major concentrations of Jewish life shifted to the Christian areas of the peninsula, and for almost three hundred years most of Spanish Jewry developed within a Christian society. When the Jews were expelled from Spain in 1492 by the Christians, most of them returned to the Islamic world: to North Africa, the Balkans, and western Asia (see figure 1.1).

The world of the Sephardim has its parallel in the world of the Ashkenazim to the north. In their strict sense, the terms *Ashkenaz* (like *Sepharad,* biblical in origin) and *Ashkenazim* refer only to the first communities of Jews in northern France and western Germany. The term *Ashkenaz* first appears in Genesis 10:3 and I Chronicles 1:6, referring to peoples descended from Japhet through Gomer. Jeremiah (51:27) identifies the term as the name of a kingdom near Armenia. Most scholars place the original Ashkenaz with the Scythians. In the Talmud (Yona 10a), the biblical Gomer, father of Ashkenaz, is called Germania, which really refers to Germinikia in northwest-

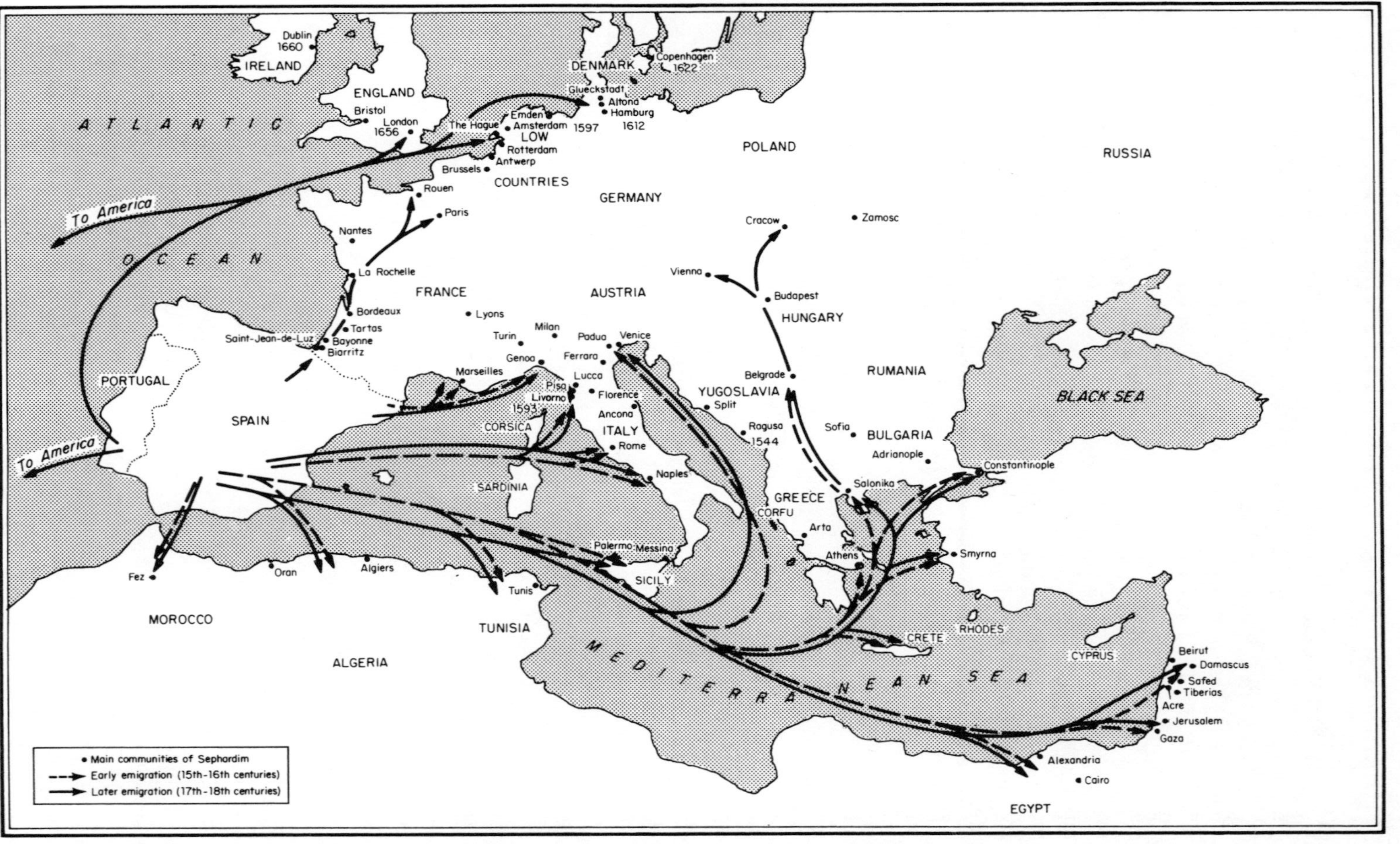

FIGURE 1.1
Sephardic emigration from the Iberian Peninsula after the expulsion of 1492, with dates of establishment of new communities where known.

ern Syria. The term was first used to refer to Germany and the Jews there in the eleventh century (see Rashi's commentary to the Talmud: Sukkah 17a, Gittin 55b, and Baba Metziah 73b).

By the end of the thirteenth century, *Ashkenaz* took on its present meaning, a subgroup of the Jewish people, in the *responsa* (*halakhic* decisions) of Asher ben Jehiel (who died in 1317). Over time, the *halakhah, mishpat,* patterns of community organization, and cultural ways of those Jews spread east and west to embrace large Jewish communities geographically far from the original Ashkenaz (see figure 1.2), the bulk of whose Jewish populations reached them from outside the Ashkenazic core area. Among these Jewish communities there were many internal differences, but they all shared a common Ashkenazic heritage, which was significantly influenced by being located within Christian civilization, particularly in the Germanic and Slavic cultural areas.

From the late tenth and early eleventh centuries, when the Sephardim and Ashkenazim emerged as the two main groupings of the Jewish people, until the twentieth century, each developed its own world within the larger Jewish whole. This does not mean that over the years Jewish unity has not prevailed above all else. The occasional stories of internal discrimination among Jews are the exception; generally, Jews, whatever their origins, have felt—and continue to feel—responsible for one another. They share a common fate, honor the same Torah, even if in the breach, and are even more alike genetically and culturally than they are different. Nevertheless, within that context this twofold division dominated the Jewish world for approximately a millennium.

What of the differences within the Sephardic camp itself—differences between Moroccans and Iraqis, Spaniolim and Egyptians, and even between Halebim (Jews of Aleppo and Aram Tzovah or northern Syria) and Jews of Damascus? These differences do exist, just as there are differences in the Ashkenazic world between Litvaks and Galitzianers, between Yekkim (German Jews) and Poilishers (Polish Jews). In the twentieth century, however, the Ashkenazim became more internally integrated a generation or two before the Sephardim, largely as a result of their earlier emigration from their original lands of settlement and earlier integration into their new worlds. The Sephardim are only now beginning to reach that stage, having begun their emigrations a generation or two later. But the trend is obvious. The emergence of such bodies as the World Sephardi Federation and forums in Israel for Sephardim from all countries of origin speaks of a common identity that Sephardim are now busy discovering.

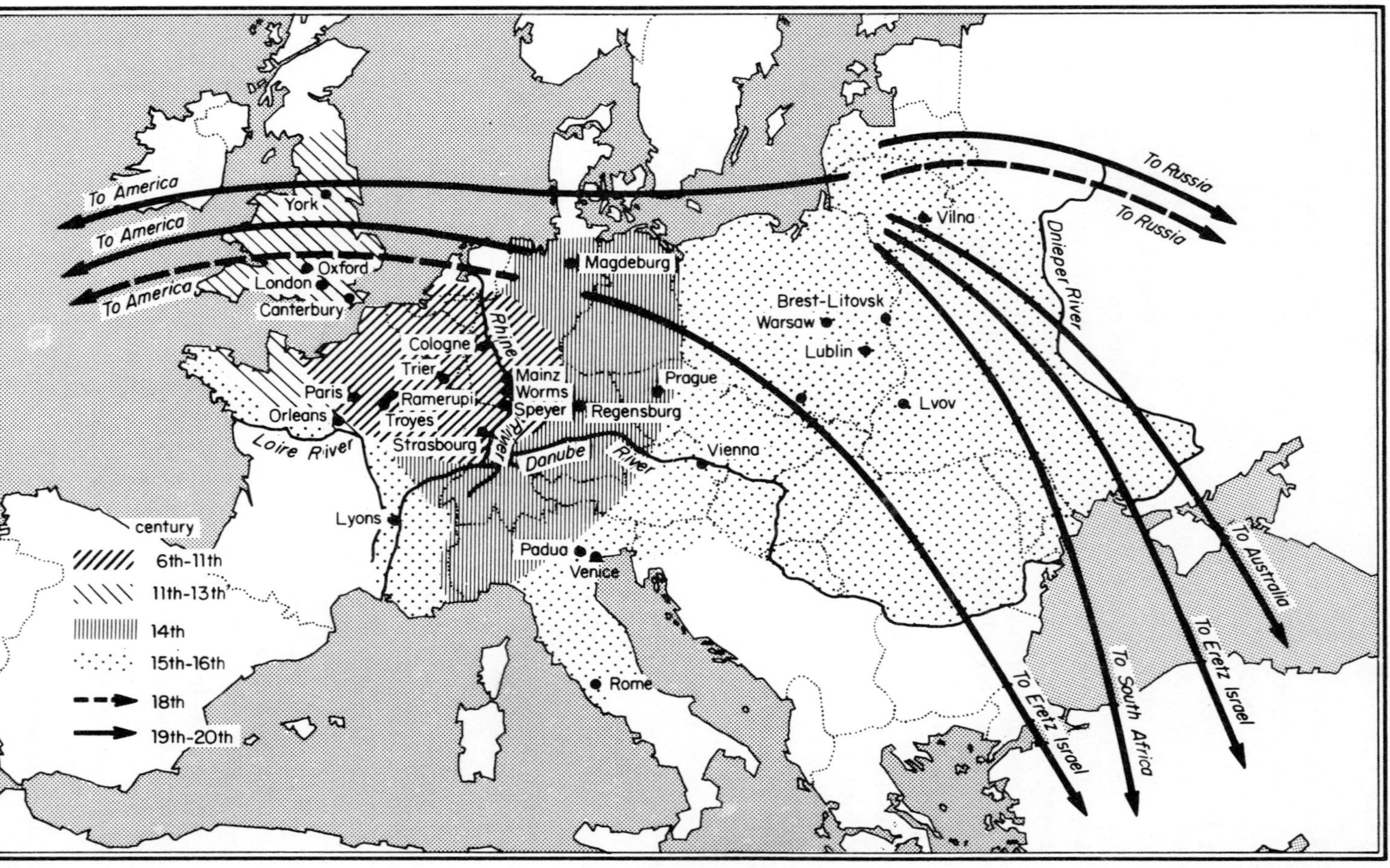

FIGURE 1.2
Ashkenazic settlement and paths of later emigration.

Migrations

Let us look more closely at the "one world" of the Sephardim. How is that world to be defined? Why, for instance, are Babylonian or Yemenite Jews, who have never called themselves Sephardim and who apparently share little of the heritage of Mediterranean culture, properly included in the Sephardic world? We begin with the evidence of history. South of the mountains that divide the north and south of Europe, from the Caucasus to the Pyrenees, became the world of the Sephardim, and to the north became the world of the Ashkenazim. With three exceptions—a handful of Jews crossed the Alps with the Romans in the days of the empire; one thousand years later another handful of Jews from Italy crossed the Alps to plant the seeds of the Ashkenazic world; and in our own times, after another millennium, Ashkenazic Jews recrossed the Alps in a return to Eretz Israel—the significant migrations in Jewish history have been between east and west. These migrations were regular features of Jewish history, encouraging the division between Sephardim and Ashkenazim.

The separation of these two groups was intensified by the fact that, with the exception of Christian Italy and Spain, all the lands where the Sephardim lived before the seventeenth century were under Islamic rule. All the lands in which the Ashkenazim lived until the seventeenth century were dominated by Catholicism.

There were, of course, cross-migrations of individuals and groups, but the newcomers generally were assimilated into their new environments rather than retaining the cultural ways that they brought with them. The many Jewish families bearing the surname "Ashkenazi" who are indisputably Sephardic, and the fact that such Ashkenazic names as Shneur Zalman, Peretz, and Sprinzak are corruptions of Spanish words, attest to migrations in both directions. Thus, in terms of cultural influence, the two worlds absorbed their immigrants, thereby managing to maintain overall Jewish unity *and* subcultural autonomy.*

Cultural development, then, occurred internally in the two separate groups. Perhaps the most significantly Jewish manifestation of this was to be found in *halakhic* development. Again, what is most remarkable about the Jewish people is the overall *halakhic* unity that was maintained

* Concerning overall Jewish unity, it should be noted that biologists have come to recognize that the similarities and differences in the Jewish genetic pool do not follow a division between Ashkenazim and Sephardim.

despite their exile and dispersion to all corners of the world. But within that unity, two clear patterns of *halakhic* development emerged, based on the division between Sephardim and Ashkenazim. Both their unity and diversity are reflected most clearly in the *Shulhan Arukh* (literally meaning the "set table"). Compiled by the Sephardi Rabbi Joseph Karo in the sixteenth century, it became the universal *halakhic* reference for the Jewish people, but the Ashkenazim would accept it only after Rabbi Moses Isserles added the *Mapah* (literally, the tablecloth), which adapted it to Ashkenazic custom. The areas of *halakhah* and *minhag* (religious ritual) are so important that perhaps the distinction between Sephardim and Ashkenazim today—despite the fact that most Jews no longer follow the *halakhah* in *private* life—should be based on which *halakhic* tradition particular Jews use on *public* occasions.

Transmission of Law

Owing to historical research of recent decades, it is now possible to trace the transmission of Jewish law from community to community since the time of the completion of the Talmud, in the sixth century, itself the result of cooperation between "proto-Sephardic" Jews of Eretz Israel and of Babylonia. After the law was initially taken north via Italy, the founding communities of Ashkenazic Jewry were mostly left to their own devices at a crucial moment in their historical development, early in the eleventh century. On the other hand, Sephardic communities from Afghanistan to the Atlantic Ocean regularly communicated with the Babylonian Jews, then the leaders of the Jewish world, sending *she'elot* (queries) and receiving *teshuvot* (*responsa*). In this way the basic *halakhic* data were transmitted. To take one example, the basic order of Jewish prayer, the *siddur tefilla* of Rabbi Amram, reached the Jews of Barcelona in response to a query they posed to Babylonian Jewry. Another example is the case of the Jews of Yemen who turned to Maimonides, the quintessential Sephardi, then living in Egypt, as their authority in both *halakhic* and political matters.

In addition to such correspondence, authoritative figures traveled to the regions involved. At that time, the brisk trade between the Mediterranean world and southern Asia, which was principally in the hands of Jews, also fostered communication from one end of the Sephardic world to the other.

These transmissions of law are important because the unity of the Sephardic world begins with them, from Babylonia westward to Egypt,

North Africa, and Spain itself in the eighth through the eleventh centuries. Between the eleventh and fifteenth centuries, the culture of Mediterranean Jewry acquired an Iberian character as Spanish Jewry came to the fore. The Jewish exiles from Spain moved eastward in the sixteenth century to the Ottoman Empire, which then became the center of the Sephardic world. Through the Sephardic *halakhic* authorities in the Ottoman heartland (what are today northern Greece, southeastern Yugoslavia, southern Bulgaria, and European Turkey), a common Sephardic *halakhah* spread throughout the empire, including Babylonia and Yemen, and beyond to the Jews of India. Other Sephardim carried it to Amsterdam and northern Europe, and even to the New World.

The migration of the Spanish exiles and their influence as *halakhic* spokesmen continued to bind the Sephardic world, even as the physical boundaries of that world expanded. Nowhere is this more evident than in the order of prayer and customs surrounding the *siddur tefilla*. As with the *halakhah*, the unity of the *siddur* among all Jews is more impressive than the differences, although there *are* clear differences between the Ashkenazic and Sephardic *siddurim*, especially regarding those elements not canonized earlier in Babylonia: the *piyyutim* (religious poetry) and the *mahzor* (prayer book) for the High Holy Days. But most Sephardim (excluding the Yemenites) share a common *minhag* (religious ritual) and forms of aesthetic expression touched by regional variations. (See table 1.1 for variations in religious terms between Sephardim and Ashkenazim.) The major differences among Sephardic subgroups are found in the liturgical music of the various communities, although the differences are not as great as those between Ashkenazic and Sephardic liturgical music.

Community Organization

Through the centuries the Sephardim were able to maintain a basic unity in community organization, largely for three reasons: one, the influence of the *Askamot* of Valladolid, the fifteenth-century codification of the communal ordinances of Castilian Jewry, which became the basic constitutional referent for Sephardic communities; two, Sephardic communities usually were without a professional rabbinical class, which led them to emphasize leadership by notables; and three, the Sephardim rejected the Ashkenazic-style chief rabbi and emphasized instead the authority of rabbinical judges. (The rabbinical class and chief rabbi have

TABLE 1.1
Comparable Sephardic and Ashkenazic Religious Terms

Sephardic	Ashkenazic	English
Arvit	Ma'ariv	evening prayer
bar minan	lo aleinu	used to refer to a tragedy
(h)ekhal	aron	ark
haggadah	seder	Passover service
ḥakham	rav	rabbi
hashkabah	hazkarah	prayer for deceased
ḥazak ubarukh	yishar kohakha	blessing and congratulation
Kippur	Yom Kippur	Day of Atonement
nahalah; años	yahrzeit	anniversary of death
pizmonim	zemirot	religious songs
ribbi	rabi	rabbi, Mr.
Sefer	Sefer Torah	Scroll of the Law
(e) snoga	shul	synagogue
tefillot	siddur	prayer book
tevah	bimah	reading desk
zemirot	pesukei de-simra	preliminary readings in the morning service

been part of Ashkenazic community organization from at least the fifteenth century.)

Sephardic communities for the most part had to develop in more complex environments than those of the Ashkenazim, as they had to live together with several different ethnoreligious groups, each empowered to conduct its own affairs. Thus, in Spain, Muslims, Christians, and Jews lived side by side within the same cities, each with separate municipal governments. In the Ottoman Empire, such ethnically different Christian communities as Greeks and Armenians maintained their own separate institutions as well.

In addition, a long tradition among Sephardim allowed Jews leaving one area to establish their own unique congregation in their new community. Thus, in eleventh-century Egypt, for example, the same city was likely to contain different congregations loyal to the *yeshivot* (talmudic academies) of both Babylonia and Eretz Israel. Contacts among them ranged from informal communication to formal confederation. The same pattern existed throughout North Africa and, most especially, in the Ottoman Empire after the Spanish expulsion. Rather than being transient phenomena of the immigrant generation, these separate congregations persisted for centuries.

Within the Sephardic communities, leading families played a special role. For most of the period, the major Sephardic communities were urban and, for the times, quite large, so that the Sephardic leaders were groups or families of notables rather than the single individuals who led the small towns of Ashkenaz. This family leadership often involved complex patterns of power distribution and sharing.

Moreover, at least from the time of the publication of *Sefer HaShetarot* (*Book of Contracts*) at the end of the eleventh century by Rabbi Judah HaBarceloni, and most especially after the adoption of the *Askamot* of Valladolid in 1432, most Sephardic communities were organized under a common set of constitutional referents that set forth the basis of their civil organization and persisted until the end of the traditional Sephardic community in the twentieth century.

Finally, living as they did in the warm and sunny Mediterranean world, the Sephardim were, in their general culture, much the opposite of the Ashkenazim in many ways. The Sephardic aesthetic is one that celebrates color and visible beauty, thereby adding a highly sensual dimension to their very traditional Jewish life. As a Mediterranean people, their lives were oriented to the green and golden outdoors for much of the year. Also, Ashkenazic food tends to partake of a certain plain heaviness (in the United States known erroneously as "Jewish cooking") that is characteristic of Eastern and Central Europe, strongly influenced by Slavic cooking. Sephardic food, however, is light and sophisticated in the manner of the fine cuisines of Spain, Italy, and Greece.

Sephardim, *Not* Edot HaMizrah

In contemporary Israel it has become conventional to refer to the Sephardim as *edot hamizrah*—usually translated as Oriental or Eastern Jews. This term, however, is a distortion based on false premises, furthering the myths concerning the Sephardim.

The term *edah* as used in this context is a distortion of a classic Jewish term with a very different meaning. From biblical times, the word *edah* commonly described the Jewish people as a body politic. Jews have constituted and continue to constitute a single *edah*, in the sense of a political and religious assembly. That is the meaning of the word in the Torah and how it has been used throughout all generations until the present. In proper usage, *Am Yisrael* (literally, the people of Israel) in its corporate dimension is constituted as *Adat Bnei Yisrael* (literally, the congregation of the children of Israel), which contrasts with *edah* because *edah* emphasizes the fact that being Jewish involves both kinship and consent. Jews may be born into their *am*, but in a very real sense they consent to being part of the *edah* by actively taking part in its business. However, the modern sociological use of *edah*, as in *edot hamizrah*, is just the reverse; it eliminates the dimension of consent and emphasizes kinship on the basis of country or region of origin. This has led to the incorrect English translation of the term as "ethnic," as if Jews—who are perhaps more than any other a single *ethnos*, or people—were divided into different ethnic groups. Because this is untrue and is, therefore, a denial of Jewish unity and peoplehood, its usage does a disservice to the Jewish people. A semantic barbarism and a national disgrace, this usage of *edah* and *edot* should be eliminated.

As for *mizrah* (east) in *edot hamizrah*, its use is prejudicial. (Even if it were used in a purely geographic sense, it would also be confusing; are the Jews of North Africa "Easterners" when all of Morocco is located farther west than London, and most of North Africa is farther west than Poland?) Obviously, the word refers to cultural differences, and implicit in that usage is that Sephardim as "Easterners" are "Oriental." Ashkenazim are "Westerners." This represents the mobilization of loaded terms to advance a convenient Ashkenazic myth in a situation where to be "Western" is often synonymous with being "modern." And since virtually everyone wants to be modern, this myth gives the Ashkenazim a significant psychological advantage over the Sephardim.

The labels of Westerner and Easterner or Oriental reflect certain assumptions with regard to culture and modernity. Unfortunately, such assumptions are often far from accurate. A case in point is former President Yitzhak Navon, acknowledged as a man of broad culture, the perfect example of what Shlomo Avineri seems to mean by European, middle class, and liberal. But Navon is a Sephardi, born in Jerusalem into a family that, before immigrating to Israel, lived in Morocco and other parts of the Ottoman Empire. The former president, then, is not only Sephardic but a member of the Afro-Asian group by any definition.

Navon is only the most visible example of how erroneous certain assumptions and stereotypes can be. There are many others like him, including dozens of old Jerusalemite families, Jews whose ancestors were part of the civic elite in Iraq, sophisticated individuals of French culture in North Africa, and heirs of the Young Turk revolution in Turkey. Indeed, before the establishment of the state, many of the older generation of Sephardim in Israel looked down upon the Ashkenazim, including the Zionist pioneers, as uncouth and lacking all cultural refinement—for reasons that Oz puts so positively, namely, the pioneers' rejection of bourgeois refinements.

What are the facts concerning "East" and "West"? Were the Eastern European lands of Russia, Poland, and Rumania, from which most of the Ashkenazim came, any less Eastern in culture than the Arab lands? Not to those who were born and raised in what are regarded as the true countries of the West. The self-proclaimed bearers of Western culture in the Middle East are those same *Ostjuden* who were once victims of stereotyped generalizations similar to those they now make about the Sephardim. Moreover, no one would dispute that the Sephardim of the Netherlands, Great Britain, and the United States are Western. As a matter of fact, the Judesmo-speaking Sephardim of the Balkans and the eastern Mediterranean see themselves as far more "Western" than any of the Jews of Eastern Europe, many of them since the nineteenth century having been educated in the schools of the Alliance Israelite Universelle, where they mastered French language and culture. Eastern European Jews seeking secular knowledge at that time still had to hide "Western" books in their *gemarot* (Talmud folios) in the *yeshiva*.

What most strikes settlers in Israel from the English-speaking world is how "Eastern" the vast majority of the Israeli population is—Ashkenazim and Sephardim alike. That, indeed, is a cultural designation. Any differences between the groups are largely differences with regard to the timing of modernization, which usually means that certain groups of Ashkenazim reached secular schools and acquired indoor plumbing a generation earlier than certain groups of Sephardim. Even that is not entirely true, since the Jews of Algeria were emancipated before the Jews of the Russian Empire. And it is often overlooked that many Eastern Sephardim—of Palestine, Iraq, Egypt, Turkey, and the Balkans—encountered Western civilization at least at the same time as did their Ashkenazi brethren in Russia. It is well known that in Western Europe and the United States the Sephardim were the first Jews to enter the mainstream of Western life.

Sephardic Pioneering in Eretz Israel

The Western-educated Sephardim are not very visible in today's Israel because the Ashkenazic Zionist establishment had no room for them. Some justify this exclusion on the basis of the Ashkenazim being the *halutzim* (pioneers) who singlehandedly built the country from the days of the Second Aliyah (1904–14) and before, whereas the Sephardim came only after 1948. In truth, the roles of those Zionist pioneers in the development of the kibbutzim and the labor movement and their great influence on the institutions of modern Israel can hardly be overemphasized. Yet, that fact does not erase the roles played by many Sephardim who entered Eretz Israel at the same time as the Ashkenazim and were involved in different forms of pioneering.

Waves of immigrants from Sephardic communities paralleled each of the *aliyot* from Eastern Europe. Sephardim from the Balkans, Yemen, and Bukhara arrived in the 1870s and 1880s, at the time of the First Aliyah, and Syrian Jews were a majority in the Sephardic immigration during the Second Aliyah. The Third Aliyah, after World War I, saw a large mixture of Sephardim from all parts of the Sephardic diaspora, and the *aliyot* of the 1930s brought Jews influenced by Zionist educational work, particularly from the Balkans and North Africa. Although the absolute number of Sephardic immigrants was not huge, their ratio to the total number of Sephardim in the world exceeded that of the Ashkenazim. Before 1948, Sephardim accounted for about one-eighth of the world Jewish population; they provided about one-sixth of the immigrants to Palestine.

These prestatehood Sephardic *olim* did much—if not most—of the urban pioneering. When the history of urban *halutziut* in Israel is written, the role of the Sephardic community will finally be revealed for what it was.

Sephardim have been especially involved in rebuilding the Israeli capital, from the first settlements outside the Old City of Jerusalem by Spanish and Bukharan Jews (financed by an American Sephardi, Judah Touro, and administered by an English Sephardi, Moses Montefiore) to the present concentration of construction activities in the hands of the Kurdish Jews. In one sense, the Sephardim have been merely building on a tradition begun in the fifteenth century, when Jewish exiles from Spain reestablished a significant Jewish presence in Eretz Israel by settling in Safed and its surrounding villages, and continued in the seventeenth century when Sephardic Jews from Syria founded modern Tiberias. Salonikan Jews built the Jewish port of Haifa in the 1930s, and Sephardim were heavily engaged in entrepreneurial activities in early Tel Aviv.

After 1948, this involvement continued in the development towns that opened Israel's postindependence urban frontier. Without minimizing the role of the agricultural settlements in the development of the state, or the Sephardic role in the *moshav* (farming village) movement after 1948, the fact that Israel has moved into the age of urbanization lends even greater importance to the work of these successive generations of Sephardic *halutzim*. Unfortunately, the role of the urban pioneers passes largely unnoticed in Israeli textbooks (mainly written by the Ashkenazic heirs of the Russian Zionist back-to-the-land movement) and in most public acknowledgments of the pioneering generation, which are managed (perhaps unwittingly) by the establishment in such a way as to exclude any pioneers but their own.

Involvement with Zionism

Sephardic immigration was no less motivated by Zionism than was Ashkenazic. Sephardim were active in the Zionist movement from its beginnings, not only as individuals—Theodore Herzl and Max Nordau, the founders of the Zionist movement, both affirmed their Sephardic descent—but as entire communities as well. Salonika, the leading city of the Sephardic diaspora, had Zionist clubs and newspapers from the time of Herzl, before the turn of the century, and the Zionist organizations in Yugoslavia and Bulgaria were important forces in the Jewish life of those two countries. The North Africans, Iraqis, Iranians, and Yemenites had less formal Zionist organization because of their more traditional societies and the often murderous opposition of the ruling powers to what was seen as a foreign movement; however, Zionist groups did exist in North Africa and Iraq in the interwar period.

The Sephardic role in Zionism has been minimized because most of the Jews who entered Israel after 1948 (largely Sephardim) were not formal members of Zionist organizations. Yet there is no evidence that Moroccan Jews, for instance, were less interested in Zionism than Rumanian Jews. In fact, Sephardim came to Israel of their own free will because they saw the state as the beginning of Jewish redemption, not as refugees from a Europe soaked with the blood of the Holocaust.

Not surprisingly, the Zionists from Russia and Russian Poland, who were the driving force of the pioneering effort, have dictated Israel's patterns of cultural, social, political, and economic organization, at least since the 1920s if not since the Second Aliyah. An especially energetic group imbued with a strong ideology is likely to lead the way, as they have, particularly if that group has managed to preempt the status of founders. These pioneers of the Second and Third Aliyot were not actually the first founders of the new *yishuv*; before them were the pioneers of the First Aliyah, and before them, the migrations that, although technically part of the old *yishuv*, really began the process of the redemption of Zion. These *aliyot* had been coming at virtually generational intervals since at least the middle of the seventeenth century.

Zionist history books tend to neglect the history of the pre-Zionist *aliyot*. The first stages reestablished Jewish communities in Jerusalem (fifteenth century), Safed and Hebron (sixteenth century), Tiberias (seventeenth), and Haifa and Jaffa (nineteenth). Sephardic Jews established Safed as the spiritual center of the Jewish world for two generations in the sixteenth century, briefly restoring primacy to Eretz Israel for the first time since the fifth century. It was in Safed that the *Shulhan Arukh* was composed and published by Rabbi Joseph Karo and where the Jewish order of service reached its present form. A new Jewish theosophy—Lurianic kabbalah—was developed, which reshaped the Jewish world, ultimately providing the intellectual and religious foundations for Hassidism two centuries later.

In the latter half of the nineteenth century, Sephardim initiated the development of the new city of Jerusalem and were involved in the first agricultural enterprises and settlements—Mikveh Israel, Petah Tikva, and Rosh Pina—initiating Jewish settlement of the lands along the coast and in the Galilee. They also tried to settle the Judean hills and the Golan, but failed to gain the support of the Zionist establishment for their efforts (thereby leaving Jerusalem exposed to Arab attacks in 1948). The support of the Sephardic communities in Jerusalem, Jaffa, Haifa, and Safed was crucial for the Zionist *halutzim*, even though the Ashkenazi settlers of the old *yishuv* for the most part wanted no part of the new movement, and many actively opposed it.

Long the established group in the old *yishuv*, the Sephardim lost their majority status during the First Aliyah, but they maintained political power until World War I. They were then replaced by the Zionist movement. The ideologies and actions of the Zionist camps reshaped Jewish life in Eretz Israel. Members of the old *yishuv* had to join the new or retreat into isolation.

The Zionists also controlled the allocation of immigration certificates, which they used to bring their compatriots from Eastern Europe, according to the Zionist party key—the share of each party's vote for the Zionist congresses. Thus, at the time the state was established, the Jewish community in Israel was virtually an extension of the communities of Eastern Europe. Nonetheless, Sephardic Jews entered the country throughout the period in disproportionate numbers and stayed in even more disproportionate ones. It has been said that of every ten Eastern European Jews entering Israel, nine left and one remained; of every ten Sephardic Jews, one left and nine remained. Even so, the Sephardic Jews fell farther and farther behind as a percentage of the total population of the *yishuv*; they represented only some 10 percent of the world Jewish population to begin with. Moreover, their pioneering efforts were largely ignored, with the official Zionist emphasis on land settlement or the building of Tel Aviv as the only real *halutziut*. The fact that the development of the new cities of Israel (including much of Tel Aviv), even before the state existed, was disproportionately a result of the efforts of Sephardic Jews simply has been ignored as somehow representing an inferior bourgeois indulgence.

As noted earlier, the myths concerning the Sephardim have been perpetuated to the detriment of Israel and Jewish unity. The relatively small number of Jews who came to Israel from primitive circumstances have been painted as representing all of the Sephardim; this is particularly so in fund-raising propaganda directed to Jews overseas. In the end, many Israeli Ashkenazim, including the leadership whose only direct contact with the Sephardim was on a patron-client basis, came to believe their own propaganda. In discussing the Sephardim, peripheral considerations came to be more important than central ones. Thus, in the 1950s and 1960s Israeli leaders could make statements in public that they had nothing in common with their Oriental brethren who did not know how to use toothbrushes, tables and chairs, or indoor plumbing, and that their only common ground was their Jewish heritage.

Jews from Arab countries were referred to as Arab Jews, as if they were more like Arabs (implicitly a put-down in the Israeli context of the time) than the Jews from Poland or Russia were like Polish Catholics or Russian Orthodox Christians. There is an outrageous quality to this assumption that if a Jew comes from an Arab land, he must be more of an Arab than a Jew, while a Jew from a Christian country would have remained more a Jew than a Christian. One of the significant points to come out of the Israeli response to the Beirut massacre was that the Jews of Israel, Sephardim and Ashkenazim alike, felt that such behavior was against all Jewish morality, and that it reflected the problems of becoming involved with Arabs—even Christian Arabs—who operate according to a different moral code.

To recapitulate, the term *Sephardic* describes the Jewish religiocultural heritage of the Sephardim—the *halakhic* chain that binds them and the cultural traits that make them distinctive—just as *Ashkenazic* does for the Ashkenazim. Both are authentic Jewish terms, rich in historical associations rather than imposed sociological categories. Both worlds are compounded of many country-of-origin groups, each with its own distinctiveness. The internal links binding each are precisely their Jewish dimensions; Jews should define themselves in no other terms. The real difference, then, is not between Eastern and Western Jews, but between northerners and southerners. The Ashkenazim are the Jews of the north and include people of both Eastern and Western culture. The Sephardim are the Jews of the south and include people of both Western and Eastern culture.

Classical and Romantic Traditions in Jewish Civilization

Every civilization has its mix of classical and romantic elements, and must have both to be complete. Within Jewish civilization, for one thousand years, Sephardic Jewry has been the embodiment of the classical tradition, and Ashkenazic Jewry, the romantic. This is evident in their respective styles, logic, and fields of focus. The Jewish people were most enriched when these two groups were vitally alive, recognized for their individuality, and encouraged to interact with one another.

Abraham Joshua Heschel recognizes these classical and romantic divisions and discusses them in some detail in *The Earth Is the Lord's,* a celebration of what he refers to as "the inner world of the Jew in East Europe." In chapter 3 of that work, "The Two Great Traditions," Heschel contrasts the Sephardic (particularly the Spaniol) and Ashkenazic (particularly the Hassidic) world views and ways over the past millennium with the intention of showing the Ashkenazic to best advantage. Among his points are that the "intellectual life of the Sephardic Jews was deeply influenced by the surrounding world," while in Ashkenaz, "the spiritual life of the Jews . . . was lived in isolation." Also, the "culture of . . . Sephardic Jews was shaped by an elite . . . which drew inspiration from classical philosophy and science and whose point of view was aristocratic," while that of Ashkenazic Jewry reflected "the archaic simplicity, imaginative naivete and unaffected naturalness of the humble mass."

Heschel continues:

The Ashkenazim did not write *piyyutim*, the elaborate and often complicated liturgical poems favored by Sephardic authors; they wrote mostly *selichoth*, simple penitential prayers and elegies. They drew their style from the homespun prose of Talmudic sayings rather than from the lofty rhetoric of the Prophets.

The Sephardic world produced the classic books of Jewish civilization, while "classical books were not written in Eastern Europe."

Writes Heschel: "Sephardic books are distinguished by their strict logical arrangement. Composed according to a clear plan, every one of their details has its assigned place, and the transitions from one subject to another are clear and simple." On the other hand, he says,

The contours of the thoughts of Ashkenazic writers are irregular, vague, and often perplexingly entangled; their content is restless, animated by inner wrestling and a kind of baroque emotion. . . . The former favor the harmony of a system . . . the latter impulsive inspiration. The strength of the Sephardic scholars lies in their mastery of expression, that of the Ashkenazim in the unexpected overtones of their words. A spasm of feeling, a passionate movement of thought, an explosive enthusiasm will break through the form.

The Sephardim aspired to personal perfection and attempted to express their ideas rationally. They strove for tranquillity of soul, for inner peace and contentment. Their ethics was . . . full of prudence and practical wisdom. To follow the golden rule, to take a middle course and avoid extremes, was one of their most popular maxims. . . . Ashkenazic ethics, on the other hand, knew no perfection that was definable; its vision aimed at the infinite, never compromising, never satisfied, always striving—"seek higher than that." The Ashkenazic moralist or Hassid was exalted; he yearned for the transcendental, the preternatural. . . . Not for him the . . . gradual ascent. What he sought was boundless fervor, praying and learning without limit or end.

What distinguishes Sephardic from Ashkenazic culture is, however, primarily a difference of form rather than a divergence of content. It is a difference that cannot be characterized by the categories of rationalism versus mysticism, or the speculative versus the intuitive mentality. The difference goes beyond this and might be more accurately expressed as a distinction between a static form, in which the spontaneous is subjected to strictness and abstract order, and a dynamic form, which does not compel the content to conform to what is already established. . . . Room is left for the outburst, for the surprise, for the instantaneous. The inward counts infinitely more than the outward.

Despite some shortcomings in Heschel's highly romanticized effort to distinguish between the expressions of Jewish culture, he has indeed captured the essence of the difference between the Sephardic and Ashkenazic worlds. In so doing, he has put his finger on the distinction between the classical and romantic approaches to Jewish life. Perhaps the simplest way to see this is in his statements that Sephardic Jewry was "distinguished not only by monumental scientific achievements, but also by a universality of spirit," and that "classical books were not written in Eastern Europe." Beginning with the Talmud and concluding with the work of the Safed kabbalists, all of the great Jewish classics were products of the Sephardic milieu.

As Heschel puts it:

> Eastern European Jews did not cherish the ambition to create consummate, definitive expressions. . . . The Ashkenazim were not interested in writing literature: their works read like brief lecture notes. They were products, not of pure research, but of discussions with pupils. The Ashkenazim rarely composed books that stand like separate buildings with foundations of their own, books that do not lean upon older works; they wrote commentaries or notes on the classical works of older times, books that modestly hug the monumental walls of older citadels.

As Heschel implies, every group in the course of its history has special moments of harmonious integration, when its finest manifestations come together in something close to their ideal formulation, when the gap between the ideal and real is palpable. The longer a group's history, the more opportunities there are for such classical moments, but also the more times when the reality is far less than the ideal. In fact, two such moments can be found in the Sephardic experience: from the midtenth to the midtwelfth centuries in Spain, and from the late fifteenth to the late seventeenth centuries in the Sephardic diaspora. Those moments were strong enough to generate bridges that in the first case survived until the Spanish expulsion, and in the second, until the destruction of the Ottoman Sephardic diaspora at the beginning of the twentieth century. In both, their glory rested on the successful expression of the elements of Jewish civilization in such a way as to represent religious, moral, intellectual, and aesthetic achievements.

At the same time, these moments represented a successful synthesis of Jewish and general civilization that produced mutually beneficial cross-fertilization. From this symbiosis appeared great Jewish scholars and sages who were fully at home both in Jewish law and lore and in Western civilization, in traditions of music and cuisine that were of the highest quality, influenced by and in turn influencing the other civilizations of the Mediterranean and Western worlds.

The patterns of community self-government and political activity of those classical moments brought Jewish congregational republicanism to the peak of its development, and gave Jews the highest levels of political efficacy in all their centuries of relative powerlessness and dependency in the diaspora. Perhaps for the first and only time in Jewish civilization, there was a strong emphasis on form and manner that added a whole new aesthetic dimension to the performance of *mitzvot* (biblical commandments), while at the same time, Jewish law was maintained within a framework of openness and tolerance. If this sounds like a Jewish Camelot, so be it. The disappearance of that world has not enhanced the quality of Jewish life; rather, it is a world that all Jews should learn so that ours and future generations may strive to achieve a similar symbiosis.

Classicism emphasizes form, simplicity, proportion, and restrained emotion. Each of these, with the possible exception of simplicity, Heschel labels as Sephardic, contrasting them with Ashkenazic attitudes and behavior. Let us look at each of these elements of classicism.

Form

Concerning form, the Sephardic emphasis on aesthetics, external appearance, and symmetry stands out. Sephardim have a word for it—*kavod*—which every Sephardi learns in both Hebrew and his or her own regional Jewish language (in Judesmo, for example, it is *honor*). The word carries with it a complex of attitudes, values, and expectations.

Among Ashkenazim, at least until recently, such emphases were largely rejected, being irrelevant to the intensive pursuit of salvation, religious or other, in Eastern Europe. Only assimilation to (real) Western civilization produced an interest in form. The flight of so many Ashkenazic intellectuals from Judaism to modernity, especially to modern aesthetics, reflects this. The literary works of so many assimilated Ashkenazim invariably describe the Jewish environments from which they came as vulgar, unrestrained, and overemotional. Although exaggerated for effect, the caricatures do make a point.

Among the Sephardim, of course, there are assimilated intellectuals, too, but what they retain from their environment is precisely this heritage of aesthetics and form. Their critiques of their own heritage are milder, more often emphasizing, if anything, problems of superstition. They tend to be respectful of their past, even if they reject it as premodern.

The Sephardic emphasis on form in contrast to the Ashkenazic emphasis on the inner self is particularly evident today in their different styles of prayer and ritual observance. The integral quality of the Sephardic service places emphasis on the meaning of the liturgy and the pronunciation of every word in the reading of the Torah and in most of the prayers. Indeed, the emphasis on common prayer in the Sephardic service is sharply different from the implicit emphasis on self-expression among Ashkenazim, not only the emotionally intense apparent free-for-all of the vociferous Hassidim but among the restrained Mitnagdim as well. The aesthetics of divine communion—in form, language, and style—is a central aspect of public prayer for Sephardim.

In order to understand the aesthetic approach of the Sephardim and to feel its power, one must witness, or better yet participate in, the Sephardic *minhag* (religious ritual) as it is expressed in congregational worship services and home ceremonies. Each service or ceremony is, in effect, a pageant of appropriate scale in which every component is highly integrated and appropriately paced, with an emphasis on rhythm, language, and concept—in other words, a kind of poetry in motion. The need to clearly pronounce every word of the liturgy means that every word must have meaning. It means that Sephardic liturgical poetry, in the classic style of Hebrew poetry, is evocative through both literal meaning and the arrangement of sounds and rhythms.

Moreover, these public rituals give religious expression to the basic civic equality of all Jews in the sense that all are *yihidim* (literally, individuals—the Sephardic word for citizens of congregational communities) who must play their role to make the service work. There is no single prayer leader, but rather different leaders for different portions who emerge from the congregation. The entire congregation participates fully each step of the way. Every participant must have at least a minimal mastery of the words and the music, which can be acquired with little difficulty through experience.

This aesthetic reaches its highest form in rituals and services where the separate Jewish communities have been able to embroider on a common ritual core. Such is the case of the Musaph service for Rosh Hashanah, of the evening service for the fast of the ninth of Av commemorating the destruction of both Temples (and the exile of the Jews from Spain), and also of the Kol Nidre service for Yom Kippur. Drawing on the works of the great Hebrew poets of medieval Spain, as well as on ancient melodies whose origins are probably from the same period, such services achieve an astounding aesthetic completeness, which those familiar only with Ashkenazic worship would never associate with Judaism.

Obviously, the two rituals—Sephardic and Ashkenazic—cannot be merged in practice without one or the other suffering serious loss. The issue is not a matter of harmonizing minor textual differences. That is why the so-called unified *siddur*, prepared for use in the Israeli Defense Forces by Rabbi Shlomo Goren when he was chief chaplain, is discriminatory and aesthetically deficient. His *siddur* is essentially the *Nusakh Sephard*, derived from the kabbalists of Safed, which reached the Ashkenazim of the Ottoman Empire early in the seventeenth century and was accepted by the Hassidim a century later. Its form is partially Sephardic, but its style is distinctly Ashkenazic.

This matter of form carries over into every aspect of ritual behavior. The emphasis on aesthetics, on harmonious expression, and on *hiddur mitzvah* (the aesthetic elevation of ritual behavior) leads to an aesthetic as well as a religious objection to rushing through a religious ceremony simply to get it done. For Sephardim, it is better to do less but do it well.

Simplicity

Simplicity is the second element of classicism. It might be argued that Sephardic thought is an exercise in classical simplicity, particularly as compared to Ashkenazic with its emphasis on *pilpul* (exposition of classic texts through intricate and convoluted interpretation). Heschel says as much:

> The Sephardim were unsurpassed masters at systematizing, collating, and codifying the scattered, multiplex wealth of Jewish lore . . . for the Ashkenazim it was not the final decision that was important, but the steps of the syllogism read pilpul whereby it was arrived at.

Among Sephardim, simplicity is particularly expressed in literary and intellectual activity, in the search for clarity of style and expression. It is no accident that the great Hebrew grammarians were Sephardim. Explaining the rules in a clear way that enhanced style as such was central to their search for expression. Even the emphasis on codification of laws, a particularly Sephardic phenomenon, is part of this search for simplicity and clarity.

In dealing with complex ideas, a major dimension of simplicity is system and logical structure, a characteristic of Sephardic works that Heschel notes. He is mistaken, however, in assuming that Sephardim lack the ability to engage in flights of fancy. Such flights for the Sephardim simply remain disciplined, no matter how lyrical or mystical they are. Traditional Ashkenazic thought, like Ashkenazic prayer, seems undisciplined to the Sephardim, more interested in exacerbating complexity than in ordering it.

Proportion

Proportion is the third element of classicism. Heschel comments on how the Sephardim seek proportion in whatever they do, and implicitly dismisses this as an emphasis on externals or as a lack of full commitment. In fact, Sephardim are noted for and pride themselves on being less fanatic than Ashkenazim in virtually all matters, especially religion. Sephardim are often bewildered by the Ashkenazic pursuit of *humrot* (difficult *halakhic* refinements), because they have traditionally sought to balance the requirements of observance with those of living in order to achieve a form of religious expression that takes into consideration the whole human being, to encourage and cultivate the range of human attributes.

Sephardim have also sought to balance their lives both as Jews and as a part of a larger human society. Ammiel Alcalay, a young Sephardic scholar now compiling an anthology on Sephardic civilization from its earliest days, describes Sephardic culture when it was at its height:

> Rabbis were poets, poets were doctors, judges were diplomats, mathematicians were mystics and all were grammarians—the typical curriculum fell into a program divided more or less as follows: Reading and Writing, Torah, Mishna and Hebrew Grammar, Poetry, Talmud, Theology, Philosophy, Logic, Mathematics and Arithmetic, Geometry, Optics, Astronomy, Music, Mechanics, Natural Sciences and Medicine.*

Isolation was not a Sephardic goal—that would have been a violation of proportion and balance. Rather, they sought to accept involvement with the larger world and its challenges. In his magnum opus, *A Mediterranean Society*, based on the manuscripts of the Cairo Geniza (the traditional storehouse for old Hebrew manuscripts of all kinds), S. D. Goitein, the great scholar of the medieval Sephardic world, writes:

> . . . as we know from Geniza documents coming from Fustat, Cairo, Alexandria, al-Malhalla and other places in Egypt, from Kairouan, Jerusalem, Damascus and Aleppo, Jewish houses often bordered on those of Muslims or Christians or both.

* From Ammiel Alcalay's unpublished lectures on the Sephardic heritage.

There was no ghetto but, on the contrary, much opportunity for daily intercourse. Neither was there an occupational ghetto. I have counted so far about 360 occupations of Jews, of which 240 entailed some type of manual work. There was constant cooperation between the various religious groups to the point of partnership in business and even in workshops. In order to assess correctly the admissibility of the Geniza records for general sociological research, we have to free ourselves entirely from familiar notions about European Jews. . . .

. . . during the "middle" Middle Ages, around 1050, the unity of the Mediterranean world was still a fact. This is all the more remarkable since the European shore of the Mediterranean, including Spain, as well as the African and Asian sides, were split up into many separate units, often at war with one another. However, despite the many frontiers and the frequent wars, people and goods, books and ideas travelled freely from one side of the Mediterranean to the other.

It is difficult for Sephardim to understand the isolationist trend that is dominant among so many Ashkenazim who have not broken away from their heritage, who see the salvation of Judaism only in separating it from those who do not meet the current religious standards, which seem to be always moving to the right. Sephardim see no hope or virtue in isolation; to them, the result is a warping of Jews and a distortion of Judaism.

Sephardic music also reflects the orientation toward balance and proportion. In its classic Iberian form, the links between Sephardic music and Western classical music at its most classical—Bach and Beethoven, Handel and Haydn—are clear. But even in its classic Arabic form, it is balanced and contrapuntal.

The Sephardic method of study is another reflection of balance and proportion. The curriculum of Sephardic schools was always broad, combining *limudei kodesh* (study of sacred texts) with *limudei khol* (general studies), open to the arts and sciences, disciplines beyond those emphasized by the sacred texts. Study was disciplined, analytical, and integrative. Unlike the Ashkenazim, the Sephardim placed great emphasis on the biblical text as the starting point for studying the classic works. In our time, however, when the Sephardic *yeshivot* have been "Ashkenazified," this tradition has been lost.

The classical way seeks to encompass the whole; that, indeed, is part of the concern with form and proportion. Once aware of what exists in the world, the classical approach must be prepared to cope with each part of it. Greek classicism is taken as the model for the classical tradition for that very reason. Jewish classicism is also concerned with the whole, but in a Jewish way and starting from a different first principle. The

Sephardic interest in the arts and sciences in addition to the study of holy texts, in politics and large-scale commerce and not only in the narrow cultivation of religious observance—these are all aspects of the Sephardic concern for the whole.

Restrained Emotion

The fourth element of the classical mode is restrained emotion. Jews are an emotional people. Within that context, the Sephardic way can be said to attempt to restrain Jewish emotionalism through harnessing and channeling it, that is, restraining it within the limits of possibility.

Under stressful conditions, some people from certain of the Sephardic communities seem to react with emotional outbursts. Hence, it may seem difficult to link this element of restrained emotion with the Sephardic way. But those who study them soon discover how well organized these outbursts generally are, how closely they follow the rules, and how confined they are to specific circumstances. It is only with the breakdown of the Sephardic way, when they are no longer embedded in the cultural matrix that restrains them, that such forms of emotional expression become outbursts.

Romantic and Classical Interactions

The foregoing is not to suggest that romanticism utterly rejects form, simplicity, proportion, and restrained emotion; for the romantic, however, they are not significant in and of themselves. At most, these elements are tools to achieve other, more desired forms of expression. For romantics, all these elements should not stand in the way of expressive commitment in the pursuit of the absolute.

This Ashkenazic tendency is expressed in a variety of ways, including, on the right, religious orthodoxy that rejects compromise with the outside world, and, on the left, a romantic embrace of revolutionary movements. Sephardim have been notably absent from both of these extremes. Significantly, where westernized Ashkenazim have sought to be decorous in imitation of their non-Jewish neighbors, as in the cases of the Breuer Orthodox community of German Jews or American Conservative and Reform Jews, they have introduced decorum in an exacerbated form—in other words, in a romantic pursuit of a classical mode. Conversely, when some younger Conservative Jews tried to relax the cold decorum of their parents' generation, it led to neoromantic anarchy. Ironically, one of the most precisely decorous Jewish worship services in the world is that of Shearith Israel in New York City, the Spanish and Portuguese congregation, which was taken over in the nineteenth century by German Jews who introduced German formalism into the tradition of Sephardic classicism.

The suggestion that the Sephardic way is classical and the Ashkenazic way is romantic does not mean that all Sephardim live according to the canons of classicism or that all Ashkenazim live according to those of romanticism. We are talking about ways of life more or less shared by those born or acculturated into them. Indeed, it is more a matter of acculturation than birth. Throughout the history of the Jewish people, since these two ways of life were formed, Jews from one world have frequently been integrated into the other. This continues to be the case. At the present time, the movement is more in the direction of turning Sephardim into galvanized Ashkenazim—to everyone's loss. But even so, the opposite does occur.

What of the Future?

In 1986, the government of Spain recognized the State of Israel, just six years short of the five-hundredth anniversary of the expulsion of the Jews from that country. The response in Israel and the Jewish world was thrilling. Ashkenazim and Sephardim alike treated the act as more than the mere decision to exchange ambassadors, seeing it as the completion of a historical cycle. There was little, if any, difference in the reaction of the two groups, any more than there is in the reaction of Sephardim and Ashkenazim to the Holocaust. In both cases, it is the unity of the Jewish people that is important, not their internal divisions. Still, it is a complex unity, and the intertwining of its classical and romantic dimensions represents part of that complexity.

The impact of modernism first necessitated the reconstitution of the Jewish people, and now it necessitates the reconstruction of both the classical and romantic modes of Jewish expression. Whereas the Ashkenazim have largely succeeded in reconstructing much of their mode to meet the new circumstances of the Jewish situation, their dominant position in the Jewish world has generally overwhelmed Sephardic efforts to do the same. This may stem from a lack of understanding or, more likely, from an uncritical commitment to their own ways that keeps Ashkenazim from understanding any other. This is evident when Lubavitcher Hassidim try to change Moroccan Jews into Yiddish-speaking Habadniks, or when Israel's Socialist Zionists try to transform Sephardic *olim* into Russian-style *halutzim*, or when Israel's state religious schools and Bnei Akiva *yeshivot* force Ashkenazic ways of prayer and learning on an overwhelmingly Sephardic student population. Many other examples of this phenomenon could be cited—all should be corrected.

But Sephardim are also to blame for the situation. Too many have been complacent cooperators in their own cultural dissolution, rather than learning, as the Ashkenazim did, the art of rebuilding a heritage after the disruptions of modernization. They must undertake the task; no one else will do it for them.

In all likelihood, we are living through the last generations in which the division between Ashkenazim and Sephardim will play a central role in Jewish life. After a millennium, its time has passed, and that should not necessarily be a matter of sorrow. In the long span of Jewish history, various divisions that have come into existence in response to different times have served their purpose and then faded out, to be replaced by others.

This particular division was a product of the historical circumstances of Jewish exile, after the Jewish people moved out of the confines of the ancient world, particularly its western Asian base, to relocate, principally in Europe and North Africa. With the shift of the centers of Jewish settlement away from those areas, and the reestablishment of a Jewish state, the original reasons for the division no longer exist. Today, the problem for the Jewish people is effectively to manage the transition through whatever new distinctions are emerging. Central to that management is ensuring that the romantic mode of Jewish expression does not suppress the classical, but that the two flourish side by side, recombining in the new era initiated by the restoration of Jewish statehood. This coincides with the immediate needs of the Sephardim in Israel for equality with the Ashkenazim, but it is not merely a call for integration on the basis of equality. We are not speaking of assimilation with honor into a Russian, Ashkenazic Israel, but of the creation of a new culture in which Sephardic ways play a major—even decisive—role.

Chapter 2

Israel's New Sephardic Majority

DURING THE SUMMER OF 1987, the fate of the Israeli economy rested in the hands of two men—Moshe Nissim, the finance minister in the National Unity government, and Yisrael Kessar, secretary-general of the Histadrut (Israel's General Labor Confederation, which embraces 90 percent of all union members in the country). The two were responsible for negotiating a wage-price agreement that would determine the immediate economic future of Israel.

Nissim was born in Jerusalem in 1935 of Iraqi parentage and is the son of the late *Rishon Le-Zion* (Sephardic chief rabbi of Israel) Yitzhak Nissim. Trained as a lawyer (with a degree from the Hebrew University), he became a leader in the Liberal party, a role he continued to play when Herut and the Liberals joined to form the Likud. Extremely successful as the minister of justice, he most enjoyed being involved as a lawyer's lawyer.

When fellow Liberal Yitzhak Modai was forced to resign in April 1986 as a result of a severe conflict with Prime Minister Shimon Peres, the Likud forced Nissim to accept the vacated finance post as a compromise candidate. He did so with great reluctance, much preferring the Ministry of Justice, and it was generally expected that he would not retain the post for long. Instead, Nissim's intelligence, good humor, and—so rare for Israeli politicians—ability to keep quiet and say only what has to be said made him a rapid success. He won the confidence of the ministry's staff and became a strong and successful defender of the public fiscal policy. By the spring of 1987, public opinion polls showed him to be the most popular member of the Israeli cabinet, a rarity for a finance minister in any government.

A religiously observant Jew, Nissim regularly attends the small synagogue established as part of a *yeshiva* by his father and now continued in his memory. Yad HaRav Nissim is a typically Sephardic institution that is trying to bridge the gap between the pressures of ultra-Orthodoxy in the Ashkenazic *yeshiva* world and the desire among Sephardim to maintain their own tradition of combining general and religious studies to produce well-rounded rabbis, a cause to which Nissim is personally devoted.

Yisrael Kessar was born in 1931 in Sanaa, Yemen, and brought to Jerusalem as a child. He studied at the Mizrachi Teachers Seminary and earned a degree in economics and sociology at the Hebrew University, later acquiring an M.A. in Labor Studies at Tel Aviv University. He rose through the ranks of the Histadrut to become the first non-Ashkenazic secretary-general in 1984. That same year he entered the Knesset as a member of the Labor Alignment list.

Kessar, who is married with two children and lives in Holon, is a new breed of Histadrut leader—quiet, without bluster, at home in Jewish tradition in the way of the Sephardim. He is a man who conducts negotiations in soft rather than strident tones.

If they have done nothing else together, Nissim and Kessar have substantially lowered the decibel level of political confrontation in Israel. Both avoided the intense antagonism that major negotiations normally produce, reaching agreement over the wage settlements that will determine the conditions of most of Israel's labor force for the near future, as well as the concomitant price and working condition policies to be supported by the government.

The New Demographics

At about the time of the Six Day War (1967), Sephardic Jews in Israel came to outnumber the Ashkenazim for the first time since the balance had shifted from Sephardim to Ashkenazim a century earlier (see table

2.1). This shift reflects the considerably higher birthrate among Sephardim. Since 1967, although the birthrate gap has narrowed considerably, the percentage of Sephardim has steadily increased. The trend is most visible in the elementary schools, where some two-thirds of the students are now Sephardic.

Demographics tell the story: First- or second-generation Israelis of Ashkenazic background are in the majority among fifty-five- to seventy-four-year-olds, while the Sephardim are in the majority among five- to twenty-nine-year-olds. Under the age of five, the data as collected by the Central Bureau of Statistics do not reveal the child's family's country of origin, but it can be assumed that by now most third-generation Israelis under the age of five are also of Sephardic background (see table 2.2).

TABLE 2.1

Jewish Population in Israel by Place of Birth[a]

	1985	1984	1983	1972	1961	1948
Asia						
born	747.8	748.1	740.3	655.9	818.3[c]	57.8
stock[b]	460.0	456.4	443.1	339.8	288.5[c]	—
Africa						
born	775.3	767.1	736.1	617.9	818.3[d]	12.2
stock[b]	445.1	435.1	413.3	269.1	288.5[d]	—
Europe/America						
born	1,343.7	1,348.7	1,339.7	1,187.0	1,007.1	39.3
stock[b]	568.0	559.8	537.7	437.6	335.0	—
Israel						
born	650.5	607.8	533.9	225.8	106.9	253.7
stock[b]	650.5	607.8	533.9	225.8	106.9	—

[a] Figures (given in hundreds) are not exact. The classification used in the Israeli census is: European/American born, including Sephardic Jews of the Balkans, southern Europe, and elsewhere; Asian/African born; and Israeli born (after the second generation, statistics do not identify individuals by ancestry).

[b] Father's country of origin.

[c] Includes Africa.

[d] Includes Asia.

SOURCE: Compiled from data supplied by the Israeli Central Bureau of Statistics (1986).

TABLE 2.2
Jewish Population in Israel by Age and Place of Birth[a]

Age group		Asia/Africa	Europe/America	Israel
0–19	born	29.2	63.1	804.9
	stock[b]	562.1	243.2	365.5
	total	591.3	306.3	1,170.4
20–39	born	226.2	185.2	485.3
	stock[b]	249.6	235.6	65.1
	total	475.8	420.8	550.4
40–59	born	240.1	253.7	68.6
	stock[b]	20.1	46.6	18.8
	total	260.1	300.3	87.4
60–79	born	99.5	274.3	16.0
	stock[b]	3.3	5.6	9.8
	total	102.8	279.9	25.8
80+	born	11.9	31.1	0.9
	stock[b]	0.3	0.6	0.6
	total	12.2	31.7	1.5

[a] Figures in hundreds; see also footnote *a*, table 2.1.
[b] Father's country of origin.

SOURCE: Compiled from data supplied by the Israeli Central Bureau of Statistics (1980).

The Turning Point

In the mid-1970s, with the beginning of the second historical generation of Israeli statehood, a turning point occurred in relations between Sephardim and Ashkenazim. This turning point was much like the one that occurred in the passage from the middle to the last generation of the nineteenth century one hundred years earlier. At that time, the Sephardim began to lose their hegemony to the Ashkenazim, just as the reverse is now beginning to occur. And just as the last generation of the nineteenth century was involved in a cultural-political struggle between the two groups, so, too, is the last generation of the twentieth.

For roughly six centuries—from 1268, when Ramban (Nahmanides) reestablished the Jewish community in Jerusalem, to the 1860s, when the Ashkenazic *kollelim* (communities organized around *yeshiva* scholars) gained de facto and even de jure recognition as separate communities outside the hegemony of the Va'ad HaEdah HaSepharadit (Council of the Sephardic Community)—the hegemony of the Sephardim in Israel went virtually unchallenged. Actually, except for the generation and a half following the immigration of "300 French and English rabbis" who entered the land in the Jewish year 4971 (1210–11 C.E.) and settled in Akko to help restore Jewish life after the destruction wrought by the Crusades, there was never a time when Eretz Israel was not under the control of the Sephardim or, before the eleventh century, their ancestors in the region.

Goitein describes how, in the period from the ninth through the thirteenth centuries, Eretz Israel played a central role in the Sephardic diaspora. Since it was possible to travel freely throughout the region, many families maintained two or three homes, including one in Eretz Israel. Thus, thousands of Sephardim were constantly stopping over in Eretz Israel on their way from North Africa to the Far East or from Baghdad, Aleppo, and Damascus to Egypt. These travelers included women as well as men. (Women held substantial status in the Sephardic world at that time. At the age of twelve and a half, a Jewish girl was considered a *bogeret l'reshut nafsha*—an adult with authority over her own soul—and was legally free to marry whomever she wanted. Women represented themselves in court on all matters concerning marriage and personal status.) In the tenth century, some Muslims could still complain that Jews and Christians had the upper hand in Jerusalem. In contrast to the freedom of the Sephardim, Ashkenazim in the late eighteenth and early nineteenth centuries could not openly settle in much of the country, running the risk of arrest, imprisonment, expulsion, and even death from the Ottoman authorities because of debts incurred by earlier immigrants.

The demographic situation in Eretz Israel was about the same as that in the Jewish world as a whole. Following Arthur Ruppin's calculations, in the eleventh century Sephardim represented nearly 94 percent of world Jewry and Ashkenazim less than 7 percent. By 1300, when the Sephardim regained their hegemony in Eretz Israel, they represented 85 percent of an estimated 2 million Jews in the world.

This picture slowly shifted. In 1650, at the beginning of the modern epoch, Sephardim represented 60 percent of the world's 1.75 million Jews. By 1700, the two groups were roughly equal in size, with 1 million each. This rough equality was preserved between the two groups throughout the eighteenth century, but in the nineteenth century improved conditions in Europe led to a population explosion among the Ashkenazim, which swelled their numbers and their percentage of the total Jewish population. In 1800, the Sephardim made up 40 percent of the 2.5 million Jews in the world, which meant that their number had not grown at all in the intervening century, whereas the number of Ashkenazim had increased by 50 percent. In 1840, when Ashkenazim began to settle in Israel again, the number of Sephardim had fallen to 900,000 and the number of Ashkenazim had grown to 3.6 million, making up 80 percent of the 4.5 million Jews estimated in the world at the time. In 1860, when Sephardic hegemony was broken, the percentages were almost the reverse of those in 1300, with 86 percent of the population Ashkenazim and 13.4 percent Sephardim. The Ashkenazic percentage of the world Jewish population passed the 90 percent mark in 1900 and reached its peak in 1930, at 91.8 percent of 15.9 million Jews.

Israel and the Labor Party

It was only after the British conquest during World War I and the establishment of mandatory Palestine that power passed into the hands of the predominantly Ashkenazic Zionist movement, and within the movement, to the Socialist Zionists, or the Labor camp. After the Labor victory in the late 1920s, the Sephardim tended to withdraw from politics, feeling they could not compete with what was essentially a Labor monopoly. Even the old Sephardic families who were rooted in the land and had dominated the old *yishuv* disengaged themselves from public affairs.

When the new Sephardic immigrants arrived after the establishment of the state in 1948, they had to undergo a settling-in period before they could attempt to compete in this highly organized political arena. Even so, by the late 1950s, they had begun to assume leading positions in the local governments of the development towns and rural settlements, where they formed the majority. Often they had to battle Mapai (the dominant political party in the state) "carpetbaggers" for those posts, who had been sent by the central party headquarters. By 1968, Sephardim were represented in local government roughly in proportion to their share of the total population, although Sephardic officeholders were principally confined to the development towns and rural settlements rather than the older, established communities. In less than a generation, they had achieved a political base and a jumping-off point for what, in the last few years, has become a major move into state politics.

During this period, Mapai, and its succeeding Labor party, made a major error in judgment. Although party leadership sooner or later began to encourage Sephardic officeholders in the local arena, recognizing that they had no other choice, they discouraged Sephardim from advancing beyond that, except for a few token Sephardim chosen by the established power holders. It is true that more Sephardim began to appear on the Labor lists in the beginning of the 1960s, but these people were essentially without independent political power and relied on the party hierarchy for their offices. As younger people sought places within the Labor party organization, they were directly or indirectly discouraged. Most of the bright, young Sephardic Knesset members in the Herut party today were originally rejected by the Labor party. Herut, being an opposition party with a weak local base, welcomed these Sephardim and gave them the opportunity for political careers, thereby forming a cadre that is now beginning to gain power and that will soon play a major role in the government of Israel.

In the meantime, the Labor establishment was getting tired, as all establishments do, and even a bit corrupted by power, in the way of the world. Moreover, it was making enemies, as every ruling establishment must in due course. Beginning with the 1965 elections, there were defections from Labor's ranks, both in the form of unsuccessful splinter parties within the Labor camp itself and, more important in the long run, in the tendency for younger Israelis, new to the political process, to vote Herut (then called Gahal, the original Herut-Liberal alignment) and later Likud. Today, voters under the age of forty-five, Ashkenazim as well as Sephardim, are more likely to vote Likud than Labor.

At the same time, the Sephardim began to gravitate to the Likud for their own reasons. In part, the Likud offered the opportunity for younger politicians to get ahead. For the rank-and-file voters, the switch represented an accumulation of resentments that could be acted on once they became affluent enough. Whereas, according to Asher Arian, "ethnic" voting has always been a factor in Israeli elections, it became more so after 1965. Throughout the 1960s, both the Likud and Labor blocs were predominantly Ashkenazic. In 1977, for the first time a majority of the votes for the Likud came from Sephardim.

The new generation of better-educated Sephardim felt that the Labor party had excluded them from the political process for twenty-nine years. They sought access to power and resources, and saw a vote for Likud as a means to gain them. In addition, their experiences in local politics led them to reject Labor and its centrist policies. These young leaders saw the importance of decentralization in the advancement of the agendas of the development towns in which they were raised.

For rank-and-file voters, other issues motivated the shift to Likud in the 1970s and 1980s, some of them listed below:

The socioeconomic gap between Ashkenazim and Sephardim remained substantially unchanged between 1949 and 1969, despite the fact that the incomes of both groups more than doubled.

In 1981, three times as many Israeli-born Ashkenazim occupied professional, academic, or managerial positions than Israeli-born Sephardim, who constituted 34.7 percent of the blue collar workforce, against 14 percent for Israeli-born Ashkenazim.

In 1975, the per capita income of Ashkenazim was twice that of Sephardim. Family income of Sephardim ranged between 57 and 82 percent of Ashkenazic family income.

Sephardim constituted majorities in vocational schools; Ashkenazim concentrated in academic schools. On average, Ashkenazic children had three years more schooling than Sephardic children, and only one Sephardic student out of six received a matriculation certificate to enter the universities, where they made up 17.1 percent of the student body.

In 1975, 2 percent of foreign-born Sephardim were found in academic and scientific occupations compared to 13 percent among foreign-born Ashkenazim. In high status occupations, there were twice as many Ashkenazim as Sephardim; in less rewarding jobs the ratio was reversed. In construction, agriculture, and industry, Sephardim were overrepresented in the lower ranks and held mainly menial and temporary jobs.

Most Sephardim lived in government housing that was inferior to the private or Histadrut housing sold largely to Ashkenazim. Small apartments and large families characterized Sephardic neighborhoods; larger apartments and smaller families, the Ashkenazic neighborhoods. This de facto housing segregation had repercussions in the school system. Schools in Ashkenazic neighborhoods had generally better facilities and better-trained teachers.

According to Sammy Smooha:

The 29 years of Labor's rule were characterized by condescension, paternalism, and cooptation, and very little by cooperation, participation, or partnership in nation-building. The process of absorption was in the main "passive." Oriental immigrants "were airlifted or shipped, housed, educated and medicated by government representatives of the veteran European Jews who planned and managed their lives." This created a cycle of dependence and resentment on the part of the Orientals, a pattern from which they have been trying to break away. As they become more educated, more socialized in the game of politics, they become aware of electoral power as the primary means for satisfying their needs and asserting their independence.

Israel's New Sephardic Majority

Once the struggle of a sufficient number of Sephardim to achieve a solid economic base was completed, they could turn their attention to social and political issues. They did not forget the way they had been treated by Labor—whether it was the way in which the people who had received them in Israel had tried to secularize them, to remake a people with traditional leanings into followers of Socialist Zionism, or whether it was the way they tried to convince them to work in the fields instead of continuing their education, or whether it was the way their culture and habits were misunderstood by people from different backgrounds, giving them difficulties far beyond the mere facts of dislocation.

The Sephardim in the 1950s were incapable of resisting Labor pressures, or even of understanding them sufficiently to distinguish between what was real, such as the necessity to settle the country's open spaces, and what was not, such as the claim that only Socialist Zionism was the right way to express Jewish ideals and achieve modernization. Two decades later, once Labor had lost its special idealism and was simply a party like others pursuing political office, its hold on the Sephardim collapsed. This was especially true for the younger generation, which had not grown accustomed to thinking of Labor as the only legitimate ruler.

In a more positive vein, Menachem Begin appealed to the Sephardim as one outsider to others. He and the Herut party, which he had led for nearly thirty years, had been rejected by the Labor establishment as beyond the political pale—with many Labor ideologists even viewing them as fascists. He could therefore empathize with the need of the Sephardim for self-respect and embody their sense of Jewishness, as well as understand the necessity for that Jewishness to find expression in the Jewish state. So, as Sephardim became alienated from Labor, they were attracted to the Likud.

Labor's response at first was to ignore Sephardic grievances, assuming that the Sephardim could be kept in line. But, after Begin's upset victory in 1977, Labor reacted with a policy that insulted the Sephardim at home as Oz and Avineri did abroad. They all publicly denigrated the Sephardim as a group. It is not surprising, then, that Sephardic alienation turned to intense dislike of a party that acted as the only legitimate governing body and implied that anyone who did not recognize it as such was somehow deficient. The more the Labor party talked about the "good old Socialist days," the more it repudiated any religious expression of Judaism, the more its extreme elements gave vent to feelings about Sephardic "punks and bums," and the more angry the by then politically sophisticated Sephardic population grew.

The 1981 elections reflected this situation. By then it was not so much love for Begin, who was recognized for the Ashkenazi that he is, that resulted in his victory, but a sense that he could be counted on to offer opportunities to Sephardim since it was in his political interest to do so. Moreover, in the interim, Sephardim had come to constitute some two-thirds of the Herut party membership.

Growth and Political Awareness

The Sephardim began to regain ground in demographic terms before the Holocaust, and despite their own losses to the Nazi murder machine, they gained even more as a result of the Nazi destruction of Ashkenazic Europe. The Sephardim continued to gain as a result of their emigration from the Islamic countries to Israel, Western Europe, and the New World, where improved conditions lowered their mortality rate. In 1970, it was estimated that 16.4 percent of the world's 14 million Jews were Sephardim, and 83.6 percent Ashkenazim. That ratio has continued to change in favor of the Sephardim. By 1984, 20 percent of the world Jewish population was said to be Sephardic (see table 2.3), and that figure does not include Sephardim in Israel who are of European origin. More to the point, the Sephardim have become a majority in Israel. Hence, they are potentially the dominant group in the Jewish world.

As already noted, Israel faces the future with a Sephardic majority. The Jews of the United States, the world's largest Jewish community and the only counterbalance to Israel on the world Jewish scene, are overwhelmingly (approximately 97 percent) Ashkenazic (the ratio of Sephardim to Ashkenazim in the United States is roughly the ratio of Jews to the total U.S. population). In the Soviet Union, the world's third largest Jewish community remains principally Ashkenazic, but it does not function effectively as a community, whereas France, the fourth largest community, has also acquired a Sephardic majority since the 1960s, one that is growing ever more articulate in the expression of its Jewishness and its Sephardic heritage.

Given the trends, it is not surprising that the Sephardim have emerged once again on the world Jewish scene. The World Sephardi Federation,

TABLE 2.3
Estimated Total Jewish and Sephardic Populations by Major Geographical Regions (1984)

	Total Jewish[a]		Sephardic[b]		
Region	Thousands	Percent	Thousands	Percent	Per 100 Jews
United States and Canada	6,017	46.4	220	8.5	4
Latin America	454	3.5	50	1.9	11
France	530	4.1	300	11.5	57
Western Europe, excluding France	519	4.0	50	1.9	10
Eastern Europe and Balkans[c]	1,710	13.2	120	4.6	7
Asia, excluding Israel	37	0.3	35	1.4	95
North Africa	17	0.1	17	0.7	100
Africa, excluding North Africa	131	1.0	5[d]	0.2	4
Oceania	79	0.6	3	0.1	4
Diaspora total	9,494	73.2	800	30.8	8
Israel	3,472	26.8	1,800	69.2	52
World total	12,966	100.0	2,600	100.0	20

[a] See U. O. Schmelz and S. DellaPergola, "World Jewish Population, 1984," *American Jewish Year Book* 86 (1986).
[b] According to a rather comprehensive but not entirely homogeneous definition. The estimate for Israel refers to all Jews of Asian or African origin; other estimates may also include Jews of Balkan origin.
[c] Asian territories of the U.S.S.R. and Turkey included.
[d] Ethiopia's Jews not included.

SOURCE: Institute for Contemporary Jewry, Hebrew University; prepared by S. DellaPergola.

with its links to the World Zionist Organization and the World Jewish Congress, is one example of this phenomenon. Another is the new Sephardic political and intellectual militancy in France, noted above. Yet another is found among the Sephardim of Latin America, where they are seeking to play a role in formerly all-Ashkenazic community organizations. Finally, the Sephardic reawakening in North America has brought them attention far out of proportion to their numbers.

Reaction to the Beirut Massacre

What is truly characteristic of the Jews of Israel, regardless of background, is how alike they are. Studies show that Jews are more alike genetically than anyone had hitherto believed—the result of centuries of endogamy. In any case, genetic similarities and differences that do exist among the Jewish people are not along Ashkenazic-Sephardic lines. Moreover, Jews continue to be much alike in their moral standards and sensibilities. One dramatic illustration tells much: The shocked response to the Christian massacre of Palestinians in the Beirut refugee camps, in September 1982, was equally spread throughout the entire population of Israel. With the first news of the massacre, a strong feeling swept the country (best articulated by President Yitzhak Navon, who had become the premier exponent of Israel's humanist values) that a full investigation had to be conducted to learn the whole truth.

Undoubtedly, some Israelis reacted to the massacre more strongly than others, but this was not a matter of Sephardic and Ashkenazic differences. My own extensive contacts and conversations within the Sephardic community during the period immediately following the massacre convinced me of this beyond any shadow of a doubt. My perception was subsequently confirmed by the public opinion polls. In fact, the people whom I met who were least concerned were a group of Israelis originally from the English-speaking countries—presumably the most "Western" of all.

Some noted, however, that there were few Sephardim at the massive demonstration in Tel Aviv where several hundred thousand Jews gathered a week after the massacre to protest government "stonewalling" of an adequate investigation.* This is true, but the reasons have less to do with humanitarian feelings than politics; many Sephardim would not participate in the rally, despite strong feelings with regard to the massacre and the government's response, because they looked on it as a Peace Now–Labor Alignment affair.

Sephardim regarded participation in the rally as identifying politically with a group that most of them strongly oppose. Any politically aware Israeli understood beforehand that as soon as Labor party leaders were designated as the principal speakers at the rally, it would become something more than a call for an investigation and would, instead, become a call for ousting the Begin government, as indeed it was. More than that, Shimon Peres, in what even his supporters later agreed was probably a serious mistake, used the opportunity to call for public commitment to

*Just how many Sephardim attended is unknown—the very assumption that every Sephardi, or at least most, can be recognized by skin color or features is an interesting bit of crypto-racism that is not borne out in reality. Israel does not have a white-black division, except where Ethiopian Jews are concerned, although some Ashkenazim like to use that terminology in private conversation— more semantic bias.

the Labor party position with regard to the future of Judea, Samaria, and Gaza, a matter that had nothing to do with the immediate issue—calling for a proper investigation into what happened in Sabra and Shatilla—and about which Israelis are divided.

A more important indicator of where the Sephardim stood on the massacre was the fact that within the government itself, Sephardim took the lead, along with the National Religious Party (NRP) ministers, in forcing a change in the initial Begin-Sharon position—that only an internal investigation need be conducted. The Sephardim were led by David Levy, a Moroccan-born Herut stalwart, deputy prime minister, minister of Housing and Absorption, and one of the most powerful men in the Likud. (As recently as five years earlier, he had been an archetypal example of the "primitive" Moroccan in the minds of most Israelis.) He was joined by the minister of Labor and Social Welfare, Aharon Uzan (also of North African birth), the representative of the Tami party, which was at the time as close to a Sephardic party as existed in Israel and viewed by the Ashkenazim as the group that introduced "ethnic" divisiveness and "spoils" politics into the Israeli system for the first time. Indeed, the leaders of Tami, which was founded by Aharon Abuhatzeira and often viewed by the opposition as an expression of the worst in so-called Sephardic values, were vocal from the first. But perhaps the most thoughtful challenge to Begin's position came from Iraqi-born Mordecai Ben-Porat, heir to the leadership of Dayan's Telem party.

Although the public demonstration in Tel Aviv did much for Israel's image in the world and was important for virtually that reason alone, it was dismissed by Begin as an opposition ploy. However, the revolt within the cabinet put Begin and Sharon under severe pressure to take appropriate steps to investigate the massacre through a formal investigative commission with full powers. Although they were able to hold their coalition together in its Knesset test of September 23, 1982, it was only on the promise that within two weeks action would be taken. The promise was extracted by the NRP, Tami, and Ben-Porat as the price of their continued support.

Project Renewal

As the Sephardim become ever more vocal in their government, American Jews have begun to discover the similarity among all Jews, regardless of country of origin. This discovery is largely a result of their exposure to Sephardic Israel through Project Renewal, a massive effort on the part of the Israeli government and diaspora Jewry to rehabilitate the disadvantaged neighborhoods of Israel. American Jewish communities have been twinned with many of those neighborhoods, and American Jewish leaders have been taking an active role in their rehabilitation. In doing so, these mainly affluent Jews have come into contact for the first time not only with Sephardim but with the Jews in Israel who are presumably the lowest in socioeconomic status as well.

Some of the upper-echelon Jewish diaspora leaders, mostly wealthy, rapidly formed alliances with the people in the neighborhoods against the established bureaucracies in Israel that wanted to conduct business as usual. In the course of forging these alliances, they developed personal contacts which, while not necessarily ripening into personal friendships, certainly demonstrated to both sides that they had as much of a capacity to work together to achieve common goals as any other Jews, and that cultural differences other than those that generally separate Israeli and many diaspora Jews were not the problem. These alliances led to the neighborhood residents mobilizing influential diaspora partners to reach the upper echelons of the Jewish Agency (world Jewries' principal instrument for assisting in Israel's development) and the Israeli government to make their case.

The diaspora leadership had the satisfaction of developing personal contacts with ordinary Israelis beyond the standard United Jewish Appeal mission or the rarefied atmosphere of the Jewish Agency Assembly. In fact, so successful was this partnership that in many cases diaspora leaders who had been involved with Project Renewal had to be told that the people they were involved with were the same "Orientals" whom so many of their Ashkenazi brethren in Israel were criticizing as culturally backward and undemocratic. Of course, once confronted with this contradiction, they understood the real truth.

Studies of this encounter between Israelis and diaspora Jews in Project Renewal show how those involved found a common language, coming out of common Jewish attitudes, beliefs, and sensibilities. In some cases, diaspora Jews have begun to interpret the Sephardim to their Ashkenazic Israeli counterparts.

Sephardim in the Contemporary World

Where there are differences in the political and religious spheres, they often are to the credit of the Sephardim. The Sephardim are not among the militant, black-garbed Jews who throw stones at vehicles on the Sabbath and refuse to serve in the army. The Sephardim pride themselves on the fact that there has been no religious reformation in their world, that however individual Sephardim chose to practice their Judaism, they stayed within a common fold because they were not ideologically bound to make clear-cut divisions. In any Sephardic synagogue anywhere in the world, one can find a wide mix of worshippers and a wide range of patterns of religious observance.

The emergence (1983) of the Sephardic Torah Guardians (Shas) as a political party both confirms this and indicates how change is in the offing, and not necessarily for the better. Sephardim of all levels of religious observance voted for Shas in 1984 if they wished to vote for a Sephardic party. The ultra-Orthodox orientation (and garb) of its leaders did not put them off, especially since those leaders talked in the characteristically moderate Sephardic tones. Despite their own strict observance, they saw all Jews as reachable religiously—and reached out to them. The subsequent speech and behavior of Shas, however, have demonstrated how much some of them have acquired characteristics of Ashkenazic ultra-Orthodoxy and therefore alienated many of their erstwhile supporters.

Rightly or wrongly, Sephardim see themselves as less dominating and aggressive than the Ashkenazim, and they attribute their own perceived lack of advancement in Israeli society to that cultural difference. In the early days of the state, some Sephardim gave the impression of being more violent, which may be because they learned that they did not have to be submissive, as they had been under Arab rule; not having completely learned how to function in a moderate way in a democratic society, they sometimes reacted too strongly in a violent direction. By now that difference has almost completely disappeared.

Sephardim have been characterized as chauvinistic, militaristic, and xenophobic, although there is no evidence to support such claims. Meir Kahane's tiny band of followers—the only group in Israel that aptly fits such a description—mainly consists of immigrants from the United States. On the other hand, within the Begin government it was a Sephardi, David Levy, who was the voice of moderation throughout the Lebanon campaign.

Differences of Opportunity, Economics, and Tradition

Another set of differences between Sephardim and Ashkenazim relates to modernization. It is generally true, as noted earlier, that Jews of the northeast began the process of modernization before those of the southeast, but the differences that remain are mostly differences in equality of opportunity. Thus, the Ashkenazim, because they arrived before the Sephardim or could turn to relatives who had arrived earlier, advanced more rapidly up the economic ladder than did the Sephardim, most of whom arrived a little later and had virtually no personal links to the existing establishment. Although it is true that 90 percent of those living in disadvantaged neighborhoods today are Sephardim, only 30 percent of all Sephardim live in such neighborhoods. In other words, 70 percent of the Sephardic population is well integrated into Israeli society at all levels. This includes IDF Chief of Staff Moshe Levy, Histadrut Secretary-General Yisrael Kessar, and members of the Recanati family (principal owners of the Israel Discount Bank, which is one of the country's three largest), as well as storekeepers and professionals, university professors and taxi drivers.

Despite this level of integration, however, statistics show that most Sephardic children are in need of special educational assistance, but that is, in great part, a self-fulfilling prophecy since the definition of who needs such assistance includes the mere fact of Sephardic background. The fact that many Sephardim are undereducated can be attributed in some degree to their position in Israeli society in the early years after the mass immigration. Studies show that among Sephardic families that separated, some going to Europe or North America, others to Israel, those in Israel suffered educational deprivation, whereas those who went to the West became doctors, lawyers, and academics in the same proportions as other diaspora Jews. Native Sephardim whose families lived in Eretz Israel before World War II occupy the same socioeconomic positions as their Ashkenazi brethren.

One cause of Sephardic resentment toward the Labor party goes back to the days when the majority of Sephardim were still in immigrant camps, and social workers sent by Mapai or the government pressed them to leave school after the seventh grade to work in the fields and orchards. The social workers often had the best of motives; they sincerely believed in the Amos Oz type of Zionism, which held that Jews should become agriculturists. The fact that the same people who advocated the agricultural life for others were sending their own children to high schools and colleges reflects some of the absurdity of the human condition, but it was no laughing matter to the Sephardim, who were often relegated by these good intentions to the bottom of the economic pyramid.

A wider economic gap was created from a source that could not have been foreseen. Some ten years after the mass immigration that followed the establishment of the state, German reparations to Holocaust victims began to flow into Israel. The reparations, which directly benefited so many of the Ashkenazic Jews in Israel, came at a crucial point in the economic growth of these still relatively new immigrants. The Ashkenazim acquired these resources at an opportune time, helping to create an economic gap that still has social and political consequences.

The Sephardim in the main are not Socialists, but are middle class in orientation (as Jews historically are) and connected to Jewish tradition to greater or lesser degrees, creating a gap between them and Labor. The many secularists in the Labor camp, particularly the intellectuals among them, have given voice to the "two cultures" issue, setting up those expectations dominant among Western intellectuals as the criteria for modern Israel. But they represent a small if vocal minority in the country. To the extent that the Labor party has accepted their vision of an ideal Israel, it has alienated itself from a large number of voters, Ashkenazim as well as Sephardim, who have turned to the Likud.

The Sephardic Majority and What It Means

Cultural and Moral Implications

What are the cultural and moral implications of the emerging Sephardic majority for the future of Israel? It should be clear that, intellectually and socially, this demographic shift is not going to bring any loss of what is perceived in the West as the Jewish character of the state. Jews, both Ashkenazim and Sephardim, will still flock to the universities in great numbers and will support their cultural institutions. They will continue to share the same moral standards and to exhibit the same willingness to defend their country. There may be some changes, however, in the style of Israeli culture, as evidenced, for example, by the struggle between new Sephardic theater groups and the Israeli theatrical establishment, which has only been open to those sharing its particular left-liberal approach. Sephardic influences on music may become more pronounced, and, if the Ashkenazi-dominated religious establishment and the Ashkenazic secularists do not succeed in squelching Sephardic self-expression in that sphere, the Sephardic religious approach may also become more influential.

In general, there will be some refinements in Israeli society as the Sephardim become more dominant. Amos Oz's Socialists rejected certain dress, social graces, and manners as "bourgeois," and these have been reintroduced by Sephardim as much as by the bourgeois elements from Central Europe. The coming Israeli society will perhaps be less abrasive but no less keen as it loses some of its Eastern European flavor to the influence of the largely Mediterranean ways of the Sephardim.

Shortly after the founding of the state, it became fashionable to blame deviations from the Socialist ideal on "Levantinization" caused by the immigrants from the Arab world. The fact that during this period those immigrants were powerless did not keep them from becoming scapegoats in this way. Actually, deviations from the ideal patterns of Socialist Zionism were indigenous to the pioneers and their descendants, members of the Ashkenazic Socialist elite. That may be small comfort to those of us who look toward a continuously improving Israel, but it does put matters in the proper perspective. In short, the moral implications of the demographic shift in Israel are no more likely to be drastic than are the intellectual and social ones.

Ashkenazic intellectuals often say that the Sephardim are antidemocratic, or at least not prodemocratic. They cite the example of the chant "Begin, King of Israel," which was popular while Begin was prime minister. Aside from the fact that this chant, derived from a folk expression, was generally used by teenagers at Begin rallies, probably organized by the local branch of the Herut party, it did not represent anyone's political ideology even then. In fact, the leading antidemocrats in Israel are people such as Dr. Israel Eldad, a native of Poland, and Meir Kahane, who favors strong-arm rule, and certain members of the extreme Orthodox camp who look to the restoration of the Davidic monarchy when the Messiah comes.

Other stereotypes depict Sephardim as "hard-line," "nationalistic," "anti-Arab," and "antipeace." But studies such as one conducted by Professor Asher Arian of Tel Aviv University indicate that Ashkenazic-Sephardic differences are negligible in determining attitudes toward security and defense issues among Israeli voters. For example, the same percentage (57) of Ashkenazic and Sephardic voters favor greater emphasis on peace talks rather than shows of military strength. Twenty-six percent of both Ashkenazic and Sephardic voters support an Israeli military initiative aimed at strategically important areas. Virtually the same number of Ashkenazic voters (36 percent) and Sephardic voters (38 percent) support first use of nuclear weapons by Israel under certain circumstances. There seems no basis for the designation of hawkishness or ultranationalism associated with the Sephardim.

Both Ashkenazim and Sephardim share the same attitudes toward and expectations of democratic government. The Jews who gathered in Israel from all over the world brought with them the political cultural influences of their respective environments. Those from Eastern Europe and the Arab world, with few exceptions, had little or no experience with the idea of citizenship, whereas those who had been exposed to continental European politics arrived with Jacobin views of what a state should be.

But all Jews share a common Jewish political culture to a greater or lesser degree. That tradition has been republican since the earliest beginnings of the Jewish people, and often a democratic tradition at that. Jewish communities in the diaspora, no less than Jewish states in Eretz Israel, functioned along republican lines throughout the ages. With the exception of Herod, who reached the throne legitimately and then usurped power, backed by the Romans who controlled Judea, the Jewish people have never known autocratic rule.

The Jewish political tradition is founded in covenant. According to tradition, the ground rules of civilization were established in God's covenant with Noah (Genesis 9); then God and the Jewish people covenanted with each other to constitutionalize God's relationship with His people (see especially Exodus 19). Historically, the Jewish people have used covenants as necessary to establish or change their political organization.

Aside from the daring aspects of the covenant idea, which require God voluntarily to limit Himself—to withdraw and leave space for human activity in partnership with Him—thus making humans at least junior partners with Heaven, the covenant idea also emphasizes the basic equality of all people. Only those sharing a fundamental equality, at least in relation to the purposes of the pact, can enter into covenants with one another. The parties to the covenant retain their individual integrity and a share in their common governance. This is clear in all the great biblical covenants, from Abraham to Ezra and Nehemiah; to the medieval communal covenants that gave individual Jewish communities the authority to govern themselves under Jewish law; to the founding covenants of modern Zionism. The very act of founding the Jewish polity and subsequent communities within it required the assemblage of *all* Jews—men, women, and children—to participate in the covenant. Only if *all* consented was the act valid.

Another aspect of the Jewish polity is the division of power among three domains—*ketarim* (crowns) is the Hebrew term: *keter Torah*, the crown of Torah, the domain of prophets, sages, and rabbis through which God transmits His message to the Jewish people; *keter kehunah*, the crown of priesthood, the domain of priests, Levites, and synagogue officiants, through which the people initiate their communication with God; and *keter malkhut*, the crown of civil rule through which the people conduct their everyday business of self-government. These crowns are always present in varying degrees in every proper Jewish polity. Each is empowered directly by God according to tradition; hence, each is equally legitimate. Whereas they can contest among themselves for power, each must respect the existence and integrity of the others, ensuring that power will not be concentrated in the hands of any single person or even any single group, but rather will be divided and shared.

Thus, the Jewish political tradition emphasizes constitutionalism. The Torah, its constitution, is comprehensive in the manner of ancient constitutions, dealing with every aspect of life. Every Jew is to know the Torah just as those who rule in the Jewish polity are bound by its constitutional laws. Hence, Jewish political culture cannot be other than republican. Even its deviations tend to be oligarchic within a republican framework and to rest on a democratic base. That, indeed, is the secret of Israel's success as a democracy, and it is a secret shared by all Jews whatever their country of origin. The political culture of Israel has not yet taken full shape, but it will continue to be republican and democratic.

With regard to Arabs and Israel's future, there may be differences in attitude between Sephardim and Ashkenazim. Sephardim from Islamic lands are more at home with Arabic culture than the Ashkenazim, and therefore perhaps more realistic about Arab intentions. They are no more inclined to hate Arabs than to love them. Europeans tend to have less experience with, and therefore less understanding of, Arabic culture or the Arabs themselves.

This does not mean that all Sephardim or all Ashkenazim are of a single mind regarding Arabs. In both groups there is a full range of opinions, but the basis for arriving at them differs. Realistic Sephardic assessments of Arabs tend to negate extreme views in either direction. The few Sephardic extremists are generally young people who have already lost direct contact with Arab culture. Ashkenazim, because they have had less contact, are more apt to make either harsher or more charitable assessments of Arab intentions.

Sephardim from Arab lands enjoy Arab culture in ways that Ashkenazim cannot. The Ashkenazic rejection of the Eastern aesthetic has led to the development of a group of Sephardic intellectuals who seek their identity by emphasizing their connections with Arab culture. Oddly enough, however, schoolchildren of both groups show a definite antipathy to learning Arabic, a compulsory subject in Israeli schools. But perhaps that should come as no surprise when it is considered that these young people inevitably face army service, and the Arabs are a very real enemy. Consequently, even children from Arabic-speaking homes avoid acknowledging that they know the language.

Political Implications

As noted earlier in this chapter, until the late 1970s, the Labor Alignment enjoyed political hegemony in Israel. From the mid-1930s until its defeat in 1977, Labor effectively had no rival, so much so that political scientists classified Israeli politics as a multiple-party system with one dominant party.

Beginning with the 1965 elections, the new voter trend toward the Likud grew ever more visible, and over the next sixteen years, those voters became the majority. In that respect as in others, the 1977 and 1981 elections can be viewed as critical in Israeli history.

An estimated three-quarters of Sephardim voted for the Likud or other parties in the Likud-led coalition of 1977–84. About the same percentage of Ashkenazim voted for Labor. Although Labor claimed that only the less educated, lower-economic-status Sephardim voted Likud, evidence shows that the coalition drew from all levels of the Sephardic population.

The Labor Alignment did show an increase in Knesset seats between 1977 and 1981; however, the increase was due mainly to the return to the fold of traditional Labor voters who had supported Yigael Yadin's Democratic Movement for Change, plus Arab voters who decided to vote for a mainstream party instead of separate Arab lists. But in the 1984 election, despite Likud's failures in governing, the Labor Alignment won only forty-four seats, a loss of four—almost as many as the six the Likud lost. If demographic inertia were the only factor involved, the Labor Alignment would lose an additional 1 percent of the electorate from election to election. Hence, Labor may have reached its peak strength for this political generation in 1981 unless other circumstances bring about a reversal of the trend.

Labor may also have turned away moderate voters who were not strongly allied with the pro-Likud, pro-Begin forces in 1981 by its show of arrogance, which came through at every turn in its campaign. Electioneering in such a small country as Israel tends to be quite straightforward; the small size of the population creates a feeling of intimacy between politicians and voters, so that the truth will out. Television spots and speeches by the Labor Alignment showed how the party saw itself ruling by right, indicating to many how little had changed as a result of its defeat four years earlier.

Labor's arrogance further alienated the Sephardim. Uncomplimentary expressions were often directed against them as a group, associating them with undesirable, lower-class behavior and election violence. These expressions were excused as slips of the tongue, but as videotapes shown after the election revealed, the overall tone of Labor leadership toward the Sephardic population was patronizing at best and often downright hostile. A documentary series analyzing the election, prepared and narrated by television commentators believed to be pro-Labor, showed extensive footage of Shimon Peres, Haim Bar-Lev (Labor's defense minister–designate during most of the campaign), Haim Ben Shahar (finance minister–designate), and other party members in confrontation with predominantly Sephardic audiences, and their manner was obviously patronizing and contemptuous.

During this period, a strong sense of nostalgia permeated the Labor party, manifesting itself clearly at the party convention and in some of the popular songs of the time. Labor seemed to be saying that somehow Israel had lost its way, presumably because of changes during the past thirty years of statehood and implicitly because of the introduction of a group that did not share the country's pioneering and Socialist ideals. Nostalgia for the Socialist idealism of an earlier time could not be separated from nostalgia for the days when the overwhelmingly Ashkenazic Labor establishment ruled.

Other examples of this tendency were sad, such as when Eliahu Nawi, the long-time mayor of Beersheva, and of Iraqi origin, was promised a safe place on the Labor Alignment Knesset list by Shimon Peres. But Peres overpromised seats when he assumed that the Alignment would win more than sixty, and Nawi's name was very far down on the list. Nawi asked Peres why he had effectively been excluded, and was told that the list was already overloaded with Iraqis. Nawi's response was, "I arrived in Israel seven years before you, yet you are an Israeli and I am still an Iraqi."

Perceptive political observers, watching the conflicts and bickering among Labor leadership and mindful of the scandals that had brought down the Labor Alignment in 1977, could only be struck by the irony of this nostalgia, in the sense that the failures of Labor rested on the shoulders of the generation that had been born in Israel during those "treasured" years, including Dayan and Rabin, or those who had immigrated to the country at that time, such as Peres and Bar-Lev, and who were, therefore, the products of Socialist Zionism—in other words, those considered the best and brightest children of the best generation of the Zionist enterprise. This made it easy for Begin and the Likud to capitalize on their greatest strength, namely, their role as spokesmen for the "outsiders."

Labor did learn from its 1981 failure and was less provocative and nostalgic during the 1984 election campaign. The party leadership attempted to reach out to the Sephardim. Their efforts, however, were so clumsy and counterproductive that they were abandoned in mid-campaign. As they had in 1981, Labor believed the reports of the early polls that they would win big, despite warning signals—apparently they just could not believe the extent of Sephardic alienation from the Labor camp. Convinced as they were of Likud's failures in the economic sphere and in the Lebanon war (which were indeed great), they could not understand why the people would not automatically fall into their laps. As a result, many Sephardim who wanted to vote for change opted for one of the minor parties while new voters continued to support Likud.

In the 1984 election, Labor took approximately one-third of the Sephardic vote, up from one-quarter three years earlier, but not enough to alter the basic orientation of the Sephardic electorate. Likud lost six seats and Labor lost four, thereby continuing the new regime of two leading parties competing for control—a change brought about primarily by the Sephardic electorate. In the process, the Sephardim developed many legitimate channels through which to express themselves and advance in public life. What the elections of the 1980s have highlighted is both the true character of Sephardic grievances—not economic but cultural and political—and the ability of Sephardim and Ashkenazim alike to forge alliances to gain political power.

Realities and the Future

Whatever the problems, Israel as a democratic society has given the Sephardim great opportunities to advance in a number of areas. Sephardim, for instance, are gaining leadership posts in the Israeli Defense Forces. According to Sammy Smooha, there were no Sephardim among the six major generals in 1955, and none among the twenty-one major generals in 1973, but by the late 1970s some 30 percent of all army officers were from the Sephardic community, and by 1982 three of the twenty-four major generals were Sephardim. Other sources indicate that in 1983 Sephardim headed at least five IDF corps and filled many other senior staff positions and division commands as well, including thirteen brigadier-generalships.

The Israeli police force has generally been viewed as being made up of Sephardic "troops" and Ashkenazic "commanders." In 1955, barely 4 percent of all commissioned police officers were Sephardim. By 1969, Sephardim numbered 25 percent; and the situation has continued to improve, reaching into such top posts as chief of police operations, commander of the Tel Aviv district, and head of the quartermaster's division.

In 1956, there were no Sephardim on the thirteen-member central committee of the Histadrut; in 1973, 5 of the 20 members were Sephardim. Ten years later, there were 12 Sephardim among the 42 members. Figures for the executive council are: 8 Sephardim out of 91 members in 1956, 34 out of 163 in 1970, and 84 out of 198 in 1983.

The Sephardim have also increased their numbers in Israel's political parties. In 1983, about 30 percent, or 1,200 out of some 4,000 members, of the central committees of the five major political parties were Sephardic. In 1950, only 8 out of 104 members of the same governing bodies in the five major parties had been Sephardic. In 1973, 14 out of 130 members of the executive committees were Sephardic. By 1983, it was estimated that 35 out of 170 were.

The present struggle between Sephardim and Ashkenazim over political power in Israel is in a transitional phase. It is unlikely to continue past the end of this generation—a testimony to the vitality of Israeli democracy.

Sephardim and Likud Leadership

Beyond the headlines, one can see a new political synthesis developing, built around a group of young Sephardic leaders in the Likud who have emerged from the development towns. David Levy started out as head of the works committee in a textile mill in Beit Shean, a small development town in the Jordan Valley, far from the center of Israeli life, and is now in the running for the leadership of the Likud. He has long since transcended the bigotry that mocked his Moroccan background to become deputy prime minister and minister of construction and housing, and the No. 2 man in the Herut party. He has also become an accomplished and moving speaker, sought after for his clarity of expression. He seems to value, as many Sephardim do, a clear, elegant, and precise Hebrew—a matter of overt Sephardic pride at least since the Sephardim systematized Hebrew grammar and formulated the Sephardic version of the prayer liturgy nearly a millennium ago.

Levy is not alone. Moshe Katzav, former mayor of Kiryat Malakhi, who became Levy's deputy minister of housing, responsible for Project Renewal, in 1981 and minister of labor and social affairs in 1984, is looked upon by many as a future prime minister. David Magen, mayor of Kiryat Gat, and Meir Shitrit, former mayor of Yavne, both Knesset members, are new and capable leaders. Each of these men initially tried to enter the ranks of the Labor party but in the end joined Likud, having been rejected with prejudice by a shortsighted establishment.

This is a sign of the times. Having achieved economic stability and having gained power in local communities where they represent majorities or substantial minorities, the Sephardim are now taking an even greater leap forward in public life.

What all this means to Israel is that the Likud may well remain the majority party, at least for the present generation. This does not preclude periodic Labor victories, especially since Likud has yet to demonstrate an ability to govern commensurate with its ability to draw votes. But Israel now has a political system in which the two major parties compete for control of the government.

Sephardim and the Religious Camp

What of the Sephardim and the religious parties? In 1981, the religious camp as a whole dropped from a maximum strength of seventeen to thirteen seats in the Knesset—a significant loss for what was generally considered the most stable bloc in Israeli politics. The NRP absorbed the entire loss; its strength was cut in half, losing seats to the Likud and to its offshoot, Tami. Agudath Yisrael, on the other hand, held its own with the help of Sephardic voters who were totally unrepresented in the party forums, and because of the virtual tie between the two largest parties plus the skills of its own leaders, it much enhanced its bargaining power.

In other words, 1981 was a turning point for the religious camp as 1977 was for Labor. The religious parties are now undergoing internal realignment, with the Sephardim playing a catalytic role. The NRP has a particularly difficult future. After winning twelve seats in 1977 under the effective dominance of the young guard, headed by Zevulun Hammer and Yehuda Ben Meir, its new leadership began to think of expanding its base to become the Israeli equivalent of the European Christian Democratic parties: in other words, a broad-based, religiously oriented political alignment capable of competing for full government power. The NRP went so far as to welcome a delegation from the Christian Democratic Union in 1980 as part of its exploration in that direction. Their hopes were severely dashed in 1981, however, and completely destroyed in 1984.

Meanwhile, after 1981 Sephardic members of the NRP who had not left when Aharon Abuhatzeira broke away to form Tami demanded their rightful share of places on the list and of the party-controlled offices. Some 70 percent of registered NRP members are said to be Sephardim, yet after Tami, there were no Sephardim in top positions in NRP leadership or in senior government positions within the party's control. Sephardim demanded parity and received it on the NRP Knesset list in 1984. Unfortunately for the party, the Sephardim chosen by the party leadership were old-timers with no constituency among nonregular Sephardic voters. They no doubt held the remaining Sephardic NRP members in line, but they were much overshadowed by Shas, which became the cutting edge of the Sephardic revolt within the religious camp.

Shas, the Sephardic Torah Guardians, first appeared as an independent list in the Jerusalem municipal elections of 1983 and surprised everyone by winning four seats on the city council. Its origins lay in two sources. The first was the dissatisfaction of ultrareligious Sephardim with Agudath Yisrael because of their lack of representation in the party's forums, which indeed were usually conducted in Yiddish to the complete exclusion of the Sephardim. The second source was the struggle between the *Rishon Le-Zion*, Sephardic Chief Rabbi Ovadia Yosef, and Ashkenazic Chief Rabbi Shlomo Goren. Goren had made a deal to give both himself and Yosef a single ten-year term instead of having to stand for reelection every five years with the right to indefinite reelection, because Goren feared he would lose after his first five-year term, whereas

Yosef would likely have been reelected again and again. Since Goren was allied with the NRP, Yosef, furious over being replaced because of Goren's deal, had to look elsewhere. He lent his support to dissident elements in order to establish a new power base for himself, and Shas emerged.

This fledgling party submitted a list for the 1984 Knesset elections. They were surprisingly successful, gaining four seats in the Eleventh Knesset, a number equal to the NRP and two more than Agudath Yisrael, which lost half its strength. Shas was successful in part because it was able to capitalize on the failure of Tami to provide a Sephardic alternative for those who did not want to vote for any Ashkenazi-dominated parties, so it attracted many votes from Sephardim who were far from being normal supporters of Orthodoxy.

Shas was also strengthened by the alliance between Rabbi Yosef and Rabbi Shach, the leader of the "Lithuanian" *yeshiva* community, who led his constituency out of Agudath Yisrael into Shas. Both the Sephardim and the Litvaks had been denied power by the mainstream Hassidic groups, which traditionally dominated Agudath Yisrael. Hence, theirs was a natural alliance. So, whereas Shas again demonstrated that to succeed a party had to draw voters from more than one country or region of origin, this was the first time that a Sephardi-dominated party was able to attract an Ashkenazic group in a secondary role. At the time that the party was formed, the two rabbis also took the lead in establishing a Sephardic-plus-Litvak counterpart to the Council of Torah Greats, which gives direction to Agudath Yisrael. The new body, named the Council of Torah Sages, institutionalized Shas in the religious and political spheres.

Sephardim and the Jewish-Democratic Synthesis

Tami's failure was the key to the success of Shas. Its origins were something less than noble, involving the personal ambitions of Aharon Abuhatzeira, who even then was in trouble with the law, and of Nissim Gaon, a wealthy diaspora Jew of Sephardic background, as well as a barely disguised appeal to the grievances of the North African segment of the Sephardic population. In one respect, however, Tami hit upon an important theme in its efforts to justify its place in Israeli politics. Tami advertised itself as the movement for tradition in Israel, appealing to Sephardim who are traditional rather than Orthodox. As such, it was the first to recognize the *masorati* (traditional) Jews as a potential political force. Its emphasis on positive involvement with Jewish tradition on something other than an Orthodox basis, plus mutual respect among all the communities in the state, was telling. In the end, however, the problems of its leaders brought it down, and in 1984 many of its voters supported Shas.

No one, however, should underestimate the power of the idea that Tami embraced. Begin certainly did not; he embodied it in his desire to become a classic "Jewish democratic" leader. His emphasis on Jewish tradition as the cornerstone of Israel's "civil religion" was one of the dominant elements in his public stance (and one of the bases for his appeal to Sephardic and religious voters). It betrays a serious concern—derived from Ze'ev Ja otinsky, Begin's mentor—for the continuity of Jewish tradition in the Jewish state on other than Orthodox religious grounds through a synthesis of civil and religious elements. None of the other Likud leaders of Begin's generation or the Labor leaders reflects that synthesis. The new Sephardic leadership does, however—another reason why Likud is more popular among the Sephardim.

The emergence of an articulated and well-formed civil religion, which draws heavily on traditional Jewish sources and expresses them in a traditional manner, is a striking aspect of Israel since the late 1970s. This civil religion differs significantly from that fostered under Labor leadership. At that time, the Socialist Zionists tried to infuse traditional Jewish forms with clearly secular content. This emerging civil religion, however, takes traditional forms with their traditional content and selectively attaches them to the civil society. This trend reflects the end of the old ideologies that flourished during the last generations of the modern epoch and that have become increasingly irrelevant in postmodern times, as well as reflecting the revival of concern for traditional religion that is also characteristic of our times. In this respect, the contemporary Israeli experience is simply a Jewish version of a worldwide phenomenon.

What, then, are the aspirations of the new Sephardic majority? Simply, to have an equal voice in Israeli society, whether in the form of an equal ratio of political power or equal expression of Sephardic culture as part of the evolving culture of Israel.

The present struggle between Ashkenazim and Sephardim is simply a normal struggle for power among "ins" and "outs," and should be read as no more than that. Yet, it is a crucial struggle for current Israeli politics. Those who would understand Israel and communicate with the Israelis who will come into power should understand this and begin to build bridges to the emerging Sephardic leadership.

We may even see the maturation and influence of a Sephardic understanding of Zionism, which will reflect a more traditionally Jewish outlook regarding the necessity for and purposes of a Jewish state than did the Socialist Zionism brought from Russia three generations ago. This renewed understanding of Zionism will more closely reflect the aspirations of the first founders of modern Israel, principally Sephardim who began their work in the 1840s and Ashkenazim who came in the 1880s, whose history and contributions are now being rediscovered. That, in turn, could lead to a new vision for Israel.

Chapter 3

Decline and Revival in Europe

RENE SAMUEL SIRAT was born in 1930 in Bône, a small seaport in northeastern Algeria, where he was raised and schooled. He continued his education in France at the universities of Strasbourg and Paris, and also studied at the Hebrew University in Jerusalem. During that time he became a rabbi and served in Toulouse, France, from 1952 to 1955. Following that, he was the chaplain of Jeunesse Juive and then a professor at the Institut Nationale des Langues et Civilisations Orientales (Enlov), where he was the director of Hebrew studies. He also became a professor at the École Rabbinique de France.

Between 1972 and 1980, Sirat served the French Ministry of Education as inspector general and sat on various Hebrew-language examining boards. He was elected chief rabbi of France in 1981, the first Sephardi to reach that position in many years and the first of North African origin. After leading a fight to maintain traditional Jewish standards, Sirat decided not to stand for reelection in 1987; his successor is also a native of North Africa.

Sirat's election reflects the power shift in French Jewry and symbolizes change throughout Europe. Today, Sephardim constitute some 18 percent of world Jewry and should exceed 20 percent by the end of the century. There are more Sephardic Jews in the world at present than ever before. But the real power of the Sephardim on the world Jewish scene stems from the fact that the major centers of world Jewry are now fairly equally divided between Sephardim and Ashkenazim.

Outside of the major centers, Sephardim are also increasing their numbers. They remain dominant in the Mediterranean basin and Asia, and they constitute some 20 percent of Latin American Jewry.

The Sephardic world is in ferment for two reasons: first, all but a few Sephardim are excluded from positions of power and influence in the mainstream of public affairs in many Jewish communities throughout the world; and second, the Sephardic heritage is excluded from contemporary Jewish culture (even from that taught to Sephardic children in the schools), the media, and other public institutions.

Although Israel is in transition, with the Sephardim gaining ground, the situation in the diaspora is somewhat more complex. The history of the Sephardic communities in the Balkans—the heartland of classic Sephardic life and culture after 1492—encapsulates the rise and decline of the Sephardim from the time of the Spanish exile to the end of World War II. The destruction of these communities during the Holocaust, and more generally by the forces of modernization, ended the most creative era of Ladino Sephardic culture, just as the same factors in Eastern Europe ended the most creative era of Yiddish Ashkenazic culture. Both still survive—principally in Israel—but as no more than remnants.

Balkan Jewry

No region of Europe has a longer history of organized Jewish life than the Balkan Peninsula, which includes the Jewish communities of contemporary Bulgaria, Greece, Rumania, Turkey, and Yugoslavia. Turkey is not usually considered a Balkan country, but the overwhelming majority of its Jews are part of the Balkan group and live in European Turkey, which *is* part of the Balkan Peninsula. Rumania was originally settled by Balkan Jews, but in the nineteenth century an influx of Eastern European Jews brought the community within the Russo-Polish orbit.

The first diaspora communities outside of the Fertile Crescent (from the north coast of the Persian Gulf to the east coast of the Mediterranean) were probably located in the Balkans, and Jewish settlement there has continued at least since the days of the Second Temple. Through the centuries, Balkan Jewish communal life has had good and bad periods and undergone several transformations. It has survived under Hellenistic, Roman, Byzantine, and Ottoman rule, and most recently has been subject to the authority of new states that reflect local national majorities.

The Jewish communities of the Balkan Peninsula have, themselves, been in the hands of different segments of the Jewish people as war, economic and political change, and migration overtook them. As the seat of the first great European diaspora, the Balkan Jewish communities were in the middle of the great conflict between Judaism and emerging Christianity. Throughout the Roman and Byzantine periods, the Balkans were under common imperial suzerainty, and as a result their Jewish communities took on common characteristics. At the same time, however, years of isolation led to the development of a Jewish life that was separate in many ways from the mainstream of Jewish history, with separate rituals and customs, if not communal institutions. Isolated examples of these oldest Jewish patterns survived in small mountain communities until World War II.

The last great tide of Jewish migration into the Balkans came from the Iberian Peninsula beginning in the fifteenth century. The fall of Constantinople to the Ottoman forces in 1453 and the resulting consolidation of Ottoman rule throughout the region, nearly forty years before the Jews were exiled from Spain, provided Sephardic Jews with a place of refuge that allowed them to exercise their considerable talents.

The Balkan Peninsula became the center of the Sephardic world. Hundreds of thousands of Jews found a place for themselves between the Black Sea and the Adriatic, from the Danube to the Mediterranean. They became the most productive and energetic people in the Ottoman Empire, at the same time developing a vigorous Jewish life and culture that flourished for four hundred years. The Sephardim entered into a virtual alliance with the imperial authorities to stand against the common Christian foe and to build a strong internal society. Their communities were given protected status within the framework of the empire, and their own power within existing communities was enhanced because of their relationship with the imperial authorities.

By their sheer numbers, not to speak of their cultural power, the Sephardim overwhelmed the indigenous Balkan Jewish communities and, in effect, assimilated those communities into the Judeo-Hispanic cultural and social framework they had brought with them. Judesmo became the Jewish language of the Balkans as Yiddish became the Jewish language of Eastern Europe. Moreover, exile from Spain—their beloved second motherland—seemed to release great pent-up energies among the Sephardim that found an outlet in the Balkans.

The result was a flourishing age of Jewish culture, bearing a distinctive Sephardic imprint, whose impact shaped the entire Jewish world for two centuries. The cities of the Balkans, with Salonika in the lead, became bastions of Jewish life and creativity. Sephardic creativity in *halakhah* and *kabbala* flourished and shaped Jewish life and thought from Russia to Latin America. It produced in time the last and greatest theopolitical movement of premodern Jewry, the midseventeenth-century messianic movement of Izmir-born Shabbetai Zvi. Sabbateanism, with its expectation of messianic redemption, was a product of the Balkan Sephardic world, yet it influenced English Puritans as well as Jews everywhere.

Even after the region's decline and the passing of its leadership role to Eastern European Jewry, Balkan Jewry continued to enrich Jewish life and to add to the store of Jewish learning. Sages, teachers, and statesmen continued to emerge and to make an impact, at least locally. Even today there remain many great works of Balkan Jewish scholarship to be rediscovered, and no adequate history of the region's Sephardic age has ever been written.

With the decline of the Ottoman Empire in the eighteenth century, Balkan Jewry also declined to some degree. Actually, the extent of its decline has been exaggerated; as major centers of Jewish life passed to other regions, general historians of the Jewish people tended to neglect the Balkans.

In the nineteenth century, Balkan Jewry underwent something of a renaissance, which was unfortunately cut short by the emergence of new nation-states from the European ruins of the Ottoman Empire. In its early stages, the renaissance featured the transformation of Judesmo into a secular literary medium which paralleled that of Yiddish in the lands to the north. It emphasized the modernization of Jewish education and, increasingly, a new political consciousness among Jews—whether in connection with local nationalisms or Zionism. The Balkan Haskalah (the renaissance was part of that universal Jewish enlightenment) gave rise to a modern literature, over 250 newspapers and journals, the systematization of Judesmo grammar, and more.

The economic condition of the Balkan urban communities also improved during this century, accompanied by substantial population growth especially resulting from country-to-city migrations. Finally, constitutional and administrative reforms within the empire led to the restructuring of local Jewish communal organization and to the creation of a central authority for all Jews. Although the Western principle of individual citizenship was still in the future, during the nineteenth century Jewish and other minorities were made increasingly equal in status with the empire's Muslim subjects.

Life changed drastically during the revolutions that tore the empire apart in the years before World War I. A Jewish world that had been united for at least four hundred years was suddenly forced to reorganize from the ground up. The breakup of the empire had far more impact on Balkan Jewry than did the breakup of the Russian Empire on Eastern European Jewry. Constantinople and Salonika, the Ottoman Empire's principal cities, were also its principal Jewish communities, unlike Moscow and Leningrad, which were not central cities in Jewish life. Cut off from their centers when the new nation-states were formed, and from the other Balkan countries, many small communities were completely isolated from their spiritual and cultural sources.

The Jewish communities within the new states, which had previously not been linked together in any real way because they were all part of the same imperial polity, now had to forge bonds. In doing so, they modernized their community structures, learning from the experiences of the nation-states of Central Europe that had undergone similar reorganization two to three generations earlier. In this way, some version of the French *consistoire* (a hierarchy of religious congregations) or German *Kultesgemeinde* (a federation of religious communities) pattern was reproduced in all of the new Balkan states, although more often than not its external forms masked the continuation of older patterns.

Structurally, the new Jewish communities achieved a high level of organization. But, as has often been the case, organization was no indication of communal health. Quite the contrary was true of Balkan Jewry. Successful reorganization occurred with the beginning of extensive assimilation and widespread loss of interest in things Jewish. Pressures from host nations and modernization began to change Jewish life. In some cases, as in Bulgaria, Zionism revived communities that had been based on a common religious faith and Sephardic culture, but elsewhere, as in Turkey, Zionism was itself opposed by the state as against the interests of its newfound nationalism.

World War I intensified nationalistic opposition to anything that spoke of Jewish separatism. With the last vestiges of the Ottoman Empire swept away, the modern Turkish state displayed the same nationalism—in some respects even more xenophobic—as the old Balkan heartland, and the Jews themselves were ambivalent about their own status. Although they welcomed their new rights to individual citizenship and assimilated into the larger society in most ways, they also wished to preserve certain elements of Jewish life. During the 1920s and 1930s, they tried to create new ways to combine both assimilation and preservation, often in the face of considerable opposition.

But whatever the local conditions, for most Balkan Jews, World War II mooted the question. The Jews of Greece and Yugoslavia were destroyed in the Holocaust. Bulgarian Jewry survived only to be engulfed in the Communist takeover, resulting in mass emigration to Israel. Turkish Jewry was physically least affected, but the government's wartime economic measures brought severe hardship to most Jews and stimulated a mass emigration after the Jewish state was established. Thus, the once powerful Jewries of the Balkans were drastically reduced, with most of their survivors reunited in Israel.

The dissolution of Balkan Jewry had actually begun before the Holocaust. The upheavals of the late nineteenth century caused a substantial emigration of Jews from the region. Tens of thousands emigrated to the Western Hemisphere, settling in North and South America. Thousands of others moved to Eretz Israel before the establishment of the state to take part in its rebuilding. At the turn of the century, the Balkan countries in the Ottoman Empire had contained over one-third of a million Jews, more than the present Jewish population of Canada. Today, no more than fifty thousand remain, equal to the Jewish population of Pittsburgh, Pennsylvania, or a medium-size Israeli city.

But Jewish communities do not so easily disappear. In the years following 1949, those Balkan Jews who remained rebuilt their communities on a smaller scale under conditions of restricted religious practice, where even the most committed Jews were assimilated linguistically and culturally. The political and organizational scope of these communities has become central to Jewish survival more than ever before. In this respect, Balkan Jewry is in much the same situation as most other world Jewries.

Ironically, as the Jewish communities lost their separate status, organizational ties have come to occupy a disproportionate place in preserving their Jewishness, exceeded only by the steadfastness (somewhat diminished by intermarriage) of family ties. Jewish religion and culture may count for relatively little in these lands, but the urge to survive persists. Whether such conditions as exist can ensure their survival is open to question, but the evidence at this point is not encouraging.

Yugoslavia

As a multinational society with no single nation in the majority, Yugoslavia has given the Jewish community the most room to maneuver by at least tacitly recognizing it as a semiautonomous nationality, although without an indigenous territorial base. Still, life is not easy. The complexities of maintaining Jewishness must vie with the complexities of Jews living freely in Yugoslavia. The Jewish community there need not fear the government, or their non-Jewish neighbors; consequently, it may be the first to assimilate completely.

Of the seventy-one thousand Jews in Yugoslavia in 1939, approximately fourteen thousand survived the war and returned. The Federation of Jewish Communities officially resumed its activities on October 22, 1944, a few days after the liberation of Belgrade by Tito's partisans. Within a few years after the war's end, Jewish life had resumed to some extent in fifty-six communities throughout the country. During the four years following the establishment of the State of Israel in 1948, about eight thousand Yugoslav Jews emigrated to the new state. The number left behind remained relatively stable for years, but it has declined and is now estimated at about five thousand; approximately half are Sephardim. Some 80 percent live in Belgrade, Zaghreb, and Sarajevo.

The Yugoslav Jewish community has almost no religious life. Not only is religion discouraged by the country's Communist leadership, but the Jews who remain in Yugoslavia are themselves overwhelmingly secular and have not sought to preserve it. There are some Jewish cultural activities, and Jewish education is provided through preschool and summer camp programs, including a program in Israel. Activity in the Federation of Jewish Communities is the principal form of adult identification. There are no restrictions on Jewish activity, however, other than those imposed by the Jews themselves.

Bulgaria

Unlike Yugoslavia, Bulgaria is a textbook example of a Communist regime. Totalitarian to the core, its drive for internal homogeneity is reinforced by the existence of a clearly dominant national majority. There is no strong non-Bulgar minority, and Jewish community life is further hampered by the intensely antireligious aspects of Bulgarian communism. However, the Bulgarians have proved relatively tolerant toward "their" Jews. Most of Bulgarian Jewry survived the war because Bulgaria was a German ally, and therefore did not come under direct Nazi control until it was too late to carry out the Final Solution. Despite the fact that the Bulgarians had more or less protected the Jews during the war, most Jews understood what awaited them under the new Communist regime. Within two years after Israel was established, Bulgarian Jews resettled there en masse. As the first community to become fully Zionist, half a century earlier, this was a natural step, and it was encouraged by the Bulgarian authorities. All told, approximately forty-nine thousand Bulgarian Jews have settled in Israel.

Of the fifty thousand Jews in Bulgaria in 1948, only five thousand remained by 1951. It was estimated that there were slightly more than three thousand Jews registered with the Bulgarian Jewish community in 1965; there are probably at least five thousand today.

For a time, the Bulgarians allowed Jewish community organization to continue in its previous form, but in a series of steps in the 1950s and early 1960s, the community was reduced to a puppet committee that the government could manipulate to add a Jewish voice to Communist propaganda themes. In recent years, however, there has been a revival of Jewish life in Bulgaria, a new sense of ethnic if not religious feeling, and new possibilities to resume contact with Jews throughout the world. The government has so far allowed these leanings to develop, but the future of Judaism remains bleak in Bulgaria.

Greece

The emphasis on Greek nationalism and cultural uniformity since the Greek revolt against the Turks in 1821 has had a negative influence on Jewish life throughout Greece. In the ensuing century of wars against the Turks (1821–1922), Jews were massacred, expelled, or encouraged to emigrate simply because they were different, not for any particularly anti-Semitic reasons.

Because the most heavily Jewish areas of Greece remained in Ottoman hands until the last of the Balkan wars (1912–13), the Jewish population in the Greek state remained small. After the Greek capture of Macedonia, however, it grew to one hundred thousand. Salonika was included in the transfer, and the Greeks immediately began a major effort to Hellenize the city. Emigration from 1890 on, which had been stimulated by the wars, was now further stimulated by the decline of the economic and cultural base of the Jewish community in Salonika. After the Greco-

Turkish Treaty of 1923, which led to an exchange of populations between the two countries, one hundred thousand Greeks from Anatolia and Asia Minor were resettled in Salonika in a deliberate effort to end the dominant role of the Jewish community. Forty thousand Jews left the city, half emigrating to Eretz Israel, where many became stevedores in Haifa and helped build the port of Tel Aviv, and half to the West.

When World War II began, there were only seventy-seven thousand Jews in Greece, mostly in Salonika. They served valiantly in the Greek army, resisting first the Italian and then the German invaders. The Jews' heroic role in the war was a major influence in changing Greek attitudes toward them in the postwar period. Under the German occupation, all captured Greek Jews were transported to the death camps. The Salonikan community was totally destroyed; over forty-six thousand Jews were deported between March and August of 1943. The much smaller Athenian Jewish community, representing about one-tenth of that of Salonika, was warned of impending danger by Greek neighbors, who were able to hide three-quarters of them. The surviving Jews fought with the Greek partisans throughout the war.

At liberation, about ten thousand Jews were in Greece; half of them left over the next decade. Approximately thirty-five hundred settled in Israel, and the rest in the United States or other New World countries. The remaining Jewish population, approximately five thousand, is located in eighteen communities, about 60 percent in Athens and over 20 percent in Salonika. Athens is now the center of Jewish life in Greece, although Salonika retains a strong sense of its historic role.

The Jewish community in Greece, reorganized in November 1944, has reemphasized the religious dimensions of Jewish life, in keeping with the Greek interest in deemphasizing ethnic pluralism. At the same time, very few Greek Jews are religious; except for the High Holy Days, synagogue attendance is very low. There are few rabbis and teachers, and, in general, communal life is weak.

Greek Jewry was preserved in the generation after the war by the law forbidding intermarriage among religious groups without conversion. Recently, that law has been changed, and it is now possible for Jews to intermarry without converting to Greek Orthodoxy, which has led to a rise in the rate of intermarriage. The Greek Jewish community today is almost entirely dependent on Israel for spiritual and cultural sustenance and technical assistance.

Turkey

Turkey's neutrality during World War II saved Turkish Jewry from the devastation of the Holocaust; however, the Turks enacted anti-Jewish measures that brought the community to economic ruin. Thus, when the State of Israel was established, Turkish Jewry, which had been emigrating for economic reasons since the late nineteenth century, was ready to seek greener pastures. Some thirty-seven thousand Jews left for Israel between 1948 and 1955, reducing the community to about forty thousand. The number continued to decline through emigration to Israel and the West, and is now said to be twenty-one thousand, although this number is probably an underestimate since it includes only those Jews who are formally affiliated with the community. All told, over fifty-three thousand Turkish Jews settled in Israel.

Turkish Jewry has preserved the old forms of community organization, incorporating only those changes forced on it by post-Ottoman Turkish governments. The Hakham Bashi (chief rabbi) still sits in Istanbul, supported by the government and surrounded by his aides and bodyguards in the old Turkish style; his official government automobile flies his flag along with that of Turkey. But it is in truth a shabby survival and reflects the decline of the office and of the community.

All is not lost, however. Jewish schools and synagogues still function. Jewish communal affairs are handled through the B'nai B'rith lodge, which encompasses the local notables. Over 95 percent of the Jews are Sephardim, and although Turkish has become their first language, Judesmo survives among the older generation.

Eighty percent of Turkish Jews live in Istanbul, another 10 percent in Izmir, and the rest scattered throughout the country. Jews maintain a network of social welfare institutions. As in Greece, Jewish religious identification is preferred over ethnic self-expression; this is further complicated by the fact that the country is Muslim and subject to the pressures of the Islamic world, including in recent years Islamic fundamentalism. Although the Jews are under less pressure today than in the days of the militantly secular regime, their future depends on the balance of forces with regard to Turkey's relationship to Islam and the Islamic world.

Survival of the Four Communities

All in all, organized Jewish life in the Balkan countries of Yugoslavia, Bulgaria, Greece, and Turkey survives by living within the local limitations. Jews are a nationality in Yugoslavia, strictly a religious group in Greece and Turkey, and no more than a Communist cultural association in Bulgaria. What is clear is that these four communities cannot undertake any common action that could mobilize the resources of all their members, most of whom share a common heritage. The governments of the four countries are too hostile toward one another to allow that.

Each of the four communities must depend on outside assistance to survive. At least eight Jewish organizations have made some inroads in one or more of these Balkan communities in the twentieth century. The Alliance Israelite Universelle was the first. Its schools played a major role in the modernization of Balkan Jewry at the end of the nineteenth century. Education, however, became a highly sensitive issue in the states that experienced a wave of nationalism, and the Alliance was forced to withdraw. Even locally sponsored Jewish schools have had difficulties; in some countries they have been forced to close altogether.

The B'nai B'rith was the second outside group in the Balkans, leading to the development of meeting places for the local Jewish notables. As the most prestigious of modern Jewish associations, B'nai B'rith lodges became places for decisions that shaped local communal life. Although most of the lodges have since disbanded, partly because of government opposition to their ties with a foreign organization, a few have been turned into independent local clubs and continue to be important in Jewish life.

Zionism is generally regarded as an Ashkenazic movement, but the World Zionist Organization (WZO) very early on became an important presence in all of the Balkan states. Zionist societies antedate the first Zionist Congress (1897), and emigration to Israel to rebuild the land has long been a goal of Balkan Jews. The Bulgarian Jewish community was the world's first to be dominated by organized Zionism and was more thoroughly Zionist in orientation and politics than any other. But the nationalism of all four countries has eliminated organized Zionism.

The World Jewish Congress serves as the point of contact between world Jewry and the Balkan communities that is most likely to be tolerated by the governments. Even so, formal links are discouraged or forbidden, except in Yugoslavia. More recently, the European Council for Jewish Community Services has stepped in to fill part of the vacuum.

The distributive organizations of world Jewry have all played some role in the Balkans. The Joint Distribution Committee, the Claims Conference, and the Memorial Foundation for Jewish Culture helped in the reconstruction of communities damaged in World War II. As sources of funds and, in some cases, technical expertise, they are substantially responsible for whatever exists today in the way of Jewish services in the Balkans, at least outside of Turkey.

In recent years, Israel has assumed a central, if usually unofficial, role in the maintenance of Jewish life in the Balkans, with the Jewish Agency as its operative arm. Its impact on Balkan Jewry is an outstanding example for those who argue in behalf of Israel's centrality in Jewish life. If the Balkan Jewish communities do survive as active entities and participate in contemporary Jewish life, it will be due in no small measure to Israel's existence and its efforts in their behalf.

Sephardic Life in Western Europe

Western Europe was the original Ashkenazic heartland. From the mid-eighth to the late fourteenth centuries, Ashkenazic Jewish culture took form in northern France and western Germany with offshoots in England and Switzerland. Then, in a series of massacres and expulsions in the thirteenth and fourteenth centuries, those Jewish communities were swept away. Their survivors migrated eastward to rebuild a new Ashkenaz in Central and Eastern Europe that became the greatest center of Jewish life from the nineteenth century to the Nazi era. Sapped and weakened in the aftermath of the Holocaust, European Jewry lost its influence in the Jewish world. Indeed, in the first postwar generation, Europe was in many respects a joint protectorate of the United States and Israeli Jewry, relying on the Joint Distribution Committee for much of the reconstruction work and on the Jewish Agency to give tone to the communities in a historic demonstration of Jewish partnership.

In the second postwar generation, European Jewry has moved from being a bystander to, at the very least, becoming a way station between Israel and the United States, with a growing number of Israeli and American Jewish leaders going regularly to Europe to participate in common activities. If it can build internal unity, Western Europe may soon become a more active partner in world Jewish life.

One source of renewed energy for European Jewry is the recent arrival of Sephardic immigrants. In the 1930s, Sephardic Jewry represented less than 5 percent of the total Jewish population in Europe. Today, Sephardic Jewry constitutes approximately one-third of the Jews in Europe outside of the Soviet Union.

The Netherlands

The Sephardim reestablished Jewish life in Western Europe some two to three hundred years after the medieval expulsions. The first open Jewish communities appeared in the Netherlands in the late sixteenth century after the Dutch revolt against Spanish rule. Marranos (Jews who outwardly accepted Christianity while secretly practicing Judaism), principally from Portugal, who sought refuge from the Inquisition in the Low Countries prior to the rebellion, moved to the new United Provinces of the Netherlands, particularly Amsterdam, and openly returned to Judaism with the support of the Calvinist Dutch government, which was strongly opposed to Catholicism, especially in its Spanish form.

The history of Amsterdam's Jewish community in the seventeenth and eighteenth centuries is one of the glories of the Jewish diaspora. The city became known as the "Jerusalem of the North," and for two centuries was one of the main centers of world Jewry. It became a major hub for Jewish scholarship, politics, philosophy, culture, and economic life. Its Jewish scholars were aided by a major Jewish printing industry that flourished from the seventeenth century on and helped to spread their knowledge to the far corners of the world.

Many of the scholars also engaged in politics to advance Jewish interests alongside those of the Dutch, as the Netherlands expanded into the new worlds of the Americas and the Indian Ocean. As a result, economic opportunities were presented to the Jews, who became leading figures in the newly created Dutch trading companies, which in turn brought prosperity to Dutch Jewry. The same Dutch Jews who carefully preserved every form of Jewish observance also produced the first Jewish freethinkers in Western Europe, including Uriel Da Costa (1585–1640) and Baruch (Benedict) Spinoza (1632–1677), one of the founders of modern philosophy. In addition, the Amsterdam Sephardim spawned Jewish settlement in the New World, establishing communities in South

America, in the Caribbean, and the first organized Jewish community in North America, in New Amsterdam (now Manhattan).

The success of the Sephardim in the Netherlands opened the doors for Ashkenazim to settle there as well, and by the time of the French conquest in the 1790s, Ashkenazim outnumbered the five thousand Sephardim by about ten to one. By then, the Sephardic community had lost its vigor and was open to assimilation, although it retained equal power with the Ashkenazic community until reforms were introduced in the nineteenth century. The Holocaust wiped out most of Dutch Jewry. Today, a small Sephardic community numbering in the hundreds survives and has no impact on Jewish life outside of the country. It is organized as the Portuguese-Israelite congregation, one of the three recognized communities of Dutch Jewry.

Great Britain

Marrano refugees, particularly from Portugal, established Jewish life in England secretly at the end of the sixteenth century and openly from the middle of the seventeenth. The modern Jewish community in Great Britain formally dates back to 1656, when Oliver Cromwell allowed the Marranos to organize a congregation and maintain a house of worship. A small Sephardic community at first, by 1701 it was sufficiently well established to build the Bevis Marks synagogue, the first building constructed expressly for Jewish worship in modern England. The congregation controlled the Jewish community for nearly a century, and its *hakham* remains the chief rabbi of the Sephardim in Britain to this day. Nevertheless, Sephardim ceased to be the Jewish majority early in the eighteenth century.

Violent public reaction against legislation to improve the Jewish condition led to the establishment of the London Committee of Deputies of British Jews in 1760, which ultimately became the Board of Deputies. The London Committee replaced the *Deputados* of the Sephardic community, who had acted unilaterally to represent English Jewry before the Crown. It brought together representatives of Sephardic and Ashkenazic congregations, which meant the end of the hegemony of the Sephardic minority. Shortly thereafter, representatives of the congregations in other cities and in the British colonies were brought into the committee. The Sephardim retained dominance throughout the eighteenth century, but at the beginning of the nineteenth century, major Ashkenazic families, particularly the Goldschmidts and Rothschilds, became increasingly important. They led the struggle for full Jewish equality in Britain, which was finally achieved piecemeal rather than by any single legislative act.

During the nineteenth century, British Jewry was dominated by the "cousinhood," which resulted from intermarriage between leading Sephardic and Ashkenazic families.

Since World War II, a modest number of Sephardim from Asia and Africa have settled in Britain, mainly in London. Most are Jews from former colonies who had prospered under British rule. Jews from Morocco and Iran have also immigrated to London and Manchester. Today, there are approximately sixteen thousand Sephardic Jews in London and about one thousand in Manchester, plus others in the smaller cities of England and Scotland. They constitute about 5 percent of British Jewry.

The Sephardic community in Britain currently consists of the Bevis Marks congregation; several other smaller congregations; Montefiore College, a rabbinical seminary; and a small group of Sephardic notables, most of whom entered Britain after World War II, either descendants of Baghdad families that made legendary fortunes in the Far East, such as the Sassoons and Khadouris, or refugees from the Middle East who came with or rapidly made fortunes, and on that basis assumed leadership in the local community. The Sephardic community continues to have its own *hakham* as spiritual leader who is parallel to the chief rabbi of the Ashkenazim.

The distance between Ashkenazim and Sephardim in Britain has increased because so much of the Sephardic community consists of first- and second-generation immigrants and their children who retain a strong sense of Sephardic culture and a close connection to Sephardic networks. What is also unique about these Sephardic Jews is the speed with which they entered British Jewish high society, being both monied and easily assimilating into the system.

The New French Jewry

The greatest European center of Sephardic Jewry today is in France. Portuguese Marranos settled mainly in the southwest, around Bordeaux and Bayonne, in the sixteenth and seventeenth centuries. They lived in relative freedom, although France as a Catholic country forbade Jewish settlement, forcing them to maintain a nominal Catholicism. By the middle of the eighteenth century, they emerged openly as Jews and prospered as the "Portuguese nation." They took the lead in the fight for Jewish emancipation before the French Revolution. Most of them assimilated in the nineteenth century, while the influx of Ashkenazim from Alsace and Eastern Europe soon overwhelmed the Sephardic component of French Jewry.

It was not until the turn of the century, when France became a haven for Jews fleeing the Balkan wars, that a real Sephardic presence was reestablished. These Balkan Jews were joined by a few from North Africa. Together they formed a minority within French Jewry until the French evacuated Algeria in 1960 and most of the Algerian Jews fled to metropolitan France.

During those years, the Jewish population of France almost doubled. French Jewry was transformed. The Algerian Jews, joined by others from Tunisia and Morocco, became the new majority. They brought new vigor to the community and planted Jewish institutions throughout the country in a way unknown since the Middle Ages. French Jewry took on a North African character.

Except for Alsace, modern French Jewry had been concentrated in the major cities, overwhelmingly in Paris. Now one hundred thousand Jews have settled in smaller communities, creating the need and the means for organized Jewish life in those locations, all Sephardic.

A new French Jewish politics emerged from the Sephardic influx, pitting those Jews who sought to maintain their Jewish identity against those who wished to assimilate. The former developed a Zionist-based ideology that negated the possibilities of a rich Jewish life in the diaspora and focused on Israel as the only real hope of the Jewish people, yet which only marginally promoted *aliyot*. These diaspora-based Zionist ideologues challenged the community's ruling establishment and were aided by Israeli emissaries in the country, to the intense discomfiture of the established leadership. Their efforts are reflected in the work of Renouveau Juif (Jewish Renewal), a movement led by Sephardim.

By the end of the 1970s, the position of chief rabbi of France was held by a North African Jew, as was the post of executive director of the Fonds Socials Juifs Unifiés, the principal organization of the French Jewish community. Nevertheless, the presence of the Rothschild family with its special status kept major policymaking in Ashkenazic hands. This led in turn to a radical challenge headed by young Sephardim but principally based on a division between those who practice old-style Jewish politics and those who wish a more active, new style. The young leaders charge that the old are still bound by the norms of *shtadlanut* (used in the pejorative sense of Jews seeking favors from the government rather than standing up and demanding their rights).

A new visibility and militancy has become evident in French Jewry, which has always been very subdued because of its understanding that the French do not like ethnic politics or emphasis on separate ethnic identity. Unlike the pluralistic United States, where Jewish involvement in politics is accepted as an expression of normal group interest, in France such activities have been frowned on as challenging French national unity. The willingness of certain Sephardic Jews to make it clear to the powers-that-be that their vote is influenced by Jewish issues marks a radical departure from earlier Jewish patterns and has brought about a schism between them and leaders of the older community.

Yet the Sephardim have produced their own paradox. While a significant percentage have become active on behalf of Israel and Jewish causes, many others are rapidly assimilating. The former have brought about an intellectual renaissance as well as a political one. A new generation of philosophers and ideologists has emerged, a powerful factor in the French context with its strong emphasis on intellectualism as the highest human endeavor. These intellectuals have influenced French culture generally, as well as Jewish life.

On the other hand, the intermarriage rate among North African Jews has become dramatically high in less than a generation. Relatively few children of these immigrants have been sent to Jewish schools or receive any supplementary Jewish education, opening the door to even further assimilation.

Despite these divisions, French Jewry, some 535,000 strong, is by far the largest Jewish community in Western Europe, as well as the fourth largest in the world, after the United States, Israel, and the Soviet Union, and it is now dominated by the Sephardim.

Italy

The Jewish community in Italy is the oldest in Europe after that of Greece. It is the only Sephardic community in Western Europe that has remained in continuous existence since the beginning of the diaspora and under Sephardic leadership (in the broadest sense) throughout. Its special Italian character has made it unique in the Sephardic world.

There were Jews in Rome in the last days of the Republic, and during the imperial period they constituted perhaps as much as 10 percent of the Roman population. Hence, the Roman Jewish community sees itself as continuous since the days of the Hasmonean kings. Although there were occasional expulsions, they were relatively few and far between and did not last long. It may be said that except for the years in which the Byzantine Empire made its fanatic Christian ideology a matter of public policy, leading to persecution of the Jews, Italian Jewry had a relatively easy time of it. Italians themselves are not particularly given to displays of group hatred, and only when the Church acted against the Jews settled within its domain did they suffer.

For as long as the Roman Empire existed, the Jews were citizens and protected as such. From the fall of the empire until the unification of Italy in 1860, Jews were no more than protected subjects. But because the country was divided into a number of small states, even in bad times Jews could find refuge somewhere. As a result, Jewish life in Italy flourished in a unique way. Italy was a crossroads for Jews from east and west, north and south, part of the route for the Jews of Eretz Israel moving to Ashkenaz one thousand years ago and for Iberian exiles fleeing to the Ottoman Empire five hundred years later.

The Italian Jews developed their own customs and sense of worth, contributing as Jews to the Italian Renaissance and leaving a legacy to Jewish culture that is only now becoming fully known. Hence, it is not surprising that in modern times Italian Jews threw themselves wholeheartedly into the Italian effort to attain national unity. Jews were to be found in all political movements once the ghetto walls fell. After the unification of Italy, the Jews were granted full citizenship in the new state and their communities were organized along modern lines. In 1911, the Consortia della Comunità Israelita Italiana was established to link these communities. Membership in the Jewish community was made voluntary.

The Italian Jews did not need to break sharply with their past in order to modernize, but they did so along with the rest of Italy. By and large, Italian Jews left the ghetto as a result of the impact of the French Revolution and the Napoleonic conquest, so that by the midnineteenth century they were already active in Italian life. By the end of the century, many had quietly begun to assimilate without developing an ideological basis for that assimilation, as happened with the Jews north of the Alps. Others sought to develop a Jewish life that simultaneously enabled them to fit into modern Italian society, again with little ideological backing. Nevertheless, a unique ideology of modernization was developed by the Jews of Italy beginning as early as the eighteenth century, reflecting their links with the life of the general community.

Between World Wars I and II, Italian Jewry went from full integration to maximum exclusion and persecution. At first, Mussolini's Fascists did not discriminate against Jews. Indeed, many Jews were active in the Fascist movement and distinguished themselves in the Italian army in the Ethiopian War of 1935–36. Mussolini established the Unione della Comunità Israelita Italiana as an obligatory organization for Italian Jewry in 1930, the year after his *concordat* with the Vatican, which established the Catholic Church as the state church. But when Mussolini allied himself with Hitler and adopted the Nuremberg Laws, the Jews of Italy were first segregated, then persecuted.

World War II brought deportations, though with the reluctant support of the Mussolini government, and then only after the German occupation of northern and central Italy in September 1943. At the end of the war, just under twenty-nine thousand Jews remained in Italy. Nearly eight thousand had been deported and killed in the camps; six thousand had converted to other religions; and approximately six thousand had left the country.

In 1943, Italy surrendered to the Allies, Mussolini was deposed, and the new Italian government restored Jewish rights. Hence, neither the local Jewish community nor world Jewry viewed Italy as a pariah state with a Nazi past, as they did Germany and Austria. Rather, most of the Jews who remained in Italy or who returned after the war began to rebuild their lives along prewar lines.

Although few of the Jews who fled Italy as a result of the Nazi persecutions returned, there was no mass postwar exodus. Moreover, the indigenous Jewish population was supplemented by displaced persons. Continued, if moderate, additions to the Jewish community occurred as wealthier Libyan Jews took advantage of their Italian citizenship to follow the Italians when they evacuated that country. A small number of Soviet Jews relocated to Italy and some Israelis arrived. This has been sufficient to keep the Italian Jewish population more or less stable at thirty-two thousand.

After the war, the Unione, which is in fact a federation of communities, regained its legal status. The country's rabbis are attached to the Unione and through it are authorized to perform marriages. As a result of the 1930 law, all those considered Jews *halakhically* automatically belong to the community unless they make a formal renunciation of their membership, and the Unione receives a portion of the state taxes paid by its members. The shape of the Italian Jewish community may change as a result of the 1987 agreement between the government of Italy and the Jewish community, formulated in the wake of the disestablishment of the Roman Catholic Church. Under the new agreement, membership in the Jewish community will be strictly voluntary.

Rome and Milan are the main centers of the Jewish community, with fifteen thousand (44 percent) and ninety-five hundred (28 percent) of the Jewish population, respectively. The Roman Jewish community retains a strong commitment to its ancient traditions. It is the stronghold of the Italian *minhag* (religious ritual). Milan's newer community has large Lubavitcher Hassidic and other Ashkenazic components. It also has a North African congregation and a congregation of Jews from Meshed (Iran). Four communities—Turin, Florence, Trieste, and Livorno—have more than one thousand Jews each. They and most of the smaller communities represent the old Sephardic heartland of northern Italy.

The general openness of Italian society and the absence of serious anti-Semitism have stimulated intermarriage and assimilation, so that although the communities are nominally strong because of their legal status, they are in fact quite weak. The most Jewishly committed of the Italian Jews tend to emigrate, and most who leave settle in Israel. The Italian Jewish community is in a holding pattern, sustaining itself primarily through its organizational structure, a structure that will have to change as a result of the disestablishment of the Jewish community. Already, the social definition of who is a Jew relates more to personal identification and activity than to *halakhic* canons. The Italian Jewish leadership fears this change and what it will mean to Jewish life and survival in Italy.

Jewish Revival on the Iberian Peninsula

Spain

Somewhat ironically, nearly five hundred years after the Spanish expulsion, the Spanish Jewish community is one of the few growing Jewish communities in Europe, primarily as a result of the immigration of Jews from Spanish Morocco after the Spanish abandonment of its protectorate. Today, Spain has some twelve thousand Jews organized in local congregational community centers in five cities, principally Madrid and

Barcelona. The communal leadership is vigorous by European standards and optimistic about the future of Jewish life in the country.

Although since 1492 there always have been Marranos in Spain, Jews began to live openly as Jews only in the nineteenth century. The present Spanish Jewish community goes back to the 1868 Republican edict of religious tolerance, but it was actually only quasilegal until just after World War II and has gained formal status as a community only in more recent times. There have been repeated government revocations of the 1492 edict of expulsion, mostly at the instigation of Jewish groups interested in making a public relations point, although it was finally removed from the statute books only in 1968.

Spain's recognition of Israel in 1985 highlighted once again the ambivalence between that country and the Jews descended from families once living there. The 1985 announcement created an outpouring of sentiment in both countries, with the press and television recalling the long, checkered past connecting Spain and the Jews. Indeed, ambivalence has existed in Spain since the midnineteenth century when Spanish scholars first discovered the existence of Sephardim speaking Judeo-Spanish in the eastern Mediterranean and included them as part of the Spanish cultural world. Spanish interest in Sephardic culture has been high ever since. On several occasions, the Spanish government offered Sephardim Spanish passports. During World War II, several thousand Sephardim in the Balkans were saved in this way. After the Six Day War of 1967, Spanish passports were granted to the remaining Jews in Egypt who wished to flee.

The government's relations with the new Jewish communities that have grown up on Spanish soil in this century have also long reflected ambivalence. The Franco government helped many Jews to escape from the Nazis via Spain, but it did not encourage them to settle there. It was only after the Catholic Church ceased to be the dominant force in Spanish society, as it had been for centuries, that the government extended full rights and recognition to the Jewish communities. Full freedom of religion was reaffirmed in a 1967 law, and the Spanish parliament is now preparing legislation to give the Jewish community legal status commensurate with that of the Catholic Church.

At the core of the present Jewish community are the descendants of a small cadre of Sephardic Jews who returned to Spain from the Balkans before and during World War I. They concentrated in Barcelona, the most liberal and progressive part of Spain, then as now. A larger contingent of Ashkenazic Jews, seeking refuge from Hitler, passed through the country; three thousand stayed and built a modest Jewish community in Madrid. An even larger number of Moroccan Jews, who arrived in the 1950s and early 1960s, took over the Madrid community and lead it today. They make up 70 percent of Spain's present Jewish population. These Jews have been joined by Latin American Jews seeking a Spanish-speaking country that would be more secure for them, and by English Jews looking to retire in the sun not too far from Britain.

The Spanish communities are principally congregational, offering some Jewish educational and social services as well. Madrid and Barcelona have had rabbinical leadership since the communities were organized. Jewish elementary schools have been maintained in both cities, and the communities maintain regular contact with the European Council of Jewish Community Services, the World Jewish Congress, and Israel; however, these are communities that, whatever their formal structure, are actually led by a handful of notables. In addition to Madrid and Barcelona, there is a small Jewish community in Seville, and another in Málaga that maintains a synagogue and a school.

More problematic is the case of the Balearic Islands—including Majorca, Minorca, Ibiza, and Formentera—and their Marrano communities. Perhaps thousands of people, conscious of their Jewish background and still kept separate from other Spaniards who continue to discriminate against them because of their Marrano heritage, live on Majorca. There is also evidence of secret Jewish life on other islands nearby, especially on Ibiza, where the Jews never formally converted to Catholicism but lived semisecretly until the Spanish Civil War. Jewish life on Majorca, such as it is, has been bolstered by tourists and English Jews settling there. They have been licensed to establish a community, have opened a kosher restaurant, and have tried to develop a kosher hotel.

Occasionally, Jews from the Marrano communities seek to return openly to Judaism. Some effort has been made to encourage them, at least on Ibiza. As the five-hundredth anniversary of the 1492 expulsion approaches, more signs of a continuing Marrano consciousness are appearing.

Gibraltar

The oldest Jewish community on the Iberian Peninsula is that of Gibraltar, reestablished shortly after the British conquest in 1704. Although Jews were originally forbidden to settle under the terms of the 1713 Anglo-Spanish treaty ceding Gibraltar to the British, a 1729 treaty with the sultan of Morocco allowed Moroccan Jews to settle temporarily for business purposes. This led to a permanent community whose legal rights were recognized in 1749. By then, the six hundred Jews constituted one-third of the total civilian population and had two synagogues.

The Jews soon formed the merchant class on Gibraltar, paralleling the British military class and the Spanish working class. Sephardic Jews, principally from North Africa, arrived in Gibraltar by the hundreds to take advantage of its excellent commercial location. Subsequently, when the British granted self-government to the colony, the Jews were in the best position to acquire political power since they were both the educated elite and the middlemen between the Spanish and British. Gibraltar's first chief minister was a Jew—Sir Joshua A. Hasson, who held office from 1964 to 1969.

At its peak in the midnineteenth century, the Jewish population numbered two thousand. Today, with the island's drop in commercial importance, it has declined to approximately six hundred, although Jews constitute nearly 2.5 percent of the local population, making it the largest in continental Europe in terms of percentage. They are organized into four congregations and various community organizations.

Portugal and Malta

Portugal and Malta contain only remnant communities. Malta, with 50 Jews, is a true remnant; Portugal has approximately 450 Jews, down from 1,000 a generation ago, basically in one congregation in Lisbon, which was organized at the beginning of the twentieth century and expanded to include wartime refugees, most of whom have left. Its population is declining. In addition, there are other congregations in northern Portugal composed of Marranos who returned to Judaism in the 1920s but who remain isolated from the rest of the Jewish world by choice.

Sephardim in Northern and Central Europe

When the Marranos left Portugal for other parts of Western Europe in the sixteenth and seventeenth centuries, some found their way to the German and Scandinavian states along the North and Baltic seas, particularly Hamburg and Copenhagen. The Hamburg Sephardic community lasted until World War II. The community in Copenhagen assimilated, as did most of the other Sephardim who reached those regions singly or in small groups. None of those communities remains today.

About the same time, small groups of Sephardic Jews from the Balkans moved into the Austro-Hungarian Empire, pioneering Jewish settlement in Transylvania and establishing small outposts amid otherwise Ashkenazic communities in Vienna and Budapest. They were soon outnumbered by Ashkenazim, who easily moved into those German and Magyar areas from nearby regions. By and large, the Sephardim quickly assimilated among the dominant Ashkenazim.

At present, there are scattered groups of Sephardim in all of these countries, but Geneva is the only place with an organized community. Formally, the Geneva synagogue is for both Ashkenazim and Sephardim, but the congregation is dominated by Sephardim: wealthy immigrants from Islamic countries who settled in Switzerland. They are led by Nissim Gaon, president of the revived World Sephardi Federation, who erected the synagogue building and provides for much of its maintenance.

With the exception of France, and perhaps Spain, the status of Sephardim in Europe today is the same as that of European Jewry in general. The Sephardim bring new vitality to those communities where they form the majority, and are virtually invisible where they do not.

Chapter 4

Sephardim in Africa: North, Central, and South

The Last Days of North African Jewry

Jews settled along the southern coast of the Mediterranean in the earliest years of the diaspora. The Jewish community on the island of Djerba, now part of Tunisia, supposedly dates from the First Temple period. Whether or not this is true, it is known that Jewish exiles reached Egypt at the time of the destruction of the First Temple, and by the time of the Hellenization of the Mediterranean world they had spread westward to the Atlantic. The first period of flourishing Jewish life in North Africa had come to an end in 115–17 C.E., when Jewish communities joined in the diaspora revolt against Rome and were destroyed.

At the height of the Hellenistic era, there were massive conversions to Judaism among the North African Berbers, who then ranged eastward well into what is now Libya. These Berbers practiced Judaism until the Islamic conquest in the seventh century, which they fiercely resisted. Upon losing, many converted to Islam, but others retreated into the interior of the Maghreb (the area of North Africa from Tunisia westward), where they intermingled with other Jews to become part of the Jewish people as a whole.

After the Islamic conquest, the communities flourished again, becoming centers of Jewish learning until repressed by waves of Islamic fundamentalists who eventually took over the governments of the Maghreb in the twelfth century.

Throughout this period, Jewish communities of North Africa and Spain regularly interacted. Most of the Jews who originally settled in Spain were from North Africa. During periods of Spanish persecution prior to the expulsion, and even before the Muslim conquest, Spanish Jews fled to North Africa, where they assimilated into the local Jewish populations.

The massive wave of Jews from Spain who found refuge in North Africa after 1492 did not assimilate so easily. As in the Balkans, they came to the region with a firm belief in their own cultural superiority and wanted to maintain that Judeo-Spanish culture on North African shores. They did so until almost the twentieth century, partially relying on periodic additions of Sephardic Jews from Italy and the Balkans. The Iberian *megurashim* (those who were expelled) often stayed separate from the local *toshavim* (literally, residents) and *mugrabim* (people of the Maghreb), but over time their differences disappeared and contemporary North African Jewry emerged. (See table 4.1 for Jewish populations in Muslim countries.)

Although North Africa was nominally under Ottoman suzerainty, the local rulers were actually quite independent, so the fate of the Jews varied with the whims of individual sultans, beys, or pashas. This created less stable conditions than existed in the Balkans, and Jewish life and culture suffered accordingly. Even so, the Jews preserved a rich culture until they were engulfed by European colonialism.

The proximity of North Africa to France, Spain, and Italy led to its colonization in the nineteenth century. The French seized Algeria as early as 1830 and by 1860 had incorporated it into metropolitan France. It was easier for the Jews seeking to modernize to identify with the Europeans than with the Arabs, which led to the abolition of the old communal institutions—which had served the Jews as a nation within a nation, with their own legal and political systems—and to the restructuring of the Algerian Jewish community as a synagogue-based religious community along the lines of the French consistorial system. Emphasis was placed on acculturation, Gallicization, and the general abandonment of

TABLE 4.1
Estimated Jewish Population in Muslim Countries of the Middle East and North Africa

	pre-1948	1985
Afghanistan	5,000	70
Algeria	130,000–140,000	300
Bahrain	400	10
Egypt	75,000	250–300
Iran	90,000–100,000	30,000–35,000
Iraq	125,000	250
Lebanon	5,000	100
Libya	38,000	7
Morocco	265,000–300,000	18,000
Sudan	400	40
Syria	30,000	4,500–5,000
Tunisia	105,000	3,500
Turkey	80,000	18,000–22,000
Yemen (including Aden)	55,000	1,000–2,000
Approximate totals:	1,003,000–1,060,000	76,027–86,577

SOURCE: Based on material from George E. Gruen, ed., *The Resurgence of Islam and the Jewish Communities of the Middle East and North Africa* (New York: American Jewish Committee Institute of Human Relations, 1985).

traditional ways. Morocco and Tunisia became French protectorates; hence, French influence, although great, was less pronounced in those countries. However, by the turn of the century Jews were undergoing modernization in those countries as well.

The Spanish were less concerned about changing the people in the part of Morocco they occupied. What did occur, however, was the return to Spain of Spanish-Moroccan Jews, and by the midnineteenth century Jews were moving freely in and out of the country that had expelled them 350 years earlier, although not always admitting to the Spanish that they were Jewish.

Italy annexed Libya in 1912, after its influence there had already become great. Once again, especially with the Italians, Jews responded strongly to the opportunity for Europeanization.

By the midtwentieth century, North African Jewry was divided into two groups: the acculturated urbanites and those who were still relatively isolated in the interior villages. It was the latter in particular who emigrated to Israel after 1948 at the instigation of the Zionist movement. Zionism had reached North Africa much earlier, as early as the first Zionist congresses, and North African Jews had participated in the nineteenth-century pre-Zionist *aliyot* as well, but the mass immigrations after 1948 drew heavily upon those who had not been touched by the Zionist movement.

Few of the better-educated and more Europeanized North African Jews left for Israel. In the period between 1948 and 1960, most of them stayed in North Africa, and it was only as decolonization progressed that they began to leave. Most of them went to France, where they transformed the French Jewish community, and a much smaller number went to Spain, where they took over that Jewish community. Some went to other European countries or to the New World.

The situation in North Africa deteriorated after each Israeli victory, with 1967 being another turning point: the number of Jews in each country steadily decreased. Virtually none remained in Libya, where they would have been prey to an unpredictable and unstable ruler. (Over thirty-four thousand Libyan Jews emigrated to Israel.) Morocco is the one exception, where a friendly monarch continued to extend his hospitality, although a steady emigration is taking place even there, and no more than very small remnant communities are likely to remain. In the meantime, communal life proceeds, including religious observance, increasingly limited opportunities for Jewish education, and a few select social services.

Egypt: The Final Days

There was no more illustrious Jewish community in the history of the diaspora than in Egypt. It is one of the oldest, dating at least to the destruction of the First Temple, when the prophet Jeremiah was carried along by Judeans fleeing their destroyed country to the land of the Nile. A flourishing Jewish community developed, so well rooted that they built the only temple ever to exist in the diaspora. The Egyptian Jews were the first to translate the Bible into a foreign language (the Septuagint, in Greek), and Jewish philosophy had its beginnings in Alexandria.

This golden age of Egyptian Jewry came to an end in the revolt against the Romans in 115–17 C.E. The community recovered slowly but did manage to flourish again. It was particularly strong from the time of the Fatamid conquest in 969 until the Mamluks took power in the mid-thirteenth century. Those centuries, well documented in the Cairo Geniza, include the age of Maimonides, who headed the Jewish community in his time.

Jewish life was difficult under the Mamluks, but it improved after the Ottomans conquered the country in 1517. Overall, the Ottoman rulers were tolerant toward the Jews, but there was much capriciousness among them; they relied, for example, on Jews as financial agents, but closed down synagogues.

At this same time, a sprinkling of Spanish Jewish exiles reached Egypt and revived the cultural and religious life of the community, which, as a result, divided into three subcommunities: the Musta'arbin (the indigenous, Arabic-speaking Jews), the Sephardim (exiles from Spain), and the Mograbim (settlers from North Africa). This followed an old pattern in Egypt, whose community had earlier been divided between those who followed the Babylonian *yeshivot* and those who followed the *yeshivot* of Eretz Israel.

As Egypt declined along with the rest of the Ottoman Empire, so did the life of its Jewish community. Quasi-independent after 1768, its most distinguished nineteenth-century ruler, Muhammad Ali (1805–1848), initiated a series of modernizing reforms. The prosperity he brought to Egypt led to growth in the Jewish population. Many Jews came from European countries, particularly the Balkans, and modern schools were established. The Jewish community had originally been centered in Cairo, but from the nineteenth century on, Alexandria became its rival; by 1897, nearly ten thousand Jews lived in Alexandria, while only about nine thousand lived in Cairo.

Each European Jewish group founded its own community, albeit under the rabbinical authority of the existing ones. Even the Ashkenazim had a community in Alexandria. Alexandria's rabbinate was particularly modern and emphasized Western as well as traditional education. Hence, they played a major role in developing a *halakhic* response to the new technology of modernity, a response that was subsequently neglected, but which is now being recovered.

The upheavals of the Balkan wars and World War I brought more Jews to Egypt, especially from Salonika and smaller Turkish towns. The 1917 census showed 59,581 Jews in Egypt with a slight majority in Cairo, the figure rising to 63,550 in 1937. Jews entered public life, including two members of the Egyptian parliament and one minister. Although some Jews joined the Egyptian nationalist movement, Zionist organizations were also established. During World War I, many Jews from Eretz Israel who had been expelled by the Turks found temporary refuge in Egypt. A Jewish press developed in Arabic, Judesmo, and French.

In 1947, on the eve of the establishment of the State of Israel, 65,600 Jews lived in Egypt: 64 percent in Cairo, 34 percent in Alexandria, and the rest in the provincial cities of Tanta, Port Said, Mansour, and Ismailia—making Egypt the most urbanized Jewish community in the Afro-Asian world. The people were generally well educated, studying in both government and foreign schools. But even before the establishment of Israel and the problems that it generated for Egyptian Jewry, the handwriting was on the wall. Egyptian nationalists organized anti-Jewish riots in Cairo as early as 1945. In 1947, the Egyptian parliament passed the Companies Law, which required not less than 75 percent of employees of companies in Egypt to be Egyptian citizens. Since only 20 percent of the Jews in Egypt were citizens (most retained the passports of the European country from which they came, or were stateless), this was a hard blow for the Jewish community.

The day the State of Israel was declared, Jews were prohibited from leaving Egypt without a special permit and their leaders were arrested. There were bombings and riots in Jewish neighborhoods. The Jews began to lose whatever privileges they had accrued. Between 1950 and 1954, the restrictions were eased and many Jews were able to move to Israel. When Gamal Abdel Nasser seized power in 1954, however, conditions worsened for those who had remained.

The final period in the history of Egyptian Jewry began with the Sinai Campaign in October and November of 1956. Hundreds of Jews were arrested, about three thousand were interned in detention camps, and thousands were ordered to leave the country in a matter of days, abandoning all their property, which they had to sign over to the government. Some eight thousand Jews left under the auspices of the International Red Cross. These Egyptian Jewish émigrés scattered throughout the world: thirty-five thousand to Israel, some fifteen thousand to Brazil, ten thousand to France, nine thousand each to the United States and Argentina, and four thousand to Great Britain. Egypt's 1957 census counted less than nine thousand Jews; a decade later the number would be reduced to three thousand.

With the outbreak of the Six Day War, the last Jewish public officials in Egypt were dismissed and hundreds of Jews were arrested. As a result of intervention by Western countries, particularly Spain, most were allowed to leave. By 1970, only a remnant of the original Jewish community remained. All told, approximately thirty-eight thousand Egyptian Jews settled in Israel.

Jewish community organization continued in Egypt after 1948 as long as a community existed. There was even a well-organized Zionist underground, able to distribute shekels denoting membership in the movement prior to the Zionist Congress of 1951. The last Jewish newspaper was closed in 1953. Synagogues, social welfare organizations, and schools were closed in the 1950s, although both the Cairo and Alexandrian communities at least formally maintained governing committees. The last chief rabbi of Cairo, also recognized as the chief rabbi of Egypt, was deported in 1968.

Less than six hundred Jews (including Karaites—a schismatic Jewish sect that broke away from Rabbinic Judaism in the eighth century and developed a strong center in Egypt) remain in Egypt today, but since the initiation of the Egypt-Israel peace in 1977, this tiny remnant has received recognition out of proportion to its numbers. The opening of the borders led to poignant encounters between Egyptian Jews and Israelis either stationed in Egypt on official missions or visiting as tourists. The community has resumed contact with world Jewish organizations, and the few hard-pressed but dedicated men who lead Egyptian Jewry are carrying on the task of preserving monuments to a more resplendent past. At best, this is a valiant holding operation. With almost no young people or families with school-age children remaining, all signs point to continuing attrition and the eventual disappearance of Egypt's Jewish community.

Cairo's present Jewish population is placed at 150, while there are 133 in Alexandria. In addition, there are another 200 to 300 members of the Karaite sect in Egypt. In the provincial cities that once supported organized Jewish communities, no Jews remain.

No less depressing than these statistics on the size of the Jewish population is its demographic composition: the overwhelming majority are older people, many chronically ill. In both Cairo and Alexandria, women far outnumber men, and there are no children to fill the classrooms of the Jewish school buildings, where Muslim children are now being taught. In what was once Cairo's teeming Jewish quarter, nine Jewish inhabitants remain. Another six live in the community's old-age home, badly in need of repair, in suburban Heliopolis. The Joint Distribution Committee (JDC) has offered to pay half the $50,000 cost of renovation, but the community has said it is unable to raise its share.

The community does still own fifteen synagogue buildings as well as four schools. Some years ago during a financial crisis, the committee obtained permission from the chief rabbi of France to sell one synagogue, but it is reluctant to sell any of the others. The government has the school buildings under long-term lease for a nominal sum.

Services are held in the imposing Shaarei Shamayim synagogue whenever a sufficient number of people (not necessarily a *minyan*, or prayer quorum of ten) is available. Its emptiness is all the more striking since it has recently been renovated after years of decay through a $700,000 gift from Nissim Gaon of Geneva, president of the World Sephardi Federation. The historic Ibn Ezra synagogue, famous as the site of the discovery of the Geniza, is also being restored through donations from members of the Bronfman family. No services are held there, but a caretaker admits interested visitors.

The situation is similar in Alexandria, except that the magnificent Eliyahu HaNavi synagogue needs no restoration. The synagogue committee has been able to maintain both the exterior and interior through the lean years.

Since the last rabbi left in 1971, the Egyptian community has been without spiritual leadership. The chief rabbinate in Jerusalem now sends an Israeli rabbi twice a year. The JDC connection also provides an important link with the Jewish world at large. Affiliation with the World Jewish Congress (sanctioned by the Egyptian government) at least symbolically provides entree to world Jewish gatherings on the basis of equality. Moreover, the Israeli presence in Egypt since the peace treaty infuses the Egyptian Jewish remnant with pride and self-confidence.

Tunisia: Barely Surviving

Jews have lived in what is now Tunisia since ancient times. Many non-Jews converted before the Christianization of the Roman Empire ended Jewish proselytizing. Still, Judaism spread among the Berber tribes until the Arab conquest of the region forced most of them to convert to Islam.

The Arab conquerors founded Kairouan in 670 C.E., and it soon became a major center of Jewish scholarship. The Jewish community along the Tunisian coast flourished even after the decline of Kairouan, maintaining close contact with Jewish communities in other parts of the Mediterranean world, particularly in Italy and Spain. As in those countries, individual Jews rose to important positions in the courts of various rulers and used their influence to protect their brethren. The Tunisian Jewish community was autonomous and led by notables from the rich and well-born families.

Throughout the sixteenth century, Spanish and Ottoman invasions and counterinvasions overran the area and did not cease until the Ottoman victory in 1574. Communal life was substantially disrupted. The following century, the settlement of Spanish, Italian, and former North African Jews, who had first moved to Livorno in Italy and then to the coastal communities of northern Africa, led to the development of a separate community. These Grana (from Livorno) lived alongside the Touansa (natives of Tunisia) in a somewhat uneasy coexistence. In 1710, the Grana seceded from the main community, maintaining a separate one until 1899, when the authorities forced them to merge under a single chief rabbi, a common law court, a single kosher slaughterhouse in each local community, and a single delegation to the countrywide council.

The tension between the Touansa and the Grana was a major feature of Tunisian Jewish life in the modern epoch. The two groups united only in the face of outside danger. Beginning with the period of the French Revolution, French influence in Tunisia began to grow. The Jews were strong supporters of the revolution and its promise of Jewish emancipation. Ultimately, in 1857, they were given equality by the Bey of Tunis, at the demand of Napoleon III and the French navy. The resulting Pacte Fondamentale was abolished seven years later in the wake of a Muslim revolt against the granting of equality to infidels, but continued European intervention more or less protected Jewish rights.

The French finally made Tunisia a protectorate in 1881. The Alliance Israelite Universelle had opened its first school three years earlier. The Jewish community was reorganized along modern lines in 1888 by government decree. From 1910 on, Jews were able to apply for French citizenship. Except for periodic riots against them, the protectorate period was one of relative peace for the Jewish community. Many Tunisian Jews even fought in the French army during World War I.

During World War II, Tunisia was ruled by Vichy France from June 1940 to November 1942, and then occupied by the German army until May 1943. Under the Vichy government, Jews were subject to racial discrimination. Under the Germans, the situation deteriorated further to include confiscation of property, heavy taxation, service in labor camps, and even deportation to death camps.

Jewish public life was revived after liberation, and for a brief period Jews were able to integrate somewhat into Tunisian life. The Destour Independence party even cultivated their support. However, once independence was achieved in 1956, the new government embarked on a program of "Tunisification," which meant "Arabization." The rabbinical court was abolished in 1957; a year later the Jewish Community Council was dissolved and replaced with a "provisional commission for the propagation of the Jewish religion" whose members were government appointees. The old Jewish quarter in Tunis was destroyed, ostensibly as part of a slum clearance project. Even its synagogue, the oldest in the city, was leveled, and the Jewish cemetery in Tunis was turned into a public garden. The government stopped subsidizing the Jewish community, and when the only Jewish member of the Tunisian cabinet retired, no successor was appointed. Although Habib Bourguiba, the leader of the Tunisian independence movement and later life-president of the state, appeared on the world scene as a moderate, willing to accept Israel's existence for a price and relatively liberal compared to his Algerian and Libyan neighbors, he was actually ruthless in suppressing autonomous Jewish life; yet he did not go so far as to encourage persecution of the Jews. Although most Tunisian Jews left the country during the first years of independence, a proportionately larger number remained than in any North African country other than Morocco.

The Tunisian Jewish community has always had a rich cultural life. Jewish works were written and published in Hebrew, Judeo-Arabic, and French well into the 1960s, until stopped by government crackdowns. Until independence, there was a lively Jewish press.

Jews began to emigrate en masse around 1948, and particularly after 1957. Between 1948 and 1970, over forty thousand Jews from Tunisia settled in Israel, with nearly the same number going to France. The 1960s was a period of deterioration for the Jewish community. Tunisian Jews were accused of being unpatriotic and were discriminated against economically. During the Six Day War, there were Muslim riots and the Great Synagogue in Tunis was burned, which all led to a new wave of emigration. Only seven to eight thousand Jews remained in the country in 1968. Israel's Peace for Galilee operation gave rise to yet another wave of anti-Jewish feeling, including attacks on synagogues, and caused more emigration, particularly among the young Jews of Tunisia. All told, over forty-six thousand Tunisian Jews settled in Israel.

There are some thirty-seven hundred Jews remaining in Tunisia today, mostly on the island of Djerba and in the city of Tunis. They maintain a traditional Jewish community but are allowed almost no contact with the rest of the Jewish world. Although the Tunisian government more or less protects them, they are subject to constant harassment, and a few are killed every year in pogroms. Their numbers are decreasing as individuals and families quietly emigrate.

Algeria: A Remnant

Prior to the Arab conquest, the main Berber tribes in what is now Algeria were led by rulers who had converted to Judaism. The Jarawa, the leading Judeo-Berber tribe, actually led the resistance to the Arab conquest. When their leader, known as the *kaheena* (priestess), was killed in 693, Berber resistance collapsed and the area was conquered. Many of the Berbers converted to Islam, others fled, and the Jewish community was rebuilt principally by Jews coming in from the east.

The Algerian Jewish communities became part and parcel of the Mediterranean Jewish world, contributing great scholars and traders during the Middle Ages. The community was substantially increased by Spanish Jewish refugees from the persecutions of 1391, most from Catalonia and the Balearic Islands. The resulting community organization lasted from the fourteenth century until 1830.

At the time of the French conquest, there were thirty thousand Jews in Algeria. The French rapidly introduced measures to modernize the country, including the Jewish community. They abolished traditional communal organization, replacing it with a formal consistorial structure modeled after their own at home, and imported chief rabbis from France. The chief rabbis were to transform Algerian Jews into North African versions of French nationals of the Mosaic faith. The result was substantial assimilation for many Jews, even the complete abandonment of Judaism by some. A minority tried to maintain traditional ways unchanged, while a few influential families attempted to synthesize modern French and traditional Jewish cultures. In 1870, all Algerian Jews were declared French citizens.

In the 1880s and 1890s, a wave of anti-Semitism engulfed Algeria, leading to periodic pogroms. This anti-Semitism was essentially imported from Europe by the *colons*, French and Italian Christian colonists imported to Europeanize the country. Anti-Semitism intensified after the

Dreyfus Affair began in 1894, when a French Jewish army officer was falsely accused of treason. An anti-Semitic party was organized and actually came to power, but the Muslims did not support it and it ceased to exist after 1902.

Anti-Semitism did not cease, however, and when the Vichy government came to power after Germany overran France in 1940, the Algerian Jews, by then numbering 117,646, were deprived of French citizenship. The Algerian administration applied the Vichy laws rigorously—expelling Jewish children from the schools and cooperating with the Nazis in preparing the way for the deportation of the Jews to the death camps. The Jews became not only the leaders of the Algerian resistance movement, but almost its total membership, leading an insurrection in Algiers to coincide with the Allied invasion of North Africa on November 8, 1942. Yet, even after liberation by the Allied forces, the Jews continued to suffer indignities, including confinement in detention camps. It required the personal intervention of President Franklin D. Roosevelt to restore French citizenship to the Jews nearly a year after the Allied invasion, and it was not until 1957 that they were again given full equality.

When the Algerian civil war began in 1954, the Jewish community was caught in the middle. Once it became clear that France would abandon the territory, the Jews sought to be recognized as Europeans since they hardly identified with the Muslims. Given asylum in France, seventy thousand Jews left by the end of July 1962, and another five thousand went to Israel. All told, some 80 percent of the Algerian Jews settled in France, and virtually all who remained in Algeria after independence retained their French citizenship. Only thirteen thousand emigrated to Israel directly from Algeria after 1948.

At first, the new government maintained a correct relationship with the Jews. In February 1964, the Federation of Jewish Communities of Algeria held a general assembly in Oran to reorganize the remainder of the community. A year later, the Boumedienne regime took power and the situation began to deteriorate. Heavy taxes were imposed on the Jews and they faced discrimination in many other ways. The government stopped paying the salaries of rabbis on the grounds that they were French citizens. The Chief Court declared that Jews were no longer under the protection of the law, and an economic boycott was initiated against them. The president of the community was brought to trial on grounds that he had connections with Zionism, and one Jew was even executed. After the Six Day War, the government took over all but one of the synagogues in Algeria and converted them to mosques. By 1969, only one thousand Jews remained in the country, principally those who were too old or ill to move. By 1980, three hundred remained.

Morocco: Survival in Decline

The one Jewish community in the Arab world with any prospect of surviving is in Morocco. Although it, too, has drastically declined in size as a result of emigration—mainly to Israel but also to France, Spain, and North America—its members are under no external pressure to leave. Rather, it is their own perceptions of better opportunities or greater security elsewhere that lead them to emigrate. As a consequence, most of the community's institutions continue to function, although in more limited form than when the Moroccan Jewish population was at its peak in 1945. As in Iran, Moroccan Jews combine traditional and modern forms.

Moroccan Jewry, like other old, established Jewish communities, has traditions that go back to the most ancient times. There is archeological evidence of Jews in Morocco in the second century. The last of the Jewish Berber tribes existed into the twelfth century. In the late sixth century, there were close connections between the Jewish communities of Morocco and Spain, with Jews fleeing Spain for Morocco to escape the Visigothic persecutions, a pattern that was repeated at the end of the fifteenth century during the great expulsion. Jews were also apparently involved in the Arab conquest of Spain, which was launched from Morocco with their assistance in 711 C.E.

The history of the Jews of Morocco during the Middle Ages involves more persecution than was usual in Muslim lands, coming from various fanatical Islamic groups that gained control of western North Africa and in some instances Spain itself. This led to reverse migrations, with many Moroccan Jews moving north into Christian Spain. Although the situation improved for Jews toward the beginning of the fourteenth century, Morocco, like the rest of the Arab world, soon entered a period of decline.

The influx of Spanish exiles after 1492 led to a sharp division in the Jewish community. In southern Morocco, the Spanish *megurashim* soon came to dominate, although in integrated communities; in the north, the *megurashim* remained separate from the local Jewish residents (*toshavim*), with the exiles increasingly dominant. The *megurashim* established their center in Fez and totally absorbed the *toshavim* of Tangier and Tetuán. The two groups did not really merge until the nineteenth century.

During the sixteenth century, many Marranos fled from Spain and Portugal to Morocco where they returned to Judaism. Ironically, at the same time the Spanish Jewish exiles were helping the Spanish and Portuguese to establish footholds in Morocco in return for guarantees of rights and benefits. In part, this was because the Arab government of Morocco was growing weaker, power was being transferred to the countryside, and the Jews had to make the best deals they could. In many of the Berber-controlled areas they were able to acquire considerable local power. In other areas, however, they were impoverished and subjugated.

Throughout this period, Moroccan Jewry was very much part of the Jewish world, culturally creative, involved in the international commerce that took Jews from the Netherlands to India, and affected by the Sabbatean craze that swept the Jewish world in the middle of the seventeenth century. There was considerable cross-Mediterranean migration in all directions: Jews from Livorno and the Netherlands settled in Morocco; Moroccan Jews settled in the new Jewish communities bordering the North Sea as well as in Italy and the Ottoman Empire; and there was a steady stream of Moroccan Jews to Eretz Israel.

In the late seventeenth century, Morocco underwent a major political change. The Alawid Dynasty rose to power—assisted by the Jews. (The two forged an alliance that is still in effect today, as indicated by the role King Hassan has played in protecting the contemporary Moroccan Jewish community.) Although Morocco had an uneven history in the following generations, Jews remained leading figures in the court of the Alawid kings, serving as ambassadors, finance ministers, and confidential advisors to the sultans. In the late seventeenth and early eighteenth centuries, much of Morocco's foreign relations, particularly with the Christian states, was conducted by Jews, who used their overseas connections to protect Moroccan interests. For example, the U.S.-Moroccan Treaty of 1787, one of the first foreign agreements made by the new republic, was the work of two Moroccan descendants of Spanish exiles: Isaac Cardoza Nunes, a member of the sultan's court, and Isaac Pinto, a Moroccan Jew who had established himself in the United States.

Civil war, an upsurge of Muslim religious fundamentalism, and a series of plagues at the end of the eighteenth century all weakened Morocco and opened the door to European influence. European powers tried to use the Jews to expand their influence in Morocco, extending protection and employing Jews as their consular representatives, a sphere in which the Jews had almost a complete monopoly until the very last generation of the nineteenth century.

Near the end of the eighteenth century, many of the wealthier Jewish families emigrated from Morocco in search of better opportunities in Europe, the New World, or Eretz Israel. The poverty of those left behind worsened, becoming desperate by the time the Europeans actually occupied the country. Estimates of the Jewish population in nineteenth-century Morocco range from two hundred thousand to four hundred thousand.

By 1912, Morocco was divided: a Spanish protectorate in the north and a French protectorate in the south, a situation that lasted until 1956 when Morocco gained its independence. Until 1912, the Jewish communities were autonomous, as the Moroccan authorities had no interest in their internal affairs. After 1912, the French limited this autonomy. The Jewish community retained management of its educational, religious, and social welfare institutions, but lost the right to elect its local governing committees, which became appointed bodies *officially* chosen by the grand vizier but *in actuality* designated by the protectorate authorities. The local committees were supervised by a Jewish government official chosen by the French for his devotion to French interests. To the extent that they could, the Jewish communities tried to influence the choice of committee members to reflect local interests, but they were no longer free to follow their own political tradition as had been the case prior to the protectorate.

The wealthier Jews of the Moroccan community increasingly turned toward French culture and sought to divorce themselves from the larger Jewish population. Modern schools, which French Jews established in the nineteenth century through the Alliance Israelite Universelle, rapidly became the focus for Jews wishing to assimilate. There their children could learn French and Western ways and abandon traditional society. As a result, in most communities, with the exception of Tangier and one or two others, this Jewish upper class detached itself from communal affairs. Any limits imposed on their assimilation into the French elite came from the French themselves, who were basically anti-Semitic.

There were efforts made to organize a Zionist movement in Morocco in the late nineteenth century, but they had a difficult time gaining a foothold, partly because the French actively discouraged national movements of any kind and partly because so many modernized Jews were pursuing assimilation as an alternative. Zionist ideas, however, penetrated fully into the community between World Wars I and II, particularly into the youth movements as well as into the common ideology of those elements of the community who had become modernized but not assimilated.

Moroccan Jewry escaped the full impact of the Holocaust, although they were separated from the larger society by the Vichy-controlled protectorate government. In the process, relations with their Muslim neighbors also deteriorated. The Vichy government introduced its version of the Nuremberg Laws despite the opposition of the sultan, Muhammad V, who lived up to his family tradition and sought to protect the Jews. Once the Allies landed in North Africa and Morocco was liberated, Jewish rights, such as they were, were restored, although the French successors to the Vichy authorities did so only in June 1943 when the Gaullists came to power.

When Israel was established in 1948, there were some 265,000 Jews in Morocco. Tens of thousands emigrated to Israel. Some 43,000 left in the first three years followed by 60,000—most but not all to Israel—during the 1950s. The Moroccan Jewish population continued to decline rapidly in the 1960s, dropping from just under 160,000 according to the 1960 census to an estimated 22,000 in 1968. Since then the decline has been more gradual—to perhaps 16,000 today. Approximately 253,000 have settled in Israel.

As late as 1951, over one-third of Moroccan Jews lived in small towns and villages throughout the country. By the early 1970s, most Jews were concentrated in a few major cities, reversing the pattern of dispersal that had been characteristic of Moroccan Jewry since earliest times.

Until 1956, no serious obstacles were placed in the way of Jewish emigration to Israel, but Muhammad V, who otherwise improved the situation of the Jews in Morocco, imposed an order forbidding them to emigrate to the Jewish state. For five years emigration continued only illegally, but still some forty-seven thousand Jews left during that period. When Hassan II ascended the throne in 1961, the restrictions were lifted, and since then Jews have been free to move anywhere, although they are considered by the king to be Moroccan subjects wherever they settle.

Jewish life in Morocco underwent its greatest transformation in the postwar generation, in part because of great demographic changes. Thus, for example, in 1948 the Alliance Israelite Universelle operated fifty-two schools in the country with nearly twenty-two thousand pupils. Until 1956, it was still a growing enterprise, establishing thirty more schools and enrolling nearly twenty-nine thousand students. By 1965, however, the number of students had dropped to nine thousand, one thousand of whom were non-Jewish. Not only did the Alliance close schools that were no longer needed, but in 1960 the Moroccan government nationalized about a quarter of its schools and opened them as government institutions. At the same time, however, Otzar HaTorah (an American-based organization), Habad (the Lubavitcher Hassidim), and a group called Em HaBanim established Jewish schools in Morocco.

The coming of independence to Morocco improved the condition of the Jews as individuals but brought further restrictions on what remained of Jewish communal autonomy as the rulers of the newly independent state acted to consolidate Moroccan nationhood. All Zionist activity was gradually forbidden between 1956 and 1959, and many other Jewish organizations were also forced to disband. The World Jewish Congress managed to maintain its links with Moroccan Jewry throughout this period. A few Jews were influential in Moroccan politics at the outset of independence, but most were soon replaced. It was not until Hassan II came to power that individual Jews again became influential members of the royal court, and a select group remains so today.

Simultaneously, however, there was a rise in anti-Semitism—both verbal and physical. The publication of anti-Semitic literature and, worse, the kidnapping of young Jewish girls who were then forced to become Muslims accelerated emigration from the country. As a result, the 1960s saw the end of the old Jewish community in Morocco. After the Six Day War, even wealthy Jews began to leave the country in substantial numbers.

The All-Moroccan Jewish Council, established by royal decree in May 1945, was torn apart by internal rivalries and dissolved in 1962. During the next decade, a new body was established, which biennially convenes a Moroccan Jewish Congress, an event that has acquired symbolic importance as a sign of the well-being of Moroccan Jewry under Hassan II. In 1984, the congress was the vehicle for opening Moroccan-Israeli relations through the invitation to a substantial Israeli delegation, including Knesset members, to participate in the event along with Jews from other countries. Since then, the congress has become an important media event designed to reflect the new openness in Moroccan-Israeli relations and the improved status of the Moroccan Jewish community.

After 1967, many local Jewish institutions were closed. The lack of leadership, particularly rabbis, *dayanim* (rabbinical judges), and *haz-*

zanim (cantors), was soon felt. A basic community structure, however, remains, with schools, charitable institutions, community councils, synagogues, and the like. Most of the present institutions of Moroccan Jewry enjoy extensive aid from world Jewish sources, particularly the JDC, which supports all of the Jewish school systems in the country and certain welfare institutions as well.

The Jews had preserved their rabbinical courts throughout the period of the protectorate, even though they were limited under French rule. In 1956, however, newly independent Morocco transformed them into state courts of law, allowing only the Supreme Rabbinical Tribune to remain independent for another decade (it was abolished in 1965). Rabbinical judges were appointed to the state courts so that their jurisdiction over the Jewish community in personal status matters would come under direct state control. Morocco maintains a chief rabbi whose functions are limited.

Moreover, the community, although having sufficient human and fiscal resources to take care of itself, has come to rely on outside, principally Ashkenazic, aid, whether through the JDC or the Habad movement. Habad, with its great energy and messianic convictions, has been able to turn many Moroccan Sephardim into Lubavitcher Hassidim with olive complexions, totally disregarding the Sephardic cultural heritage—another example of Ashkenazic imperialism.

Moroccan Jewry in the 1980s is much like Iranian Jewry in the 1970s, sitting on the edge of a volcano and protected by the grace of a ruling monarch. Even the most devoted supporters of the government might not be willing to bet on the future of the Jewish community should something happen to Hassan II, or if his successor does not share his positive attitude toward the Jews.

During the first generation of Israel's statehood, the image of North African Jewry there has not been commensurate with their worth. Nevertheless, future generations will mark the contributions of North African Jewry to Israel and the Sephardic world in the decades following the breakup of their communities. For example, beginning in the early 1950s, Moroccan Jewry became the primary reservoir for both religious and civic leadership in much of the Sephardic world. Moroccan Jewry provided most of the rabbis, teachers, and *hazzanim* for Sephardic communities in the diaspora, and Jews of Moroccan background became highly visible in Jewish communal life in their new countries of settlement and in world Jewish institutions. Thus, the last years of North African Jewry as a distinctive entity have been far from barren.

Africa South of the Sahara

The existence of Sephardim in Central Africa is little known in the Ashkenazic world. As in Asia, small groups of Sephardic merchants and adventurers followed the Western colonial powers into black Africa, establishing small communities in the Belgian Congo, the Rhodesias, and British East Africa. In colonial days, the Belgian Congo and Northern and Southern Rhodesia had Sephardic communities, principally settlers from the Balkans and Syria, all of which have nearly disappeared as a result of decolonization. Some of these Jews, like their Ashkenazic brethren, have gone to South Africa and have established Sephardic congregations there.

Zaire

A Belgian colony prior to 1960, the first Jews settled in Zaire in 1907, coming from South Africa. In 1911, Sephardim arrived, mostly from the island of Rhodes and other Greek communities. They became dominant in the community, particularly after many of the Ashkenazim left during the Depression. After each world war, a few Ashkenazic refugees arrived as well.

By 1911, the resident Jews organized the Communauté de Congo Belge et du Ruanda-Urundi, which was given legal status by the colonial government. A synagogue was built in 1930 in Elizabethville (now Lubumbashi). It housed a community center as well as the other Jewish institutions in the community. From 1937 on, there was a resident rabbi. The Asociación Sionista de Congo Belga also functioned during this period. In addition to the Elizabethville community, seventy families lived in Leopoldville (now Kinshasa), with smaller concentrations in other Congo towns. Jewish children were taught Hebrew and Judaism in the government schools, the teachers paid by the colonial authorities. By 1960, there were twenty-five hundred Jews in the Belgian Congo, half in Elizabethville.

During the civil war that followed the sudden granting of independence to the Congo, many Jews left, and the Jewish population was reduced to less than one thousand, most remaining in Lubumbashi and Kinshasa. In the intervening years the Jewish population has continued to decline. In the mid-1980s, there were no more than two hundred known Jews permanently living in Zaire.

Zaire and Israel established diplomatic relations in 1960, and Israeli technical and military aid flowed into the country until Zaire broke off relations in 1973. Zaire later became the first country to restore relations with Israel, and Israeli assistance resumed. Hence, in addition to the permanent Jewish community, there are invariably a certain number of Israelis temporarily residing in the country.

Zambia

Jews went to Zambia, then Northern Rhodesia, at the turn of the century following British colonial expansion. The first two Jewish settlements were at Livingstone and Broken Hill. When the railroad reached Victoria Falls in 1905, there were enough Jews in Livingstone to establish a congregation, which by 1910 had thirty-eight members. Jews were pioneers in Northern Rhodesia, opening up the country to Europeans. They were involved in ranching, the cattle trade, transportation, and copper mining.

In 1921, forty-eight Jews lived in Livingstone, eleven in Broken Hill, and twenty-five in Lusaka. German Jewish refugees arrived in the late 1930s, increasing the size of the community somewhat, and the Jewish population reached a peak of close to twelve hundred in the mid-1950s, mainly in Lusaka and in five copper belt centers, each having a small congregation. After the breakup of the Central African Federation and the granting of independence to Northern Rhodesia as Zambia, many Jews left. The community survived in part because of Israelis temporarily in the country under the auspices of Solel Boneh, which had construction contracts with the Zambian government.

Zimbabwe

Sephardic Jews, principally from the island of Rhodes, were among the first settlers in Southern Rhodesia, now Zimbabwe, after it was opened up for white settlement in 1890. A small but significant Sephardic community developed alongside a larger Ashkenazic one. Although they maintained their own congregations, they were otherwise integrated into the general Jewish community, which was one of the best organized and most active in the world for its size.

Sephardim, like other Jews, began to leave as the civil war worsened, but most remained until Rhodesia was turned over to the most radical black group among the revolutionaries and became Zimbabwe. Subsequently, the vast majority of Jews left, most moving to South Africa, where the Rhodesian Sephardim became important in the development of South African Sephardic congregations.

South Africa: A New Community

The occasional Jews who drifted into South Africa in the seventeenth and eighteenth centuries were mostly Sephardim from Amsterdam, but they either left or rapidly assimilated. There were also a few Sephardim among the first Jewish settlers from England in the early nineteenth century after the British conquest of South Africa during the Napoleonic wars. Others drifted in throughout the rest of the nineteenth century. However, it was not until after World War II that an organized Sephardic presence emerged, the final step in the southward movement of the Balkan Jewish migration into black Africa, which had begun at the end of the last century.

There are now Sephardic synagogues in Johannesburg and Cape Town, founded initially in the 1960s by Sephardim who had left the newly independent African countries to rebuild their lives in South Africa, and reinforced most recently by the substantial Jewish exodus from Zimbabwe. These are typical Sephardic congregational communities, generally outside of the mainstream of South African Jewish life, yet likely to share whatever fate lies in store for South African Jewry.

Chapter 5

Tenuous Survival in Asia and New Frontiers in the Pacific

THE JEWISH PRESENCE in Asia is overwhelmingly Sephardic. In western Asia there are remnants of traditional Middle Eastern communities, and in Central Asia Sephardic communities in the Islamic countries overlap into the Islamic areas of the Soviet Union.

Western Asia is the birthplace of the Jewish people. Abraham, the first Jew, was born and raised in Mesopotamia (now Iraq) before settling in Canaan (now Eretz Israel). With the exception of the period of the Egyptian bondage, Jewish history was entirely confined to western Asia for its first twelve hundred to fourteen hundred years, and continued to be centered in Asia for a subsequent period of equal length. Indeed, the center of Jewish life did not pass from Asia until the eleventh century C.E., approximately three thousand years after Abraham. Thus, three-fourths of Jewish history has an Asian focus. Today, when the Jews have returned their center to Asia, it is important to recall these historical facts.

When the Jews were exiled from their land, first after the Assyrian conquest in the eighth century B.C.E. and then after the destruction of the First Temple by the Babylonians in the sixth, the other lands of western Asia were the principal places of settlement for the exiles. In the following centuries, Babylonia became a major center of Jewish life and creativity, first refounding and then interacting with the Jewish community in Eretz Israel throughout the period of the Second Commonwealth (from the end of the sixth century B.C.E. to the middle of the second century C.E.). After the destruction of the Second Temple (70 C.E.) and the disastrous Bar Kochba rebellion (132–35 C.E.), Babylonian Jewry, which included what is today eastern Syria, Iraq, Iran, and beyond into Afghanistan and Bukhara, became a coequal power with the community in Eretz Israel. Babylonian Jewry had its own comprehensive internal structure headed by the *resh galuta* (head of the exiled)—considered a descendant of King David—who shared power with two prominent *yeshivot* (in those days assemblies of scholars with decision-making powers), all under the suzerainty of the imperial power of the time. There the Babylonian Talmud, the most authoritative text of Jewish law and lore, was created, compiled, and canonized. There Saadia Gaon developed the accepted basis for systematic Jewish thought. After the rise of Islam, the *resh galuta* and *yeshivot* extended their control over 97 percent of the Jews of the world—from India to the Atlantic.

Following the eleventh century, the decline of western Asia was precipitous, stimulated by the devastating Mongol invasions that recurred over the next two centuries. Neither general nor Jewish life fully recovered from those blows. Though Jewish life on a local level continued to be rich in its day-to-day texture, the western Asian Jewish communities ceased to influence the world Jewish scene. There was some revival, especially in what is now Syria, after the Spanish expulsion when some of the exiles reached the region, but it was not until the nineteenth century and the beginning of modernization that those communities again became active forces.

In the nineteenth century, Jews from these communities were among the first to respond to the reawakened desire to return to Zion. After midcentury, Jewish *olim* from every one of them formed communities in Eretz Israel, but it remained until after 1948 for the remainder of those Asian communities to be evacuated en masse to the new Jewish state. This was the case with regard to the Jews of Iraq, Yemen, Aden, and Afghanistan. There were large *aliyot*—almost evacuations—from Iran and Syria. Only the Jewish community in Lebanon was hardly moved by the events of 1948, but it, too, subsequently left as a result of the Lebanese civil wars. In the 1970s, a substantial proportion of the Jews of Soviet Central Asia had the opportunity to emigrate to Israel, and a decade later many of the remaining Jews of Iran also emigrated, some to Israel and others to Europe and North America.

Lebanon: The Last Days

There are sporadic records of a Jewish presence in what is now Lebanon since ancient times: in the cities and villages of the mountains and on the adjacent coast. However, it was not until the late nineteenth century that a serious concentration of Jews developed. They settled in Beirut as that city became the *entrepôt* of southern Syria and the port of Damascus. The last traditional rural Jewish community, in Hasbayya on the slopes of Mt. Hermon, moved almost *en bloc* to Rosh Pina in Eretz Israel in 1888.

Among the Jews who settled in Lebanon were Sephardim from Greece and Turkey engaged in commerce. By 1929, approximately five thousand Jews lived in Beirut, with perhaps nine thousand in the entire country by 1948 with the arrival of Jewish refugees from Syria and Iraq after the State of Israel was established. The Lebanese government did not punish its Jews for the "sins" of the Zionists and even granted citizenship to some of the newcomers.

Jews did not begin to leave Lebanon until 1958, at the first outbreak of internal unrest, which became outright civil war by 1975. Only a few hundred of the emigrants went to Israel; most settled in Europe and the United States. Over the next decade, the Jewish population in Lebanon dropped to five thousand. The Six Day War convinced many of them that there was no Jewish future in the Arab world, and another two thousand left within the year. Still, the Safrah and Zilka banks, the two great Syrian and Iraqi Jewish family institutions, continued to function until the 1970s.

Throughout this period, the Beirut Jewish community maintained its synagogue and communal institutions. A community with a synagogue also existed in Sidon, as well as synagogues in the summer resorts of the mountains near Beirut. Both the Beirut and Sidon communities maintained Jewish elementary and high schools.

By 1970, the number of Lebanese Jews decreased to fifteen hundred.

The arrival of the Palestine Liberation Organization (PLO) and the outbreak of civil war accelerated the decline so that by 1985 there were less than one hundred Jews in Beirut, the one remaining community. Since 1971, community leaders have been kidnapped periodically by Syrian and terrorist organizations, culminating in the kidnapping and murder of the remaining leaders in 1985.

Syrian Jewry: Imprisoned But Functioning

Syria—ancient Aram—is Israel's oldest enemy and the home of one of the oldest Jewish communities in the diaspora, dating back to biblical times. There were large communities in the Roman period, difficult times under the Byzantine rulers, improvements under the Arabs between the seventh and twelfth centuries, and severe destruction resulting from the Mongol invasions in the thirteenth and fourteenth centuries.

The arrival of Spanish exiles in the early sixteenth century revived the Syrian Jewish communities with the influx of more cosmopolitan Sephardim. Their arrival coincided with the conquest of Syria by the Ottoman Turks, which increased trade opportunities as well as the strength of the Spanish exiles, who had particularly good connections with the regime. As a result, trade expanded from the western Mediterranean to the Indian subcontinent on routes passing through northern Syria. Communities prospered in Damascus, Aleppo, and in smaller centers. The cultural and religious life of Syrian Jewry was strongly influenced by the Jewish community in Eretz Israel, particularly the Kabbalists in Safed.

Aleppo, the center of a region known in Jewish tradition by its biblical name, *aram tzova*, declined in the second half of the eighteenth century as trade routes shifted and its economic base eroded, while the Jewish community of Damascus rose in importance. Its leaders played an increasingly important role as ministers and advisors to the local rulers, especially in finance. Throughout the nineteenth century, leading Jewish families were engaged in local political intrigues. New interethnic tensions developed, bringing blood libels against the Jews on several occasions, including the famous Damascus blood libel of 1840, which was one of the catalytic events of the reawakening of world Jewish involvement in the international arena.

The Jews were frequently caught in the middle of growing Muslim attacks on the Christian minority. In addition, the opening of the Suez Canal virtually ended Syria's share of international trade between Europe and Persia. Syrian Jews began to emigrate in substantial numbers, particularly to the Americas. The Jews remaining in Damascus began to modernize and assimilate, particularly into French culture.

Modernization was much less a factor in Aleppo, which retained traditional patterns. Although many Halabim (Jews from Aleppo) emigrated to the New World, they have been notably tenacious in retaining traditional ways generations after leaving their city of origin. Aleppan Jews also emigrated to Eretz Israel; fewer Damascene Jews did so.

At the end of World War I, the Jews of Syria and Lebanon were concentrated in three large communities: Damascus and Aleppo with approximately six thousand Jews each, and Beirut with some four thousand. Another two thousand Jews were scattered in smaller communities. During the period of the French Mandate, there was little Jewish public activity, with most Jewish life confined to traditional and family frameworks. After Lebanon was given independence in 1943, about fifteen thousand Jews remained in Syria. Ten thousand left after 1948, stimulated by the 1947 pogroms in Aleppo in response to the United Nations partition decision.

After 1948, the condition of Syrian Jewry progressively worsened. Anti-Jewish laws were periodically passed, mostly designed to impoverish the Jews by preventing the sale of their property and by freezing their bank accounts. Much Jewish property was confiscated by the authorities and turned over to Palestinian refugees. Except for brief periods in 1954 and 1958, emigration was forbidden. Some Jews who did get out, to Lebanon, were actually returned to Syria by the Lebanese authorities. Others were caught, punished, tortured, and even executed, and their families were punished as well.

Today, an estimated 5,000 Jews remain in Syria: 4,000 in Damascus and less than 800 in Aleppo. There is also a community of 150 to 200 in Quamishli. None are permitted to leave the country and all are under constant harassment by the authorities. A few do escape and a few others are released in response to special outside intervention. Jewish property is confiscated on any pretext. On the other hand, a few Jews are able to study at the universities. No countrywide Jewish organization is allowed, but each community maintains its own governing committee under the watchful eye of the authorities. The Alliance Israelite

Universelle maintains schools in Damascus and Aleppo, and somehow manages to maintain working relationships with the Syrian government.

The Jewish Handful in Iraq

Iraq—ancient Babylonia—was the site of the first great Jewish diaspora community, founded twenty-six hundred years ago. From the fifth to eleventh centuries, it was the greatest of all diaspora centers. The decline of Babylonian Jewry began before the Mongol and Tartar invasions in the thirteenth and fourteenth centuries.

Under the control of the Ottoman Empire from 1638 until 1917, the Jews did relatively well, but the general decline of the empire and the bewildering succession of regional rulers kept the community from prospering or progressing. Still, during the nineteenth century their economic situation was good. They controlled the country's commerce and exerted considerable influence in government circles. Jewish merchants traded throughout the world and, in partnership with the British, opened up the Far East, where they established Jewish communities from Karachi to Kobe. Iraqi Jews were sufficiently prominent in politics to be elected to the Turkish parliament as delegates from their country after the Young Turk revolution of 1908. Jews were among the founders of modern Iraqi literature and did much to advance education in the country.

In 1917, the British conquered Mesopotamia and ruled first as occupiers and then under a League of Nations Mandate until 1932. They installed the eldest son of Sherif Hussein of Mecca as King Faisal I. He was a liberal, and sympathetic to Jewish interests. Jews were allowed freedom of religion, education, and employment, and representation in the Iraqi parliament.

Jews rapidly advanced in all the institutions of the Iraqi government and continued to be prominent in banking and commerce. They had an advantageous position because so many of them had been educated in Alliance schools founded in the nineteenth century. Although Baghdad, Basra, and Mosul were the three great Jewish centers in Iraq, Jews were scattered throughout the country. At the end of World War I, there were probably one hundred thousand Jews in Iraq, increasing by another fifty thousand by 1947, with two-thirds located in the province of Baghdad.

At least four Hebrew language societies and a Maccabi sports group were organized in the 1920s and early 1930s. Teachers from Eretz Israel provided Hebrew and Jewish history instruction in Iraqi Jewish schools. The Jews were free enough to organize a Zionist movement and maintained it more or less openly from 1918 to 1935, including annual fund raising through the World Zionist Organization's Keren Hayesod from 1923 on. In 1929, however, the government began to attack Zionism, and after 1935 the movement had to go underground.

Much of this was a false dawn, since Jewish prosperity depended upon British government protection. Once Iraq gained its independence in 1932, the government turned against the Jews in an effort to Arabize the civil service and the economic sector. Jews were consistently discriminated against and emigration was made difficult, all this culminating in the Shavuot pogrom in 1941 when many Jews were killed and injured in Baghdad. The British intervened, mainly because the pogrom was connected with a pro-Nazi uprising against the Iraqi government, and peace was restored. As early as 1932, a Zionist underground movement had been organized to prepare for the evacuation of the Jews from Iraq, and it intensified its activities after 1941.

As the Jewish-Arab conflict over Palestine intensified, the attitude of the Iraqi government toward the Jews became more negative. In July 1948, Zionism was made a crime, punishable by imprisonment or even death. Between May 1948 and December 1949, hundreds of Jews were arrested and several hanged. This led tens of thousands of Jews to flee illegally to Iran. In March 1950, the Iraqi authorities permitted Jews to leave if they relinquished Iraqi nationality. In May, the legal exodus to Israel began, continuing until August 1951. Under the auspices of the Jewish Agency and with the help of the underground Zionist organization, 110,000 Jews left for Israel, with another 13,500 following via Iran or illegally before May 1950. Their abandoned property was seized by the Iraqi state. All told, some 125,000 Iraqi Jews have emigrated to Israel.

The Jews who remained were still aided by the underground Zionist organization for the next several months and protected by a Jewish self-defense force of some six hundred men organized by the Hagana. Both groups were broken up in December 1951, and two of their leaders hanged several months later. In January 1952, the six thousand Jews remaining in Iraq were issued new identity cards and forbidden to leave the country. In that year, the lone Jewish senator in the Iraqi parliament and the six Jewish members in the lower house resigned, ending Jewish representation in the parliament.

The government reorganized the Jewish community by law in December 1954, further restricting Jewish rights. Except for short periods, Jews were not allowed to leave the country until 1958. For the five years following, under the Qasim regime, conditions improved, but when he was overthrown the gates again closed. By that time, the Jews numbered only three thousand. The remaining Jews continued to maintain basic religious and educational institutions.

Slowly, the lives of the Jews who remained in Iraq improved, until in the 1960s life returned to normal for them. Most prospered until the Arab defeat in the Six Day War led to another round of persecutions and hangings. The climax came between September 1972 and April 1973 when at least twenty-three Jews were murdered by authorities. Others fled the country, so that by the time of the Yom Kippur War only four hundred Jews remained. About the same number live in Iraq today with a few trickling out every year. Two synagogues remain in Baghdad, but only one is in use.

Prior to 1948, a second major concentration of Jews was located in Iraqi Kurdistan. The Kurdish people are spread over sections of Iran, Turkey, and Syria as well as Iraq, but most of Kurdistan's Jews were located in the Iraqi section, particularly in the cities of Mosul, Kirkuk, Erbil, Amadiya, Zakhu, and Barashi. The Kurdish Jews are a separate group in their own right, speaking their own Aramaic dialect, closely related to that of the Babylonian Talmud, so they did not even share a common language with the Iraqi Jews of the Valley of the Two Rivers.

A traditional community to the end, Kurdish Jewish *olim* trickled into Eretz Israel from the sixteenth century on. Those under Iraqi jurisdiction were eligible for the mass emigration of 1950, and virtually all of them came to Israel at that time. There has been no organized Jewish life in Iraqi Kurdistan since then. All that remains of Kurdish Jewry outside of Israel are a few villages in Iranian and Turkish Kurdistan.

Yemen Rediscovered

The "rediscovery" of Yemenite Jewry at the beginning of the Zionist revolution led them to be treated as a lost tribe by the Ashkenazim, who had not been aware of their existence prior to the 1880s. In fact, the community, while isolated, was always part of the communications network of the Sephardic world. The community itself apparently goes back at least to the time of the Second Temple, although its own traditions date it even earlier. Its greatest period was in the sixth century when the Yemenite ruling family embraced Judaism and governed for a brief time what was, for all intents and purposes, a Jewish state.

The Ottomans conquered Yemen in the midsixteenth century and, unlike in other parts of the empire, their arrival brought great difficulty to the Jews. The Jews were caught in the crossfire between the Turkish conquerors and the local tribes, or were subject to persecution by Muslim zealots, culminating in the destruction of all synagogues in the capital, Sanaa, and the expulsion of the Jews in 1676. The local imams succeeded in expelling the Turks, thereby worsening the Jews' position. Ottoman control was not reextended over the country until 1849, and even then it remained nominal.

During the eighteenth and nineteenth centuries, the Jews' economic position deteriorated further, although even nominal Ottoman rule brought them greater physical security. Imam Yahkya revolted against the Ottomans in 1904 and captured Sanaa a year later. He ruled until 1948 and, like his predecessors, persecuted the Jews, who remained at the bottom of the Yemenite social order, defined as serfs without rights, severely restricted in their public and private lives and required to perform degrading tasks.

From the eleventh through eighteenth centuries, the only hope for Yemenite Jews was the periodic appearance of false Messiahs—promising redemption through divine intervention—climaxing in the Sabbatean episode. In the nineteenth century, three pseudo-Messiahs appeared, the last in 1893, but after that, messianism was replaced by a turning toward Eretz Israel. The first *aliyah* of Yemenites actually took place in the eighteenth century and led to the foundation of Jerusalem's Beth-El congregation, which for nearly two hundred years was the home of the city's Kabbalists. Still, it was not until the nineteenth century that regular, organized *aliyot* of Yemenite Jews began to arrive, culminating in the mass evacuation of the community through Operation Magic Carpet after the establishment of the state.

Jewish life in Yemen continued in the traditional pattern until the end of the nineteenth century. The first modern Jewish school was founded in Sanaa in 1910, leading to a struggle in the community between traditionalists and those advocating change. Since the latter did not find favor in the eyes of the imam, few changes were introduced. The local communities continued to be governed by councils and law courts, with the chief rabbi of the Sanaa community being the Hakham Bashi for all of Yemenite Jewry. The last rabbi to hold that office died in 1932 and no successor was appointed.

Between 1919 and 1948, nearly one-third of the Jewish population of Yemen, approximately sixteen thousand Jews, emigrated to Eretz Israel. Between June 1949 and June 1950, another forty-three thousand were brought by Operation Magic Carpet. Some thirteen hundred Jews arrived between 1951 and 1954.

By 1955, the number of Jews in Yemen was estimated at about eight hundred, dropping to about two hundred by 1968. Since then, the rediscovery of concentrations of Jews who did not leave after 1948 places the number of Jews in Yemen, now renamed North Yemen, at between one thousand and six thousand. Within the limits imposed by a hostile government, they maintain traditional communal and religious lives in a number of cities and towns around the country, and even continue to learn Hebrew. Schools exist in the larger communities, and in the smaller ones volunteer teachers educate the young semiprivately.

The principal institutionalized contact between the Jews of North Yemen and the outside world is through the Satmar Hassidim, who cultivate the connection as part of their anti-Zionism. Satmar Hassidim have visited communities accompanied by Yemenite government officials and members of the PLO who act as intermediaries to facilitate the contact.

Economically, Yemenite Jews are in much the same circumstances as their Muslim neighbors, certainly no worse. In some places they are even allowed to carry weapons for self-defense, although not the *jambiah*, the traditional dagger carried by male Muslims, a sign of status. Recently, there have been reports of renewed persecution, and Jews in other countries have demanded that they be allowed to leave.

What were once Hadramuth and Aden are now known as South Yemen. The Jewries in those areas were part and parcel of overall Yemenite culture. Jews had been in the Hadramuth region since ancient times, but Aden did not become a significant settlement until it was conquered by the British in 1839 and turned into a way station on the British path to South Asia and the Far East. In 1839, Jews constituted five hundred of the fifteen hundred residents of Aden. As the city grew, so did the Jewish population. At its peak, at the end of World War II, there were eight thousand Jews in Aden out of a total population of one hundred thousand.

Under the British, the Jews began as builders and ended up in middle-management and administrative positions with the British government and as merchants within the community. Since they were fully literate, they became essential middlemen in the British protectorate. Aden's Jewish community was the key in a network that stretched from Yemen to Hong Kong.

Some 70 percent (nearly four thousand) of the Jews of Aden settled in Israel between 1947 and 1969. With the British evacuation in 1968, all the remaining Jews left. Most settled in London. Others followed the earlier path of Adeni Jews to India, Singapore, Hong Kong, and Australia; only a few of the poorest settled in Israel.

The Jewish Community in Iran

In addition to the Arab states, the Muslim world includes the rest of western Asia, with its ancient Jewish communities of Iran and Afghanistan, which as Muslim countries have more or less gone the way of the Arab states in Jewish matters. The Jewish communities in Iran and Afghanistan were part of the long stream of Jewish history as frontier regions of Babylonian Jewry. They were the sources of Jewish settlement both in the Central Asian areas now under Soviet rule and in the Jewish communities of old China. They were also known for producing sectarian challenges to normative Judaism in the seventh through ninth centuries.

The Jewish community in Iran remained intact longer than those in any Muslim country other than Morocco and Turkey. Until the Khomeini revolution in 1979, it even enjoyed a protected position. Iranian Jews trace the beginnings of their community to the foundation of Persia at the time of Cyrus the Great, some twenty-five hundred years ago. It is possible that Jews lived in what is now Iran prior to that as a result of the exiles and population exchanges that began with the Assyrian conquest of the northern kingdom of Israel in 721 B.C.E. Yet the antiquity of the community bears little relevance to its present situation.

The best years of Iranian Jewry were in the early years of the Persian Empire. Subsequently, its Jewish communities suffered from periodic outbreaks of religious fanaticism that seem to be endemic to the Iranian people and that antedate their embrace of Islam in its Shi'ite version.

While there were other periods in which the community was allowed more room to flourish, including a time in the late Middle Ages when Persian Jewry produced a substantial literature in its own Judeo-Persian language, by and large Jews have lived in Iran with difficulty, and the country never became a center for sustained Jewish creativity—certainly not since the fourteenth century.

Jewish life reached its nadir in the centuries immediately prior to the present one. The situation of Iranian Jewry began to improve in the late nineteenth century after leading European Jews took note of its condition and with the backing of their respective imperial powers put pressure on Persian rulers to allow the Jews to improve their position. It was not easily done, since even when concessions were wrung from Iran's benighted shahs, everything was done to prevent their translation into action. The Alliance Israelite Universelle was finally able to open its first school in Teheran in 1898, over thirty years after the first intervention on the part of European Jewry.

The 1906 Iranian constitution granted Jews civil rights, but it was not until General Reza Pahlevi took power in 1921 that their situation began truly to improve. Reza became shah in 1925 and inaugurated a westernizing revolution similar to that of Kemal Ataturk in Turkey. He began by breaking the extremely reactionary Shi'ite clergy. The Jews were politically emancipated under his rule. Their situation further improved under the rule of his son Mohammed Reza Shah who formed an alliance with the leading Jewish families and benefited from their support in moments of crisis as well as in his efforts to develop Iran's economy. It was accepted that without his special protection the Jews in Iran would have difficulties, and when he was forced to abdicate in 1979, the Jews' political position worsened considerably.

In 1948, there were ninety-five thousand Jews in Iran. Nearly sixty-one thousand emigrated to Israel between 1948 and 1970. More than ten thousand others settled there after 1979. Of the estimated thirty thousand to thirty-five thousand Jews remaining today, about twenty-five thousand live in Teheran, the capital, which has existed as a city for little more than two centuries and became a large city only in the twentieth century. Most of Teheran's Jews settled there in the past two generations. Consequently, only the few thousand Jews in the older cities and towns (five thousand to seven thousand in Shiraz, about two thousand in Isfahan, and thirty-five hundred in other towns and villages) have maintained any ancestral connections with long-time places of residence, but these are declining communities. Despite the persistence of premodern elements in its legal status and organizational structure, the contemporary Iranian Jewish community is as much a product of modern migrations as are the other Jewries of the contemporary world.

Many of the community's problems are directly related to the fact that Jews of contemporary Iran have assimilated many aspects of Iranian culture, relatively isolated as they have been from the rest of world Jewry for centuries. The community has virtually no ancient and venerable institutions that are carried over into the present. That, too, is part of Iranian culture.

Since the establishment of the State of Israel and most pronouncedly since the Khomeini revolution, the Iranian Jewish community has shown signs of a community in dissolution, at the same time maintaining a range of institutions and commitments. Up to three-quarters of its members—including many potential leaders—have moved to Israel or the West since 1948, principally in two mass emigrations, the first to the new state in the early 1950s and the second to Israel, Western Europe, and North America in the 1980s.

For most Iranian Jews, family and personal ties are still perceived as so important that they feel no need for formal Jewish organization, which is virtually nonexistent. In the days of Mohammed Reza Shah, young people going to the university began to mix with the general population and break away from their family circles so that even those ties became less binding. Many assimilated Jews were kept within the Jewish fold only because of Iran's personal status laws, which require everyone to be a member of some religious community for purposes of marriage and inheritance.

Although the traditional separation between Jews and Muslims led the Jewish community to maintain a relatively wide range of institutions—synagogues, schools, a hospital, and social welfare services—the community did very little either to construct or support those institutions. Instead, it relied on world Jewry to initiate, fund, and sometimes even supply the personnel to operate them. This dates back to the late nineteenth century.

The grinding poverty of Iranian Jewry was such that outside Jewish aid continued to increase until, by the mid-1950s, the community was essentially a protectorate of world Jewry, led by a condominium of American and Israeli Jews through their institutions for overseas aid, principally the Joint Distribution Committee (JDC) and the Jewish Agency. These and other bodies, such as the Alliance and the Otzar Ha-Torah school system initiated by Aleppan Jews in the United States to serve the Sephardic world, provided services ranging from elementary education to a traveling rabbinical court from Israel. The Israeli connection ended with the Khomeini revolution, but the JDC, Otzar HaTorah, and the Alliance retain an attenuated presence in the country under strict government control.

The Iranian community has produced little in the way of Jewish culture for centuries. Its members are concerned with improving their economic status, which is not surprising since only some fifty years ago virtually all of Iran's Jews were desperately poor. World War II increased their opportunities for prosperity, and Mohammed Reza Shah's modernization program, to which the Jews contributed greatly, benefited them as well. Within a generation, the vast majority of the Jewish community had prospered, and a few families became very wealthy indeed. The wealthy joined the ranks of the worldwide Jewish elite, spreading their business interests and social networks far beyond Iran.

Of course, all of this prosperity was contingent on the community's good relations with the shah. His downfall, therefore, put the Jews, especially the very wealthy, in an extremely precarious position. Most of the wealthy left the country as soon as they could, many settling in southern California. What remains of the Iranian community today lives in the shadow of Khomeinism.

Although the Khomeini regime took away many privileges the Jews had under the shah and spurred mass emigration, the regime has, oddly enough, given the Jewish community something of a new lease on life. The constitution of Khomeini's Islamic Republic recognizes the Jews as one of three protected religious minorities, guaranteed "complete freedom in the practice of religious duties and functions, such as in matters of marriage, divorce, inheritance, wills and testaments." Hence, the rabbinical courts have reacquired certain powers once taken away by the previous secular regime.

Not only has the regime allowed the old institutions to continue under new leadership, but its religious tone has led to a religious revival among the Jews, if only in self-defense. In 1981, the Jewish community was given a new religious leader in the form of a chief rabbi for Teheran, a position often vacant in the past. The same year, the Jewish community elected a representative to the Majlis, the Iranian parliament, to assume the seat held under the shah by the executed Habib Elghanian. Synagogue attendance has increased, with the encouragement of communal leadership, as part of the Jewish effort to increase the legitimacy of Jewish religious observance. Public meetings at which government officials appear are periodically held at synagogues to strengthen Jewish ties with the regime.

Although the Jewish schools have been nationalized and are now under even closer government supervision than in the days of the shah, the Ministry of Religion provides financing for Jewish religious education, which is compulsory for Jews. Those children not enrolled in Jewish day schools must acquire Jewish religious education through supplementary schooling. As a result, afternoon Hebrew schools have been established, teachers have been trained and hired, and *siddurim* and textbooks have been published with the education ministry's backing. All this has ended the slow but continuing decline in Jewish religious education under the shah's more open regime.

The Anjoman Kalimian, the Jewish Community Council, has a new head. The Jewish hospital and welfare institutions continue to operate, although under some pressure to provide more extensive services for non-Jews, which was true under the shah as well.

On the other hand, most Jews in government posts and at the universities were dismissed after the revolution, and today an estimated 60 percent of the working Jewish population is self-employed, principally in retail businesses and small trades, and another 10 to 15 percent is employed as professionals. Thus, Jewish dependence on Iranian society for economic sustenance has been reduced to a minimum, involving exchange rather than employment.

Despite official protection, Jews are still subject to harassment from revolutionary guards and local workers' committees, and there are occasional executions. On the other hand, Jews serve in the Iranian army and attend universities. As a price, though, Jewish leaders are regularly forced to denounce Israel and Zionism.

Afghanistan's Scattered Families

According to Afghani tradition, the leading tribes, the Durani, Kussatzai, and Afridis, are descended from a combination of the ten lost tribes of Israel and King Saul through one of his wives. This tradition is presented as fact in the locally published tourist guidebooks, and is part of a widespread claim to Jewish descent found among Pathans in Pakistan and India as well. Jewish tradition also regards Afghanistan, known in medieval times as Khorasan, as the location of the ten tribes, and in recent years there have been those who are interested in bringing the Muslim Afghanis back into the Jewish fold.

Whatever the reality, Jews have lived in Afghanistan for several thousand years. During the days of the Babylonian Exilarchate, rejected candidates for the office of *resh galuta* were often exiled to Afghanistan because of its remoteness. Afghanistan was also a jumping-off point for Jewish excursions to China and other parts of Central Asia. From the time of the Mongol invasions, the Jews in Afghanistan were in difficult straits, but perhaps no more so than the rest of the population, since the area was in a constant state of intertribal warfare. The Jews formed alliances in order to survive, including close ties with the great Mongol leader Timur, or Tamerlane, who favored them.

Afghanistan reappears in Jewish history in the nineteenth century when many of the *anusim* (Marranos) of Meshed in Iran fled there after their forced conversion to Islam in 1839. They revived Jewish life and quickly came to dominate the community, even to the point of making the dominant language of Afghani Jews a Judeo-Persian dialect rather than Pushto, which is spoken locally. Jewish scholarship flourished in a modest way, and toward the end of the century Afghani Jews began to emigrate to Eretz Israel where they organized a separate subcommunity in Jerusalem.

In 1948, approximately five thousand Jews were living in Afghanistan, principally in Kabul, Balkh, and Herat, the largest community. From the time of the 1933 assassination of King Nadir Shah, the Jews had been subjected to pressure and indeed had been banished from some towns and forbidden to leave others without a permit. They retreated into their own walled quarters for self-protection. A few managed to flee the country to Iran or India and from there worked their way to Israel, but the government did not allow the others to depart. As soon as permission was granted in 1951, virtually all of them left.

Thus, within two years, the Afghani Jewish community all but ceased to exist. The great majority emigrated to Israel, a small minority to the United States. All told, there were some two hundred Jews in Afghanistan in 1976, on the eve of the Soviet invasion. There were fifteen Jewish families in Kabul, most of them native Afghanis and the rest from Bukhara—who had fled to Afghanistan in the 1920s after the Russian Revolution. They maintained a synagogue and a *shohet* (ritual slaughterer).

Sixteen families lived in Herat, where they maintained three synagogues. There has been no word of them since Afghanistan was invaded by the Soviets.

Soviet Asian Jewry

The original Jewish exiles who moved north from Eretz Israel spilled over into Georgia and the Caucasus to develop long-lived and substantial communities. Georgian Jewish tradition claims that the first Jewish communities established themselves after the Assyrian exile of Jews from the northern kingdom of Israel (721 B.C.E.). Through the centuries, several Jewish communities developed in Armenia, Georgia, and the Caucasus proper. The Armenian and Georgian communities lived among Christians; the Caucasus Jews among Muslims. All suffered the usual persecutions and attrition. For approximately six hundred years, from the thirteenth to the nineteenth centuries, they were cut off from the major centers of Jewish life. The Russian conquest of those territories at the beginning of the nineteenth century restored contact and brought new persecution.

In earlier days, these Jewries came under the jurisdiction of the Babylonian Jewish Exilarch and *yeshivot*. Later, after they were isolated, they had to shift for themselves. The Russian conquest brought them under Russian Ashkenazic influence. At first forbidden to settle in these Asian territories, after 1860 Ashkenazic entrepreneurs, soldiers, and craftsmen arrived, and regular contact led to a few of the local Jews traveling to Lithuania to study in the *yeshivot* there in order to serve their communities as rabbis.

Zionism easily took root among these Jewries, and hundreds settled in Eretz Israel, especially in Jerusalem, beginning in 1863. The Bolshevik Revolution enabled Georgia, Armenia, and other areas to declare independence, but they were reconquered by the Soviet army within a few years. The local Jews all strongly resisted Communist efforts to de-Judaize them. In general, the Soviets have had difficulty imposing their will on the non-Russian mountain peoples of Armenia, Georgia, and the Caucasus, and the Jews benefited from Soviet caution in dealing with the locals. By and large, they were able to maintain much of their traditional way of life for two generations after the revolution.

In 1959, the Soviet census registered 125,000 Jews in the Caucasus, which includes the republics of Armenia, Azerbaijan, and Georgia, and the autonomous provinces of Chechan-Ingush, Dagestais, Kabardino-Balkar, and North Ossetia; approximately half of those Jews were Ashkenazim. In the 1970s, Jews took advantage of a brief easing of the Soviet emigration policy to leave for Israel. Nevertheless, organized Jewish communities remain throughout the area.

Farther east are the Jews of Bukhara, once an independent khanate and now a territory in the Uzbek S.S.R. They are closely related to the Jews of Persia and Afghanistan, with whom they have maintained connections over the years. The Muslims who ruled them were particularly fanatical, and persecutions were relentless, at least from the thirteenth century on, intensifying in the mideighteenth century. Hence, when the Russians began their conquest of Bukhara in the midnineteenth century, the situation of the Jews actually improved.

Bukharan Jews have a long cultural and literary tradition. They wrote in both the Tajiki-Jewish dialect and in Judeo-Persian. They were brought within the Sephardic orbit after 1793, when the Jewish community of Safed sent Joseph ha Ma'arav as an emissary to Bukhara. He established links with the Sephardim of the Mediterranean. The Bukharan Jews abandoned the Persian Jewish liturgy and adopted that of the Spaniolim. Thus, when they began to settle in Jerusalem in 1868, they were easily assimilated among the Sephardim there. Hebrew was introduced as a spoken language by the Russian Ashkenazic Zionists at the end of the nineteenth century and soon became the language of instruction in the more forward-looking Jewish schools. It was still studied legally as late as 1924.

Beginning with Rabbi Jacob Meir's 1882 mission to Bukhara, prompted by the Council of the Sephardic Community in Jerusalem, Bukharan Jews were encouraged to settle in Eretz Israel, especially in Jerusalem, where in 1892 they founded the Bukharan Quarter. By 1936, there were twenty-five hundred in the country.

At the time of the Russian Revolution, Bukhara sought independence but was conquered by the Red Army in 1920 and incorporated into the Soviet Union. Because of Bukhara's non-Russian character, the Soviets showed the same kind of prudence in enforcing Communist ways as in the Caucasus; hence, the local Jews were able to preserve more of their way of life than was possible in Russia proper. Jewish cooperatives even had Hebrew names until they were disbanded in the late 1930s, and a Communist newspaper was published in the local Jewish language. In 1939, there were just under fifty-one thousand Jews in Bukhara, nearly doubling by 1959 as a result of Ashkenazic immigration from other parts of the U.S.S.R. Despite Soviet efforts, Jewish life persists apparently unabated. Synagogues remain open and full on the Sabbath and on holy days. Kosher meat continues to be available. Bukharan Jews were not included in the mass Soviet Jewish emigrations of the 1970s, and so the community remains more or less undiluted.

South and East Asia

One of the largely untold stories of modern Jewish history is how Sephardic Jews from Mesopotamia and the Persian Gulf moved eastward in the nineteenth century to found new communities across Asia and in the Pacific. As the bulk of world Jewry was discovering new worlds to the west, these Arabic- and Persian-speaking Sephardic Jews, mostly merchants, followed the tide of empire—particularly the British Empire—as middlemen in the new imperial society and economy. As such, they helped bridge the gap between colonial rulers and indigenous populations, establishing small communities in India, Singapore, Indonesia, the Philippines, Japan, and the coastal enclaves of China. In time these communities became more diversified in their Jewish populations and sufficiently established to acquire a permanent presence, although they all remained small and most have declined since decolonization. The fortunes of these Jews were tied closely with those of the colonial powers and most did not try to make the transition to life within the newly independent states. Nevertheless, a few of these communities remain.

Since in every epoch Jews notably gravitate to the most active centers of the world's communications network, until modern times few moved south of the Sahara or east of the Hindu Kush. Neither Africa south of the Sahara nor the rest of Asia offered them much opportunity. Two exceptions to this rule are Ethiopia and India—both immediately adjacent to ancient Jewish concentrations in western Asia—which were settled early in the long history of the Jewish diaspora by adventurous pioneers from those adjacent lands, and which in time became more or less cut off from their Jewish brethren but managed to survive as indigenous, isolated Jewish communities. Their rediscovery and reconnection with the Jewish people is part of the saga of modern Jewry. Otherwise, except for such isolated occurrences as the periodic settlement of a few Jews in China between the fifth and fifteenth centuries and the appearance of a few Portuguese Marranos in the East Indies and western Pacific in the sixteenth and seventeenth centuries, no Jewish communities were established in black Africa or East Asia until the modern epoch. The fleeting contacts with Mediterranean Jewish traders or migrants who moved into South Asia from time to time during the Middle Ages, or occasional Marranos who settled along the coasts of the Indian Ocean or on the islands of the Pacific in the fifteenth century, had left no trace. When Jewish settlement finally began, it was primarily an extension of the Sephardic diaspora southward and, most particularly, eastward. Only relatively recently have Ashkenazim become significantly involved in those areas, particularly in southern Africa.

Although they did not found great communities, as did the westward migrants, these pioneers did bring organized Jewish life to a world of ancient civilizations, which, except for two small coastal regions of India, had little or no previous contact with Jews. Disrupted by World War II and decolonization, these communities survive as outposts for Jewish businessmen. Their basic structure is congregational with a few ancillary organizations.

India: A Permanent Community

Of all the communities in southern and eastern Asia, only the Indian Jewish community has an indigenous population rooted in the land for centuries. It is also by far the largest Jewish community on the Asian continent east of Iran and one that promises to remain in existence. The overwhelming majority of the Jews of India are located in Bombay, the principal center of organized Jewish life, and its surrounding areas, including a synagogue in Poona and a declining number of Bene Israel in villages between the two cities. There are also tiny Jewish communities in New Delhi, Calcutta, and Cochin. Only the New Delhi community is stable, reinforced by Jews in the Indian civil service or the Indian army (not an uncommon phenomenon; the army was once a very attractive career for Bene Israel villagers), as well as a constant stream of Jews from other countries now stationed in the Indian capital. The Calcutta and Cochin communities are declining, with less than one hundred and fifty Jews in each. The smaller communities are organized around synagogues, and only Bombay and New Delhi even maintain the notion of Jewish organization beyond that.

India is almost unique among countries in its attitude toward its Jews. There is no known anti-Semitism nor are Jews looked upon as different in any significant way from the many Indian minority religions. The character of Indian culture—its relative placidity, its acceptance of diversity, and its inherent communalism—has given the Jews a sanctuary not known in any countries of the Western world. At the same time, Indian Jewry has acquired the characteristics of the general Indian population. Their social patterns, psychological characteristics, and culture all bear the marks of the civilization in which they have lived for so long.

The Jews of India are divided into three principal groups. The largest is the Bene Israel, located principally in the state of Maharastra, in Bombay and its environs. They number approximately five thousand today. The second group includes the Jews of Cochin, now reduced to less than one hundred and fifty and divided into two groups: the so-called white and black Jews. Both groups have been indigenous to India for centuries—according to their traditions back to the time of the First or Second Temples, and certainly at least fifteen hundred years.

The third Indian group is in the Persian Gulf region, consisting of the descendants of those merchants and adventurers who arrived with the British. Since most were originally from Iraq, they are known as Baghdadis. For a long time they remained separate from the indigenous Jews, whose Jewishness they regarded with great suspicion. They developed their own community institutions in the nineteenth century. For the most part, they left the country for Europe, particularly London, and the United States, particularly Los Angeles, when the British granted India independence in 1947.

Most of the indigenous Jews—nearly twenty thousand—also left India in the late 1940s and early 1950s, but they headed for Israel. At its high point in 1948, India may have had as many as thirty thousand Jews. Today there are probably no more than seven thousand. (The Indian census does not include questions on religion, but it does ask about caste, so Jews appear as a category.) There is no pressure from India itself on the Jews to leave. Those who left did so mainly to realize the Zionist vision or to seek greater economic opportunity. The number of Jews has been stable for several years now. Emigration to Israel has all but stopped, and no one talks about the community disappearing.

Before World War II, the old Baghdadi families essentially led the Indian Jewish community, although they were not involved in the activities of the Bene Israel, which were in any case confined to their synagogues. During the first generation of Indian independence, community leadership was divided between a few remnants of the old families and a newly empowered Bene Israel middle class, led by a remarkable Polish Jew, Hirsch Cynowitz, who reached India as a wartime refugee and stayed on to become the political "boss" of the community—in the best sense. Cynowitz, long active in Zionist circles in Eastern Europe, brought with him the organizational know-how of the Zionist movement. Although the Jews in India did not respond as had those in Eastern Europe, he did manage to keep a few communitywide organizations afloat and to build good ties with the Indian and Israeli governments, with whom he intervened in behalf of Indian Jewish interests. The community was also periodically assisted by the Jewish Agency, especially when there was still significant emigration to Israel, by the JDC, and by the Organization for Rehabilitation and Training (ORT). After Cynowitz's death, the community suffered a severe crisis of leadership, although by the early 1980s a new group of leaders was emerging.

In the 1970s, Indian Jewry received very little assistance from Israel or the world Jewish organizations. More recently, the Sephardic Educational Center, located in Jerusalem, has tried to bring Jewish education to Indian Jewish youth, bringing groups to its center in Israel and establishing a winter camp in the Bombay area. At present, it is the only Jewish body outside of India paying serious attention to Indian Jewry.

Singapore: Gateway to the Far East

Baghdadi Jews, including members of the Sassoon family, established Jewish life in Singapore in 1840, still in the early days of British development of the island. The Magen Avot synagogue did not have its own building until 1878, but services were held almost immediately in what is still known as Synagogue Street. A second synagogue, Chased-El, was built in 1904. Sir Manasseh Mayer who endowed it also endowed a Talmud Torah. The community was overwhelmingly Sephardic and has remained so, but Ashkenazim from England and the Netherlands, and later China, Russia, and Germany, also came to Singapore. The community became extraordinarily prosperous. In 1931, the census recorded 832 Jews on the island, increasing to 1,500 by the outbreak of World War II.

The Japanese interned many of Singapore's Jews along with other Europeans during the occupation. After the war many left. Yet, when Singapore became independent in 1955, David P. Marshall, a Jew, became its first prime minister.

The community is united through the Jewish Welfare Board, which publishes a monthly bulletin. It embraces the two synagogues and the Menorah Club, maintaining a single rabbi for both synagogues. The Jewish population continued to decline in the 1960s, but it seems to have stabilized now at around four hundred. Because Israel and Singapore have very good relations, there are always many Israelis visiting and working in Singapore who additionally complement the community.

Hong Kong: China's Jewish Outpost

When the Chinese ceded Hong Kong to Great Britain in 1842, members of Baghdad's Sassoon family were among the first outsiders to arrive. They already had offices in Canton, which they transferred to Britain's new island possession, and were instrumental in developing its port. The Khadouris soon joined them, and both families built companies that employed only Jewish managers and clerks, leading to an increase in the Jewish population and the establishment of the Jewish community in 1857. Those families eventually came to own a great part of the Crown Colony, retaining ownership of lands, enterprises, and public utilities even after leaving for greener pastures.

The present building of the Ohel Leah synagogue was completed in 1900 and financed by Sir Jacob Sassoon. The community was almost entirely Sephardic until World War II, when the Japanese occupied Hong Kong and interned the Jews. Community life resumed after the war when the Sephardim were joined by a number of Ashkenazim, either Jewish refugees from Europe or Jews from the United States and Australia with business interests in the Crown Colony.

In 1984, there were 252 Jews in Hong Kong, half Sephardim and half Ashkenazim. Since then the number has stabilized at around 200. While their numbers are small, Jewish investments and holdings remain extensive. Since Hong Kong is the gateway to China, Jewish businessmen from the rest of the world are frequently there. There are relatively elaborate provisions for kosher food made by a community that otherwise would not necessarily be concerned with such matters.

Now that the British have agreed to relinquish control over Hong Kong to the People's Republic of China by the end of the century, the Jewish community's days may be numbered. On the other hand, China's opening to the West may make it even more important. For example, Israeli business interests have found it an important gateway to the mainland.

The Philippines

Because the Philippine Islands came under Spanish rule in the sixteenth century, Marranos found their way to the islands and were followed by the Spanish Inquisition. At first, they were sent to Mexico for trial and punishment, but in 1580 an auto-da-fé was held in Manila itself. At least eight Marranos from the Philippines were tried by the Inquisition in the fifteenth and sixteenth centuries.

It was not until the 1870s that Jews began to settle openly in the Philippines, then still under Spanish rule. The first of these Jews were from Alsace, but they were the exceptions; most of the incoming Jews were Turkish, Syrian, Lebanese, and Egyptian. Subsequently, a small number of Jews from Russia and Central Europe found their way to the islands, generally via the Jewish communities of Harbin and Shanghai.

After the Spanish-American War and the U.S. occupation of the islands, American Jews began to settle there, and by the early 1930s, approximately five hundred Jews lived in the Philippines. Although they had conducted services earlier, a formal congregation was not organized until 1922, in Manila. Although the Philippines were occupied by the Japanese in World War II, Jewish refugees reached the islands in sufficient numbers to quintuple the size of the community by the end of the war. By and large, the Japanese did not bother the Jews, but they did use the synagogue and its social hall to store ammunition, and the buildings were destroyed when the Americans reconquered the island of Luzon. Some 10 percent of the Jews were victims of atrocities committed by the retreating Japanese.

After the war, most of the refugees moved on. The community was reorganized and the synagogue rebuilt. By the 1960s, only 250 Jews remained, approximately half Sephardic and half Ashkenazic. The wealthy, long-term residents were principally Sephardim, who dominated synagogue life. This mixture is reflected in the community's modes of self-expression. There is one congregation that encompasses all Jews who wish to join. The service generally follows the Sephardic *minhag*, but the prayers are sung to American Ashkenazic melodies. The Torah reading is according to the Sephardic style. All of this reflects the fact that those who lead the service and train the children for Bar and Bat Mitzvah are Sephardim from Syria, Iraq, India, and Hong Kong, while most of the congregants are Ashkenazim from the United States.

Sephardim in Australia

Jews were among Australia's first settlers, convicts shipped out from Britain to the new penal colony in the South Pacific. There were a few Sephardim among them. They were joined by other Sephardim from Britain in the nineteenth century who looked to Australia for adventure.

It was not until World War I that enough Sephardim immigrated to establish an organized presence. They were refugees from Eretz Israel, which was suffering under the Turks as a war zone. Most were Judesmo-speaking, principally from Safed and other Galilean communities, who settled in Perth in western Australia, where they established a congregation. There are still a few Judesmo-speaking survivors of the immigration in Perth's Jewish home for the aged.

Adelaide is the only community in which the Sephardim, principally North Africans and West Asians who arrived in the 1950s, are dominant, but it is such a small community, perhaps two thousand in all, that it carries little weight on the Australian scene. Perth's Sephardic community is also small, and the communities in Sydney and Melbourne even smaller. If the Sephardim there are active in Jewish life beyond the synagogue, they are so as individuals rather than through Sephardic institutions.

Chapter 6

Sephardim in the Caribbean and Latin America

On August 2, 1492, the ninth of Av in the Jewish calendar, the anniversary of the destruction of both Temples and the day of the expulsion of the Jews from Spain, Christopher Columbus set sail on the voyage that would lead to his discovery of the New World. Columbus noted the coincidence of the two events in his diary, perhaps not surprising for someone who was probably of Jewish background, from a Marrano family. The striking coincidence has become part of the folklore of the Jews of the Americas: the day of the greatest expulsion in Jewish history also marked the first step in the discovery of the greatest haven for Jews in the history of the diaspora.

Apparently Columbus and several of his crew, including Luis de Torres, his interpreter, were of Jewish origin. De Torres, who settled in Cuba, was probably the first Jewish settler in the New World. Three Jews later accompanied Cortés when he conquered Mexico in 1521. One of them, Hernando Alonso, later became the first Marrano to be burned at the stake in the New World for secretly practicing Judaism. Many were to follow, as Sephardic Jews who had nominally accepted Christianity but continued to practice Judaism in secret arrived in increasing numbers in the New World, hoping to escape the long arm of the Inquisition.

It was a vain hope, but throughout the sixteenth and well into the seventeenth centuries, there were substantial secret communities of Jews throughout Spanish and Portuguese America. Cecil Roth chronicled their history in *The Marranos,* and there is a substantial literature on individual cases, including the works of Martin Cohen and Seymour Liebman, which describe true events more exciting than legend, possessing an air of tragic romance rare in the Jewish history of the time but now often associated with the Marrano experience.

These Marrano communities also gave birth to the first open Jewish communities in the New World: in the early seventeenth century in northeastern Brazil after the Dutch conquest of Recife; then on the islands of the Caribbean that passed into Dutch and English hands by midcentury; and later in North America, where the Jewish community of New Amsterdam (now Manhattan) was founded by twenty-three Marranos escaping from Recife after the Portuguese reconquest in 1654.

In later years, these and other Marranos were to become known as the grandees of American Jewry, although some would say that from a Jewish point of view the real grandees were those who never abandoned Judaism, or at least returned to it and then became the great scholars and leaders of the Sephardic communities in the eastern Mediterranean. Nevertheless, out of these beginnings came the great Jewries of the Americas.

For nearly three hundred years the Jews in the New World were overwhelmingly Sephardic, to the extent that there was a Jewish presence there at all. Columbus sailed in 1492, but the first Ashkenazic congregation in any New World country, Rodeph Sholom in Philadelphia, was not founded until 1795. Until then, any Ashkenazic settlers had to live within Sephardic communities.

In Latin America, the Sephardim did not lose their dominance until well after the Latin American revolutions against Spain and Portugal early in the nineteenth century, which made it possible for Jews to settle openly in that region. Sephardim often formed the first wave of openly Jewish settlers to arrive after independence—but in the course of the century they were reduced to minorities of little influence. The few communities in which they remained the majority, primarily in the Caribbean, declined in importance on the world scene.

For the most part, today's Sephardic communities in the New World were formed early in the twentieth century as a result of new waves of immigration, first from the Balkans and North Africa at the turn of the century, then from the Arab countries of the Middle East after the establishment of the State of Israel, and finally from Israel itself. Almost without exception, they have no actual link with those original Sephardic outposts that grew in the wake of Columbus. The exceptions are some of the Caribbean communities and a few congregations in the United States (discussed in chapter 7).

Surviving Caribbean Communities

The first permanent Jewish communities in the New World were established on the islands of the Caribbean and adjacent coastal areas in Central and South America where Jewish life flourished during the seventeenth and eighteenth centuries, but which today survives only as remnant communities in serious decline. These communities appeared after Dutch and English conquests in the Caribbean allowed Spanish and Portuguese Marranos to emerge openly as Jews. The Jews brought prosperity to the region in return and built a network of organized communities that were a vital part of the Jewish world.

These Jews of the Caribbean lived through the same settlement and acquisition of rights processes as Dutch and English Jewry elsewhere. In most cases, they became more prominent in public affairs than their brethren in the Old World because they represented a larger proportion of the white population and were, perhaps, the most energetic of the Europeans as well.

In the nineteenth century, changing world markets and the abolition of slavery destroyed the economic base of the Caribbean region, and those Jews who had not assimilated began to emigrate in search of new opportunities, usually to the United States. Since then, the Caribbean Jewish communities have been in a decline that has become more precipitous in the twentieth century, as these small communities are prone to losses through intermarriage and assimilation.

Six small island communities in the Caribbean remain. They are organized primarily as local congregations. Founded by Sephardim—ex-Marranos or their descendants—most were shaped by Dutch, English, and, more recently, American Jewry, and they share their characteristics, namely, full voluntarism and identification primarily through religious institutions. Their small size and the low level of local Jewish interest keep organized Jewish life within a fairly neat framework that masks grave weaknesses of morale and commitment.

Today, there are no more than three thousand Jews in the Caribbean communities, scattered over numerous islands—each now a micro-state—and broken up into scattered groups of a few hundred at most. Their synagogues are monuments to an unusual Jewish life that flourished during the first half of the modern epoch, and the survivors synthesize Portuguese rites, local culture, and elements of American Reform and Conservative Judaism. With the rediscovery of the Caribbean as a vacation area and a haven for financial speculation, there has been a slight influx of Jews, mostly Ashkenazim from the United States, who may at some point generate new life.

Jamaica

When the British took Jamaica from Spain in 1655, they were assisted by Sephardic Jews living on the island, who then became protected subjects. The British conquest enabled the Jews to establish a community, and throughout the rest of the century there were additional immigrations from South America and England. Jews were not given full political rights until 1831, however, after which time they became quite prominent in local public life. After a hiatus in the midnineteenth century, a new wave of immigrants came from the Levant, but many Jews left the island because of the declining economic situation.

Although Jews have established congregations in various cities around the island in the past, at present about 90 percent of the three hundred and fifty remaining Jews live in the Kingston area. The first congregations followed the Portuguese rite. An Ashkenazic congregation was established later. Efforts to merge them failed until 1921, when the original congregation Shaare Shalom became the United Congregation of Israelites. In its ritual it combines Sephardic, Conservative, and Reform practices. Jamaica is a congregational community, and the United Congregation of Israelites maintains a home for the aged, a day school, and a supplementary religious school.

Netherlands Antilles

Approximately seven hundred Jews live in the Netherlands Antilles, an associated state of the Netherlands. Jewish communities exist on Aruba (the first settlement, in 1753) and on Curaçao. The Jewish population was no more than fifty throughout the nineteenth century, but after 1924 other Jews from the Netherlands, Surinam, and Eastern Europe settled there. A Jewish center was established in 1942, and in 1946 a Jewish community was officially organized. A synagogue building was dedicated in 1962. The sole Jewish functionary doubles as a *hazzan* (cantor) and a teacher.

In Curaçao, the Jewish community was founded as Mikveh Israel in 1651, but Jews were on the island from the time of the Dutch conquest in 1634. The Jewish community was linked to Amsterdam and consisted almost entirely of Portuguese Jews. It grew during the seventeenth and eighteenth centuries, but throughout most of the latter century it was involved in a series of disputes that required the intervention of the States-General in Holland as well as the local authorities. While matters improved in the nineteenth century, internal rivalries continued to divide the community and led to the establishment of Temple Emanuel in 1864 as the first Sephardic Reform congregation in the world. Mikveh Israel and Emanuel merged in 1934, joined the World Union for Progressive Judaism, and adopted the Reconstructionist prayerbook.

Small numbers of Ashkenazim settled in Curaçao after 1926, formed their own club in 1932, and established a synagogue, Shaare Tzedek, in 1959. The Jewish community has been legally recognized from the first, and the Jews have been fully active in the social, civic, and political life of the island.

Surinam

Surinam, a Dutch possession from the early seventeenth century until it gained independence after World War II, has the oldest Jewish community in continuous existence in the Western Hemisphere. Jews had settled locally by 1639 and the community already had a rabbi by 1643. Groups of Jews continued to settle throughout the seventeenth century, most fleeing from the Inquisition in other parts of Latin America or leaving the Sephardic congregations of Western Europe. In the late seventeenth century, there was a virtually independent Jewish state in Surinam centered at Joden Savanne, dominated by Jewish plantation owners who were probably the most powerful single economic force in the colony. They had their own law courts and local government, as well as a flourishing Jewish life.

The Portuguese Jewish settlers were joined by German Jews who formed their own separate congregation in 1734. While the number of

Sephardim declined, the German Jewish community continued to grow, and by 1836 it became the majority. Economic decline followed the abolition of the slave trade in 1819 and the emancipation of the slaves in 1863. Surinam's plantation economy, based on the growth of sugar cane, required cheap labor and so began to fail.

Still, the Jewish population stood at fifteen hundred at the century's end. It declined quite rapidly after that, however, to about seven hundred in the mid-1920s, and approximately five hundred today. The community remains organized into two congregations: Neve Shalom and Sephardi Sedek y Shalom, each offering minimal services.

Latin America's Larger Jewish Communities

Latin America has the greatest concentration of Sephardim outside of Israel and France, but in almost every Latin American country they represent no more than 20 percent of the total Jewish population. Moreover, they have generally gone their own way because of the divided character of Latin American Jewry. In those countries more than any others, the dominant Ashkenazic community long refused to accept Sephardim as equals, going so far as to deny the legitimacy of their *kashrut* (dietary laws and observance) on the grounds that their kosher slaughtering did not meet Ashkenazic *halakhic* standards. Hence, the Sephardim built their own communal institutions, generally synagogue-based, and remained separate even among themselves according to country of origin. Although much the same is true among the Ashkenazim in Latin America, they at least formed umbrella organizations.

The Jews who settled in Latin America found themselves immersed in a Hispanic—or, in Brazil, Lusitanic—civilization with premodern roots that had difficulty shaking off medieval influences. These countries were Catholic from the start, going through the modernization process more or less in the same manner as other Catholic countries.

The Jewish communities developed quite late, long after the host polities had been formed. The Jews missed three centuries of colonial history and the crucial first generations of national independence. As already noted, the Marranos who had settled earlier left no trace on contemporary Latin American Jewry.

When Jews began to settle in Latin America in the middle and at the end of the nineteenth century, among the first were Sephardim from the Balkans, Syria, and North Africa. Since they were basically from Mediterranean environments, they fit more easily into the Latin American society than did their Ashkenazic brethren. Those who spoke Judesmo did not even have a language problem. They organized themselves through their extended families and congregations as they had in the Old World, perpetuating the same regional and local differences. They were both more a part of the Latin American environment and more tenacious in their retention of Jewish customs and culture precisely because, for them, there was relatively little contradiction between the two.

The Ashkenazim, in organizing their *kehillot* (formally structured communities), built them on a secular basis, since most had come from antireligious backgrounds in Eastern Europe; and Yiddish was used almost exclusively as the language of communication. The Sephardim were excluded on both accounts. It took many years to overcome the resulting mutual alienation. Only recently has there been greater willingness on the part of both Ashkenazim and Sephardim to begin to build links between the two subcommunities, and these efforts are still in their early stages.

The Sephardim did not undergo the upheavals of emancipation and radicalization that had been the lot of Jews from Central and Eastern Europe, so they maintained the traditional structures that formed a basis for Jewish life in their new setting. As a result, the Sephardim have remained more Jewish in a traditional way than have the Ashkenazim, although the new generations are beginning to feel the impact of their local environments. Perhaps Sephardic assimilation was slowed by yet another factor: the tendency of many, especially those of Syrian background, to stay within the business community and not to send their children to universities, eliminating a major force that encourages the abandonment of traditional ways.

Today, there is a Sephardic revival in Latin America that is a hopeful sign for Latin American Jewry. It is most pronounced in Argentina, Brazil, and Venezuela. For the most part, it has taken the form of a new associationalism among the younger Sephardim, a movement into more modern and cosmopolitan forms of organization, beyond the traditional and highly localistic synagogue.

As noted, Ashkenazim and Sephardim organized separate communities, in some cases by country or city of origin. Just as the Jewish immigrants did not assimilate into their host societies, so, too, they did not assimilate among themselves. In time, these communities loosely confederated to deal with common problems, essentially those of immigration, anti-Semitism, and Israel. At the same time, each country-of-origin community retains substantial, if not complete, autonomy in internal matters and control over its institutions.

Argentina

The number of Jews in Argentina is a matter of some dispute. The local community has long estimated its population at half a million, but recent studies suggest something closer to 265,000. While the local figures are too high, the lower number seems to be an underestimate. Recalculations of the data suggest that the actual figure is approximately 300,000.

The organization of Argentinian Jewry follows the common Latin American pattern. As Jews reached Argentina, they established associations—synagogues, cemetery associations, *landsmanshaften* (associations of immigrants from the same town, region, or country), benevolent societies—usually based on Old Country ties. These organizations gave them a framework for settlement in their new home. However, because they also reinforced the differences among the immigrants, they made more comprehensive structures difficult to establish.

Today, six communal bodies are the building blocks of the Argentinian Jewish community: the four Sephardic communities of Buenos Aires; the Asociación Mutual Israelita Argentina (AMIA), essentially the Ashkenazic community of Buenos Aires; and the Federación de Comunidades Israelitas (known in Hebrew as the *Va'ad HaKehillot*), which serves as the umbrella group for communities in the provinces.

The oldest of the four Sephardic communities in Buenos Aires is the Congregación Israelita Latina (Jewish Latin Congregation), founded in 1891 by immigrants from Morocco and other parts of North Africa. Seriously weakened by intermarriage and assimilation, it has only three hundred registered members.

The second community, the Asociación Israelita Sefardita Argentina (AISA), was founded in the early twentieth century by Jews from Aleppo. They were joined by immigrants from the Caucasus and, in the 1920s and 1930s, from Palestine. From its inception, this community was distinguished by its extremely religious character and by the close attachment of its members to their communal institutions. The membership of the AISA is approximately twenty-five hundred.

The third Sephardic community was founded in 1913 by Jews from Damascus who wished to maintain distance from their Aleppo brethren. Although originally intended to serve only as a burial society and as a means of arbitrating disputes among its members, it now provides extensive religious and educational services. Its estimated membership is thirty-five hundred.

The fourth Sephardic community is the Asociación Comunidad Israelita Sefardita de Buenos Aires (ACIS), which grew out of the union of Judesmo-speaking congregations that had established neighborhood synagogues as early as 1914. In 1942, they united to form a single organization for immigrants from Turkey, Rhodes, and the Balkans. The separate character of each group was maintained, to the point where one of the main synagogues became Conservative while the others remained Orthodox. This community is third in size among the four in Buenos Aires, with 2,365 families representing about 7,600 people.

The Sephardim have never developed an effective organization to embrace these diverse communities. The Argentinian branch of the World Sephardi Federation has been trying to provide a common meeting ground, but most of the stimulus for that has come from outside the country. Nevertheless, today the Delegación de Entidades Sefarditas coordinates Sephardic activities on behalf of Israel, while ECSA, the Entidad Coordinacíon Sefardita, attempts to do so within Argentina.

Brazil: A Dual History

The first Portuguese landing in what is now Brazil took place in 1500, with at least one person of Jewish origin on board. Gaspar da Gama, a Jewish adventurer from Poland who had been kidnapped and forcibly baptized in 1497, is said to be one of the first two Portuguese to set foot on Brazilian soil.

Portuguese "New Christians"—Jews who, like da Gama, had been forced to convert in 1497—saw great opportunities in Brazil. In 1502, a group of them obtained a concession from the throne to colonize the land, and they are said to have introduced the cultivation of sugar cane. Subsequently, the country became a haven for Marranos, who were generally left alone since no local Inquisition was established, although after the 1581 unification of Spain and Portugal, Inquisitorial commissions were periodically sent from Portugal. The commissions did arrest a number of suspects and returned them to Lisbon for trial, but Brazil continued as a site of Marrano concentration, and New Christians contributed greatly to the foundations of Brazilian culture.

The Dutch conquest of Recife in 1630 led many of the Marranos to return openly to Judaism. They founded congregations in Recife and Paraiba, enrolled in the militia where they had their own Jewish company, and became an active part of the Jewish world. Rabbis, Hebrew teachers, and *hazzanim* came to them from Amsterdam. The Recife community was responsible for a number of Jewish "firsts" in the New World. It was organized along traditional lines, following the Amsterdam model. The Jewish population reached a peak of fifteen hundred in 1645 when it made up about 50 percent of the total European civilian population in Dutch Brazil.

The Portuguese reconquered the colony in 1654. In recognition of their role in building and defending it, the Dutch secured the Jews' lives and liberty, but they were required to evacuate within three months. Most moved to Amsterdam, some to Curaçao—also under Dutch rule—and other Caribbean islands, and twenty-three founded the first organized Jewish community in what later became Manhattan, then known as New Amsterdam.

This ended organized Jewish life in Brazil until independence, although many Marranos apparently stayed in the country. There were periodic investigations, arrests, and punishments during the seventeenth and eighteenth centuries until the Portuguese royal decree of 1773, which ended discrimination against New Christians. In time, the Marranos fully assimilated into Brazilian society.

Brazil declared independence from Portugal in 1822. Its 1825 constitution retained Roman Catholicism as the state religion but provided for religious tolerance. This allowed for open Jewish settlement. Sephardim from Morocco founded the country's first congregation in Belem in 1824. Belem has remained a Sephardic community ever since. Other Sephardim settled in Manaus, in the heart of the Amazon basin, at the end of the nineteenth century.

Few Jews settled in the southern part of the country, and organized Jewish life did not emerge there until the end of the nineteenth century. When large-scale Ashkenazic communities emerged in the major southern cities, they, too, were divided by country of origin, and the Sephardic minority founded its own congregations.

Only in 1946 and 1947 were local federations of Jewish institutions and organizations formed in the larger communities, culminating in

1951 with the establishment of the Confederación das Entidades Representativas des Colectividad Israelita do Brasil (CIB). By that time, the Sephardim were a relatively small minority of the total community and continued to maintain their own congregations and chief rabbi.

Mexico: Excluded Sephardim

The real story of Mexican Jewry belongs to the twentieth century, but the epic Jewish experience is that of the sixteenth- and seventeenth-century Marranos. The first of the Marranos arrived with Cortés himself and participated in the Spanish conquest of the Aztecs. Hernando Alonso is celebrated as the first Jewish martyr on Mexican soil (political *and* religious factors are said to have played a role in his arrest and execution). Other Marranos followed Alonso to Mexico, where they scattered from the Yucatán to the Rio Grande. Seymour Liebman has estimated that the Marrano population of Mexico reached at least ten thousand and was perhaps even greater.

The Marrano communities created a network of underground institutions. They were even able to establish contact with the Jewish community of Eretz Israel, which sent emissaries to Mexico on several occasions. But the combination of the Inquisition and assimilation finally eliminated the community, although an awareness of Marrano origins persisted well into the nineteenth century and, according to Liebman, even into the twentieth. It was only with the arrival of Jews from Eastern Europe, who were strangers to Mexican ways, that the last of the Marrano descendants abandoned their identity to avoid being grouped with the newcomers. This made the break between the two eras of Mexican Jewish history even more deliberate.

The present Jewish community dates back, at most, to the mid-nineteenth century, when a congregation was founded in 1862 by Jews accompanying the ill-fated Emperor Maximilian during the brief French occupation of the country. These first Jews were adventurers seeking their fortunes, mostly from German-speaking countries, and they assimilated even more rapidly than the Marranos. This community also disappeared.

The first substantial immigration of Jews consisted of Sephardim from the Ottoman Empire and North Africa between 1870 and 1890. These included Syrian Jews, who had earlier fled to Morocco to escape persecution in Syria, and Jews from the Balkans, particularly Turkey. The latter increased in number after the Young Turk revolution. These Jews settled principally in Mexico City and Guadalajara, and many of their descendants became wealthy and prominent. In the 1880s, two Jews became generals in the Mexican army. Most of the wealthy Jews eventually left for the United States during the 1910 revolution.

The Jews who arrived prior to the revolution opened small businesses or worked as laborers around the country, so that communities were established in at least six cities besides the two major ones. Until the 1920s, these settlers were principally Sephardim; the Ashkenazim did not become the majority until World War I. None of these communities developed, however, and in most cases the Jews who settled in them, or their children, left for the larger Jewish communities, so that by the 1950s only Mexico City, Monterrey, Guadalajara, and Tijuana had one hundred or more Jews.

Of the approximately fifty thousand Jews in Mexico today, between forty thousand and forty-five thousand live in Mexico City. Guadalajara has about three thousand and Monterrey some fifteen hundred. Many Jews are scattered around the country and do not reveal their identity for fear of standing out in a society that does not take kindly to strangers, but they do contribute secretly to Jewish organizations. Hence, only about thirty-five thousand Jews are recognized by the official institutions of the Mexican Jewish community. Overall, 65 percent are Ashkenazim and 35 percent are Sephardim. Curiously enough, the Mexican census, which asks people to list religious affiliation, registered over one hundred thousand Jews in 1960, but many of them were actually Protestants whose fear of the Catholics caused them to register as Jews. Others were self-proclaimed Jews, members of sects founded by Protestant missionaries that have become Sabbatarian and are not recognized by the Jewish community. This number also included the so-called Indian Jews, who attract much attention outside of Mexico because of their claimed descent from the early Marrano settlers.

In Mexico as elsewhere in Latin America, the Ashkenazim and Sephardim are divided. In some cases, the Ashkenazim do not even recognize the Sephardim as Jews or as observant Jews, even though Sephardim are likely to be more observant than most Ashkenazim. Until recently, there was almost no social intercourse between the two groups, even between those who engaged in joint business ventures.

In Mexico City, there are four separate *kehillot*, all grown from congregational roots. Three are Sephardic: the Alianza de Monte Sinai, consisting of Arabic-speaking Jews from Damascus, founded in 1912; the Sociedad Beneficencia del Alicencia Israelita Sedaka y Marpe, consisting of

Jews from Aleppo, founded in 1938; and the Unión Sefardita—Jews from the Balkans, founded in 1923. The Ashkenazim maintain separate *landsmanshaften* and congregations by region of origin, but they are united in the Kehillat Nidje Israel, founded in 1922 after an incident between the Sephardic and Ashkenazic members of Monte Sinai. Their *kehillah* council provides representation for those constituent bodies.

The Alianza de Monte Sinai is the oldest community in the country. Its founder, Jacob Granott, was active in the Mexican revolution, supporting its first leader, Francisco Madero, and maintaining close contact with Pancho Villa and other revolutionary leaders in the north. It is the only Jewish body that has any real identification with that crucial event in Mexican history. Its synagogue was completed in 1913. Arabic was originally the common language, but subsequent generations have shifted to Spanish. The community maintains a day school from kindergarten through the equivalent of the first year of college in the United States, and has three synagogues in different locations. It offers a full range of religious services and supervises *kashrut* for all the Sephardim. Most of the community's private life is conducted within the family circle, which is structured around extended families. The best estimate places membership at just under four thousand.

Sedaka y Marpe broke away from the Alianza de Monte Sinai when there was a sufficient number of Aleppan Jews to develop separate institutions. The community today has an estimated six thousand members. It maintains two synagogues, a day school from kindergarten through elementary school, and a *yeshiva* that meets part-time. Although it relies on the *kashrut* supervision of the Alianza de Monte Sinai, it does maintain its own burial society.

The Unión Sefardita tends to confine itself to religious services and modest social welfare programs overseen by its women's committee. It does not maintain its own school, nor does it release membership figures.

Outside of Mexico City, the communities are too small to maintain more than a single organization in which region-of-origin groups may be represented. The Comunidad Israelita of Guadalajara, founded in 1924, has less than one thousand members. The Sephardim and Ashkenazim maintained separate congregations until 1955, but the establishment of a common day school helped to eliminate differences. The community also supports the Club Deportivo Maccabi (originally founded by Sephardim), a Women's International Zionist Organization (WIZO) group, and a B'nai B'rith lodge.

Uruguay

Uruguay claims forty thousand Jews. If the figure is accurate, it would have the third or fourth largest Jewish community in Latin America—after Argentina, Brazil, and possibly Mexico. The first known Jews did not arrive until 1898, when a few drifted in from Argentina. The 1918 constitution separated church and state and protected the rights of aliens, and in that year there were an estimated seventeen hundred Jews in Uruguay, 75 percent Sephardim, most of the others Eastern Europeans.

The majority of Uruguay's present Jewish community arrived between 1925 and 1928, with another spurt of immigration from Central Europe between 1933 and 1940. Virtually all live in Montevideo, the capital. Today, the percentages are reversed from two generations ago: 70 percent from Eastern Europe, 18 percent from Central Europe, 12 percent Sephardim. The closeness of Uruguay to Argentina keeps it within the orbit of the larger Jewish community.

The first communal organization in Uruguay was Ezra, founded by the Sephardim in 1909. In 1916, both an Ashkenazic and a Sephardic *hevra kadisha* (burial society) were established. Post–World War I immigration destroyed the coherence of the small community; *landsmanshaften* proliferated, one for every group, and various immigrant aid societies were established.

By and large, the Uruguayan Jewish community is nationalist and secularist. It is built around four *kehillot*: the Ashkenazic (Eastern European) Comunidad Israelita de Montevideo, founded in 1932, with approximately four thousand members; the Comunidad Israelita Sefardita, also founded in 1932, which now has fifteen hundred members; the German Nueva Congregación Israelita, founded in 1936, also with fifteen hundred members; and the Sociedad Húngara de Montevideo, founded in 1942, with two hundred members. These four groups focus mainly on communal welfare; except for the Sephardim, the religious element is of minor importance. The Sephardic *hevra kadisha*, predecessor of the present community, founded the Talmud Torah Eliezer Ben Yehudah in 1938—one of the first two Jewish schools in the country. All four *kehillot* are united under the Committee Central Israelita (CCI), which was established in 1940 to represent the Uruguayan Jewish community in the government.

Chile

A substantial Marrano population existed in Chile in the sixteenth and seventeenth centuries, giving rise to several famous Inquisition cases. By the eighteenth century, they had all left or assimilated. Many of the prominent Chilean families claim Marrano descent. The present Chilean Jewish community dates from just prior to World War I, when groups of Ashkenazim from Eastern Europe and Sephardim from the Balkans settled there. The Sociedad Unión Israelita de Chile, the first Jewish organization, was founded in 1909, and Zionist activity began a year later, but the overwhelming Catholicism of the country led many Jews to hide their identity. Organized life was carried on through societies with names that did not reveal their Jewish character.

In September 1919, the first congress of Chilean Jewry was convened in response to anti-Semitic events in Argentina that culminated in the pogrom of the *semana tragica*. The congress was attended by both Ashkenazim and Sephardim, representatives of thirteen organizations from six cities, and Indian Judaizers as well. It established the Federación Sionista de Chile, which became the framing organization of Chilean Jewry, functioning both as a representative body and a Zionist organization.

Grass-roots Jewish organization in Chile, as in other Latin American countries, is mainly based on country of origin, with Eastern European Ashkenazim, German Jews, and Sephardim maintaining their own separate congregations, social groups, and welfare associations. The principal bodies are the Ashkenazic *kehillah*, which grew out of the *hevra kadisha* dating back to the World War I period; the German Sociedad Cultura Israelita Bne Jisroael, founded in 1933; and the Comunidad Israelita Sefardita, founded in 1935. These bodies are now beginning to lose their importance as native-born Chilean Jews take over the community's leadership, but they still form the basis for communal organization.

Venezuela

Venezuela was one of the first newly independent Latin American states to establish religious freedom, in its constitutions of 1819 and 1821. As a result, the first Jewish families settled in Coro about 1820. They were Sephardim from Curaçao, descendants of Portuguese Marranos, who retained close ties with the mother community.

A Jewish cemetery was established in Coro several years later and still serves the few Jewish families remaining there. By the 1840s, Jewish cemeteries appeared in Caracas, Barcelona, and Puerto Cabello. These Jews would hold prayer services as necessary, but no formal community was established until the eve of World War I. The children of these first settlers assimilated or left. Today, many of their family names are borne by some of the first families of Venezuela.

The contemporary Jewish community began with the arrival of other Sephardim from North Africa before World War I. Still, the Jewish population remained small: 247 were recorded in 1891 and 475 in 1917. That number nearly doubled in the national census of 1926; including an estimate of the Jews who did not openly declare their religious affiliation, there were probably about 1,000 Jews in the country.

Eastern European Jews began to settle in Venezuela between the world wars and were joined after 1934 by refugees from Central Europe, approximately six hundred during the next decade. After World War II, there were between five thousand and six thousand Jews in Venezuela, and today the Jewish population is estimated at twenty thousand. There is some question, however, as to how such an increase came about since the only mass immigration of the postwar years was in 1958, when one thousand Jews from Egypt, Hungary, and Israel were admitted into the country.

More than half of the Jewish community lives in Caracas, with other concentrations in Maracaibo, Valencia, and Maracay. The organized Jewish community in Maracaibo includes a synagogue, a B'nai B'rith lodge, and a school. The Asociación Israelita de Venezuela is the oldest Jewish organization in Caracas, founded in the 1920s by the Sephardim. Today, it has about eight hundred family members and is centered around a synagogue.

Latin America's Smaller Jewish Communities

Bolivia

There were Marranos in Bolivia in the sixteenth century, and at least a few Jews passed through the country in the eighteenth and nineteenth centuries. The first permanent settlement dates from 1905. Its members came from Russia and were followed by a group from Argentina and

Sephardic families from the eastern Mediterranean. Until the rise of nazism, the number of Jews in the country did not exceed thirty families. Seven thousand German Jewish immigrants arrived between 1933 and 1942, most leaving Bolivia as soon as they could gain entry to another country. Today there are no more than one thousand Jews in Bolivia.

Colombia

Marranos reached Colombia with the Spanish conquistadors in the sixteenth century. A substantial community developed but was destroyed by the Inquisition in the midseventeenth century. The only remnants of that early community are found in the city of Medellín, to which many Marranos fled. There are Christian families there where the women light candles every Friday night and Jewish ritual objects have been preserved for generations. They have also preserved the Jewish sense of separateness and remain the purest "Spanish" families in the country, having avoided intermarriage with the indigenous Indian population. Many have maintained Hebrew or Sephardic names. Perhaps not coincidentally, Medellín is also the center of liberalism in Colombia. Today, five Sephardic families live in the city.

Although Roman Catholicism was the only religion permitted until 1853, individual Jews began to settle in what is now Colombia by the end of the eighteenth century. They were Sephardim from the Caribbean islands. By the midnineteenth century, Jews had settled in all of Colombia's port cities and established a cemetery in Santa Marta. Cemeteries were established in other communities over the next several decades, but it was not until 1874 that a congregation was organized. Most of these early Jews were Sephardim, and most assimilated during the nineteenth century.

The Colombian Jewish community was revived just after World War I by Sephardic Jewish immigrants from the Balkans, North Africa, and Syria. They were joined by Eastern European Jews and later augmented by German Jews fleeing nazism in 1938. The Jewish population of Colombia reached a peak of eleven thousand at the time of World War II and is now approximately seven thousand, most located in the capital of Bogotá.

Until the 1940s, Jewish life remained fragmented since the Colombian government did not allow the existence of a comprehensive Jewish organization. Ultimately, however, the Jewish community was permitted to establish the Federación General des Comunidades, a representative body that unites Ashkenazim, Sephardim, and German Jews, each with its own communal institutions.

There are Sephardic congregations in Barranquilla and Cali as well as in Bogotá. Eight of the one hundred and fifty families in Barranquilla are Sephardi, and the rabbi is a Sephardi from Egypt. There are two Jewish clubs there, one for Sephardim and one for Ashkenazim.

Costa Rica

The first Jews to settle in Costa Rica came from the Caribbean islands in the nineteenth century but quickly assimilated. The present community was founded by Turkish and Eastern European immigrants after World War I, supplemented by German Jewish refugees after 1933. Organized Jewish life revolves around the Centro Israelita Sionista, but there are WIZO, B'nai B'rith, Zionist, and youth groups, and La Sociedad de Damas Israelitas de Beneficio as well. There is also a Jewish school. Despite an initial period of hostility, the government has been friendly. Today, there are approximately twenty-five hundred Jews in Costa Rica.

Cuba

Cuba is a special blend of the Hispanic and North American worlds. It has a Marrano past dating back to 1492. There was a secret community of Sephardic merchants from the midseventeenth to the eighteenth centuries whose members participated in extensive European and North American trade.

The present community dates back to the period immediately after Cuba became independent from Spain in 1898, which opened the country for legal Jewish settlement. The first settlers were Jews from Florida who had been supporters of Cuban independence or veterans of the Spanish-American War. They settled on the island to take advantage of business opportunities. The community was formally founded in 1904 with the establishment of the Union Hebrew Congregation, affiliated with the American Reform movement.

Some ten years later, Sephardic Jews arrived from the Balkans. In 1914, they established the Uniona Hebrea Shevet Ajim, an entirely separate entity, although they did receive some aid from the Ashkenazim on an individual basis. In 1952, when the Jewish population reached its peak of an estimated twelve thousand, Sephardim constituted one-third.

The Colegio Autónomo de Central Israelita, founded in 1924, served both Sephardim and Ashkenazim from the start. There were also Sephardic, Zionist, religious, secularist, leftist, and American-style English-language schools in the 1950s.

At first, the Castro revolution was viewed sympathetically by many Cuban Jews and at no point has the revolution been anti-Jewish per se. But its effort to impose communism and to destroy the middle class led thousands of Jews to emigrate, principally to the United States, where they established three Cuban Jewish communities in Miami.

The Jewish community was impoverished by the regime's Socialist doctrines, and by 1963 only 30 percent of the remaining three thousand Jews on the island were employed. The community's schools were consolidated into one in the 1960s. The Zionist movement continued until the Six Day War. Two Sephardic synagogues still function, along with three others covering the range of the communal divisions established fifty years earlier. The community's decline seems to have stabilized at twelve hundred Jews.

El Salvador

Jewish settlement in El Salvador dates back to the first half of the nineteenth century when French Sephardic Jews settled in Chialchuapa. No communal institutions were established until World War II, with the Comunidad Israelita del Salvador in 1944, a cemetery in 1945, and a synagogue in 1950. The Zionist Organization of El Salvador dates from 1945. With only 350 Jews in the country, there is no Jewish school and little beyond the life of the congregation.

Guatemala

Guatemala is the only Central American country with a real Marrano past, consisting of a few Marranos who drifted down from Mexico and thereafter disappeared. In the midnineteenth century, Jews from Germany arrived and quickly assimilated. The present community is descended from immigrants who arrived just before World War I from Germany and the Middle East, followed in the 1920s by Eastern European Jews. That community was ruined in 1932 when the Guatemalan government prohibited peddling, and many Jews subsequently left the country.

The eleven hundred Jews now in the country are divided into German, Sephardic, and Eastern European groups, each with its own institutions. The German Sociedad Israelita de Guatemala and Bet El are affiliated with the Reform movement. The Sephardim have the Magen David, and the Ashkenazim the Centro Hebreo. There is a Comité Central that links the three communities, plus B'nai B'rith, WIZO, and youth groups. All the Zionist groups are linked by the Organización Sionista de Guatemala. There is also a small Jewish school.

Honduras

Inquisition records attest to the presence of Jews in Honduras in colonial times, and a small number reached there in the nineteenth century, but there is no Sephardic community in Honduras today.

Panama

Because Panama was part of Colombia from 1821 to 1903, the first Jews who settled there were Sephardim who drifted up from the Colombian port cities. A few more arrived at the time of the California gold rush to take advantage of business opportunities created by the completion of the railroad across the Isthmus of Panama in 1855. Kahal Shearith Israel, the first Jewish community, was founded in 1876 in the city of Panama, with a synagogue, cemetery, and mutual assistance organization. A Jewish organization was also established in Colón. The Jewish community grew slightly at the time of the construction of the Panama Canal (1903–14). Kahal Shearith Israel eventually affiliated itself with the Reform movement, and many of the descendants of its first families have intermarried and assimilated.

There are an estimated two thousand Jews in Panama today. Most are Sephardim, and they maintain the largest community, Shevet Ajim. Most of its members arrived in Panama after World War II from the Balkans, the eastern Mediterranean, and North Africa, although some came from Eretz Israel during World War I.

Paraguay

The Jewish community of Paraguay was founded by Sephardim who emigrated from Eretz Israel and settled at the time of World War I. They founded the Alianza Israelita as a *hevra kadisha* and then a synagogue in 1917 when they were joined by Sephardim from the Balkans. The first Eastern European Jews came in the 1920s and founded an Ashkenazic community, the Unión Hebraica. Paraguay allowed between fifteen thousand and twenty thousand German and Central European Jews to find refuge there between 1933 and 1939, virtually all of whom left as soon as they could.

The two communities established a common Consejo Representativo Israelita de Paraguay to represent them before the authorities. They have a common school, a sports club, a B'nai B'rith lodge, a WIZO chapter, and one or two youth groups. Although Paraguay became a haven for Nazi war criminals after World War II and has a very large Arab population, the Jews have not been disturbed, apparently because the country's lifetime president, Alfredo Stroessner, protects them. Approximately seven hundred Jews remain today.

Peru

Peru, along with Mexico, had one of the two great concentrations of Marranos in the sixteenth and seventeenth centuries. An Inquisition tribunal was established in Lima for all of Hispanic South America, and there were regular crackdowns leading to frequent autos-da-fé. The greatest was in 1634, when so many people were arrested that the economy of Peru collapsed in the wake of the Inquisition's activities, and it led to the greatest auto-da-fé in the New World, in 1639. The work of the Inquisition was so effective that by the latter part of the seventeenth century, Judaism was wiped out in Peru.

The present Jewish community dates back to the midnineteenth century when Central European merchants and engineers began to settle in Peru. Sephardim arrived around 1880, principally from North Africa, and established a community in Quito that paralleled the Central European community in Lima. Most subsequently departed, leaving behind descendants who still call themselves *Hijos des Hebreos* (Sons of the Hebrews). After World War I, there was a more substantial emigration of Balkan Sephardim to Lima.

In the 1930s, an influx of German Jewish refugees strengthened the old German Jewish community. Today there are the usual three Jewish communities in Peru: Eastern European Ashkenazim, German Ashkenazim—who inherited the institutions of the 1870 community—and the

Sephardim. The Sephardim are organized under the Sociedad Beneficencia Israelita Sefardita. Each individual group has its own synagogue, rabbi, and *hevra kadisha,* but they do maintain a common cemetery. The three Jewish communities are joined together as the Asociación des Sociedades Israelitas. Today, some five thousand Jews live in Peru.

Chapter 7

Sephardim in North America

The United States

1776—Plantation-owner Francis Salvador, lieutenant colonel in the Georgia militia and member of the Georgia legislature, is killed in one of the opening battles of the American Revolution. Gershom Mendes Seixas, *hazzan* of Congregation Shearith Israel in New York City, leaves that city as it is occupied by the British, taking a Torah with him to Philadelphia where he spends the rest of the war as *hazzan* of Shearith Israel's sister congregation, Mikveh Israel. While there, he dedicates a new building for the congregation in 1782 with a prayer for George Washington and the Continental Congress.

1777—Benjamin Nones sails to America to serve as aide-de-camp to the Marquis de Lafayette, his former schoolmate. Subsequently, he is appointed an aide to Washington with the rank of major. After the revolution he settles in Philadelphia, writes one of the earliest commentaries on the U.S. Constitution as part of the struggle for its ratification, and becomes active in politics as a Jeffersonian. At the same time, he serves as president of Congregation Mikveh Israel, writing a passionate defense of Jews as republicans and democrats.

1825—Mordechai Emanuel Noah, long-time Jeffersonian political activist, U.S. consul to Tunis, Grand Sachem of Tammany Hall, editor, and playwright, proposes the establishment of a Jewish national home on Grand Island in the Niagara River near Buffalo, New York, to be named Ararat. (After his plan is rejected, he becomes one of the first proto-Zionists.)

These Sephardim are among the foremost in American Jewish history. Today, U.S. Sephardim with celebrity status are engaged in many different activities: people like Eydie Gorme (née Gormazano), Neil Sedaka, and Murray Perahia. In between the Salvadors and the Sedakas lies the history of the Sephardim in North America.

If the Sephardim established a real presence in Latin America, they were hardly visible in British North America for the 150 years of its earliest growth, despite the handful of Sephardim who were the founders of Jewish life there. Only recently has this picture changed, as tens of thousands of Sephardim have moved to the United States from North Africa and Asia to join those from the Balkans or to found new communities. They are now able and eager to express themselves, sometimes even militantly. Hence, it is not surprising that the Sephardic Jewries of North America have become the subject of increasing attention.

The U.S. Sephardic population has been built on a series of immigrations. The earliest, in the colonial period, consisted of the first Jews to settle in what became the United States. As in Europe and Latin America, they were Marranos who had emigrated from Portugal and Spain in order to return to Judaism. They moved quickly to establish their own institutions and punctiliously sought to preserve the institutional forms that combined their Iberian heritage with Jewish tradition; and they did so in a manner so aristocratic that they became known as grandees. They never numbered more than a handful, but they left a heritage of high romance, some minor institutional traces such as Shearith Israel in New York City and Mikveh Israel in Philadelphia, and a few families who trace their descent back to them. The Nathan, Cardozo, Hendricks, and Phillips families are still active in the Shearith Israel congregation.

In 1654, twenty-three Sephardic refugees from Brazil established the first Jewish community in New Amsterdam (now Manhattan). For the next three generations, small numbers of Sephardic Jews made their way to British North America. They founded Jewish communities in Montreal, Newport, Philadelphia, Savannah, and Charleston. At the time of the revolution, there were only one thousand Jews in the colonies, nearly five hundred Sephardim. Between 1730 and 1760, the Sephardim lost their numerical majority, but maintained cultural and religious hegemony in the nascent community until the 1820s. As the Ashkenazic Jews arrived, they assimilated into the Sephardic congregations, adopting their customs—at least in public. Mikveh Israel, for example, never had a Sephardic majority but still maintains the Sephardic ritual of its most influential founding members.

Sephardim continued to immigrate throughout the nineteenth century in numbers too small to have more than isolated impact. Moreover, as a result of assimilation, low birthrates, and ultimately the massive waves of Ashkenazic immigration, Sephardic strength diminished. Until the Civil War, their congregations remained among the country's leading synagogues, but they began to retreat into themselves, leaving communal and institutional domination to the Ashkenazim. Their last major impact on the American Jewish scene was the founding of the Jewish Theological Seminary in 1886.

The second wave of Sephardim followed the collapse of the Ottoman Empire, the Balkan wars, and the 1908 Young Turk revolution. They and their descendants make up one-third to one-half of the Sephardic population in the United States today. They founded the majority of existing Sephardic institutions. In the early years of settlement, they were ignored or rejected by their equally newly arrived Ashkenazic brethren, who hardly recognized them as Jews. Thus, they developed separate communities out of necessity as well as choice. The scars of those days still influence their children's relationships with the larger Jewish community.

Most of this second wave was from the Balkans, principally Greece, Rhodes, and Turkey; from Syria, principally Aleppo; and from Eretz Israel, with smaller groups from North Africa and other Islamic countries. Although most settled in New York City, they also established communities in such places as Rochester (New York), Atlanta, Birmingham, Indianapolis, Los Angeles, San Francisco, Portland, and Seattle. This second wave was dominated by those of Ladino culture who were in certain crucial respects quite different from the by now Americanized descendants of the first wave.

Only in New York City was there a direct confrontation between the "Portuguese" old settlers and the new arrivals from the Levant. Elsewhere, there were too few of the old families to make a difference. Where more than one country-of-origin group settled, they tended to found their own separate congregations, but together they founded synagogues, benevolent aid societies, and social groups, meeting for occasions such as Purim and Hanukkah.

The Syrian (actually Aleppan) community in Brooklyn was particularly successful in this respect. It established a network of congregations, schools, *yeshivot*, and benevolent associations. Postwar Syrian immigrants to Los Angeles carried some of those institutional patterns with them. Collectively, this wave built most of the present structure of the contemporary Sephardic community in New York City.

In later years, members of New York congregations joined together to found the Sephardic Home for the Aged, which soon became the major unifying force in the community. Between 1905 and 1922, assorted mutual aid societies merged. A Sephardic Brotherhood still exists, claiming membership of three hundred families throughout the New York City area.

The Sephardim also made several attempts to create countrywide organizations to link local communities, with major efforts in 1912, 1928, 1941, and 1952. However, unlike the larger masses of Ashkenazim, the Sephardim were until recently unsuccessful in such attempts. The first effort, which was encouraged by the New York *kehillah* in 1912, was an attempt by the three well-established Sephardic synagogues—Shearith Israel of New York City, Mikveh Israel of Philadelphia, and the Montreal congregation—to found the Federation of Oriental Jews in America. Dr. David De Sola Pool, rabbi of Shearith Israel, received ideological support, but lack of financial help brought about its collapse in 1918.

Rabbi Pool also tried to establish a Union of Sephardic Synagogues in 1928, among whose goals was the establishment of a unified Sephardic liturgy. It, too, lasted only a few years, although it did issue a *siddur* with an English translation by Rabbi Pool.

In 1941, the Central Sephardic Jewish Community of America was formed. It appointed a Sephardic chief rabbi and aided refugees, Holocaust victims, students, and the Sephardic Home for the Aged. From 1943 to 1957, it published a bulletin. Today, the organization survives as an active entity only through its women's division. The Sephardic Home for the Aged remains the principal unifying institution in the New York City area.

In 1952, the World Sephardi Federation was reorganized and extended to the United States, but it was not until 1972 that the American Sephardi Federation (ASF) was actually activated. Since then it has maintained a countrywide organizational structure and has been represented in the activities of the worldwide body. The ASF is also a member of the American Zionist Federation. It publishes *The Sephardi Voice* on an irregular basis. Its principal activities have been with Sephardic youth, for whom it established the American Sephardi Youth Federation. Chapters of the ASF have been founded in virtually every Sephardic community, the individual congregations recognized as affiliates.

In the aftermath of World War II, another wave of refugees arrived from the Balkan states. Some of these survivors of the Holocaust joined in already established congregations; others formed their own groups, as did the Sephardic community of Detroit.

The next waves came in the 1950s and 1960s in the wake of decolonization in Africa and Asia. Sephardim from Iraq, Egypt, North Africa, and Lebanon who did not go to Israel or France arrived in the United States. Wealthier Jews from Iran arrived, usually for business reasons. They built congregations and clubs of their own and also furnished the bulk of militant leadership among American Sephardim.

A current, fifth wave consists of an increasing number of *yordim* (emigrants) from Israel. Before 1973, relatively few Sephardim could afford to leave Israel, but their improved circumstances have made it possible. The 1973 Yom Kippur War, in particular, stimulated many to seek their fortunes elsewhere. The number of *yordim* is subject to widely ranging estimates but is no doubt smaller than the exaggerated claims that are made in the press. No one knows the percentage of Sephardim among the *yordim*, but it seems to be growing. Since most of them are recent arrivals, their impact on the American Jewish scene is not yet evident. Today, *yordim* make up most of the Sephardic immigration to the United States.

No reliable method has been found to determine the number of Sephardim in the United States today. Estimates range from 60,000 to 180,000. Marc Angel's 1973 estimate is 100,000, for which he acknowledges a high probability of error, but a closer estimate may be 150,000.

It is also difficult to ascertain who went where and when. Many Sephardim arrived individually and, if they chose to identify themselves as Jews, were often assimilated into the Ashkenazic community. For example, perhaps as many as one hundred of the principals of Conservative Jewish schools in the United States are of Sephardic origin, many educated in Israel; however, they serve Ashkenazic congregations scattered all over the country and are rarely identified with any Sephardic groups.

It is believed that the Sephardic community comprises approximately 2.8 percent of the general Jewish population, which has been estimated at 2.7 percent of the overall population of the United States. American Sephardim are a small minority within a small minority, a fact that raises concern among those interested in the survival of Sephardic group life.

Because Sephardic Jews are such a small percentage of the American Jewish population, there has been little room for them to play active roles on other than an individual basis, which some have done. The children of the second Sephardic wave have undergone Americanization as have their Ashkenazic peers. To the extent that they are active in the Jewish community, they are part of the mainstream of American Jewish life, which is dominated by Ashkenazic institutions and customs. Sephardim rarely occupy top leadership roles in major Jewish organizations, and, in some cases, there are actually Sephardic divisions in already existing groups.

Today there are organized Sephardic congregations or associations in twenty-one communities across the United States. These small enclaves, still outside of the Jewish mainstream, are detailed in the appendix, except for the New York City, Los Angeles, and Seattle communities, which are discussed in the following pages.

New York City

Today, there are an estimated sixty thousand Sephardim in New York City, not counting Israeli *yordim*. The addition of the latter would at least double that number. Shearith Israel was the leading synagogue in North America until the midnineteenth century; it is still the "mother synagogue of American Jewry" and a focal point of Sephardic Jewish life in New York City. The congregation erected its first permanent edifice in 1730, the interior of which has been transported to every subsequent location of the synagogue and serves as the current edifice's *bet midrash* (chapel).

Shearith Israel has been involved in the great events of American history from the revolutionary struggle against the British to the present. In earlier years, the history of the congregation dominated the history of American Jewry. It was not until 1824 that a second synagogue was established in New York City to serve the new Ashkenazic immigrants.

The rapid growth of the German Jewish and Eastern European populations led to the emergence of new institutions that overshadowed the relatively small Sephardic congregation. Its own membership became heavily German as the families intermarried with later arrivals, although faithfully maintaining the Sephardic ritual. As old families in New York

City, the Sephardim entered the upper levels of the city's social life and found little to link them with the new immigrants. The congregation's gradual withdrawal from community affairs was in many respects typical of the behavior of upper-class American Protestants at the turn of the century.

Eventually, Shearith Israel joined the Orthodox camp when the Jewish Theological Seminary, which it had helped to establish in cooperation with other traditional congregations, turned Conservative.

As Sephardim from the Balkans began to arrive, Shearith Israel helped them settle in. Nevertheless, relations were strained between the established, wealthy Shearith Israel Jews and the new immigrants. The latter were too proud to accept outright charity and the former somewhat insensitive to the psychosocial needs of the newcomers. Despite the great differences, however, Shearith Israel did help. A settlement house was established in 1910, and near it a synagogue, Brit Shalom, in 1912.

In the twentieth century, Shearith Israel became the congregational home for Sephardim of diverse origins. Today, the five hundred member families include Jews of Italian, Dutch, Bulgarian, Spanish, Greek, Turkish, French, North African, Israeli, and other Mediterranean backgrounds. The synagogue maintains its Talmud Torah, now nearly two centuries old. The membership supports various specifically Sephardic organizations as well as other general Jewish institutions, but it stays out of the limelight with regard to general Jewish activities. Rabbi David De Sola Pool, its senior rabbi for many years, was a figure of considerable stature on the American Jewish scene, a prime mover in American Orthodoxy before World War II. He was succeeded by Rabbi Louis Gerstein, a Jewish Theological Seminary graduate of Ashkenazic origins and a major force in preserving the congregation's Sephardic heritage, who was assisted by A. Jeshurun Cardozo, a *hazzan* originally from the Dutch Sephardic community. Its present rabbi, Marc Angel, is a native of the Seattle Sephardic community and Orthodox by training. He is a leading scholar of American Sephardic history and life.

Between 1899 and 1925, nearly twenty-five thousand Sephardim from the Balkans and the Middle East settled in the New York area. They retained their individual identities, separate from Ashkenazic communal and religious groups and also from each other. Jews from Rhodes settled on Manhattan's Lower East Side, those from Greece and Turkey in the Bronx, and the Syrians in Brooklyn.

The first Sephardic congregation of the second wave was Moses Montefiore, established in Harlem in 1885 with the assistance of

Shearith Israel. Its members came from various countries around the Mediterranean. It lasted for two decades, during which time local brotherhoods founded other synagogues, so that by 1916 there were twenty-eight Sephardic synagogues serving the new immigrant community, most quite small.

In 1924, the Spanish-speaking Sephardic community of New York was organized in Harlem. It lasted officially until 1933 when economic conditions resulted in Sephardic families leaving the neighborhood.

By 1926, most communities had moved out of the settlement house area and into their own neighborhoods, establishing eight synagogues on the Lower East Side, three in Brooklyn, and three in Harlem, as well as thirty-six benevolent associations. The Harlem communities have since moved on to Brooklyn and Queens.

Organized life outside of the synagogue began in 1899 with the founding of the Union and Peace Society, principally by Turkish Sephardic immigrants from Smyrna (Izmir), joined by a few natives of Eretz Israel and Morocco. Over the next two decades, twenty societies and congregations were organized in New York City, each based on a different city or town of origin in the Old World, although some tried to reach out to other Sephardim as well. These societies fell into three groups: Judesmo-speaking Jews, Greek-speaking Jews, and Arabic-speaking Jews from Syria. Most of these societies concentrated on providing burial services, free loans, social activities, and *tzedakah* (poverty relief). Most of them organized worship services as well, and either became congregations or developed congregations within their framework. As their members spread out, the societies developed branches in various parts of New York City. Most reached their peak in the 1920s and disappeared with the death of the immigrant generation.

Judesmo-speaking Jews also organized the Sephardic Jewish Brotherhood of America, originally founded in 1915 and reorganized in 1921 as a comprehensive group similar to the Ashkenazic Workmen's Circle. It survives in weakened form. Contrary to myth, in the early years of the twentieth century, many of the Balkan Sephardim *were* active Zionists and Socialists, especially those from Salonika.

The Greek-speaking societies early on became the bases for congregations that ultimately absorbed the societies themselves and continue to exist.

The Arabic-speaking Sephardim from Syria, far more religious in a traditional sense than their Balkan brethren, organized congregations first, and then social, cultural, and philanthropic societies. In the 1940s, the Syrian congregations and organizations established an umbrella body, the Magen David Federation, which continues to function in modest ways. Today, there are an estimated twenty-five thousand Jews within the Syrian community. They are the best organized, have the most comprehensive and best articulated community organization, do the most to provide Jewish education for their children, and remain a tightly knit group with their own chief rabbi, Jerusalem-born Jacob S. Kassin, who heads the Rabbinical Council of Syrian and Near Eastern Jewish Communities of America.

There have been a number of efforts to combine the Sephardic organizations of New York City into a single community, including the Sephardic Community of New York (1920–22); its successor, the Sephardic Jewish Community of New York, technically lasted from 1924 to 1947 but effectively ceased to be influential in the 1930s.

The first Yemenite Jews arrived in the United States in 1927. They organized a synagogue on the Lower East Side of Manhattan and, in 1936, a mutual aid society in Brooklyn, which became the Federation of Yemenite Jews in America. Despite their small numbers, by 1946 the Yemenite Jews maintained four separate, small synagogues. The population increased in the 1950s and 1960s with newcomers from Israel.

A few Iraqi Jews arrived prior to 1930, but the Iraqi community took form only after World War II. Its one congregation is Kehal Joseph in Los Angeles, although in 1971 it organized the American Committee for the Rescue and Resettlement of Iraqi Jews to help brethren still in Iraq.

Egyptian Sephardim first entered the United States after World War II, most in the wake of the Israeli-Arab wars. Some formed congregations of their own, but since many were of Syrian ancestry, they joined existing Syrian synagogues. They also formed an organization to rescue and assist their brethren in Egypt.

Lebanese Jews began to arrive after the Six Day War in 1967. Their numbers grew following the outbreak of civil war in Lebanon in 1975. Since they, too, were basically of Syrian background, they joined existing Syrian synagogues.

Although the first Jews from Morocco arrived in the United States in the eighteenth century, a separate Moroccan Sephardic community has developed only since World War II. They have organized their own congregations and social groups in New York City, Washington, D.C., Los Angeles, Miami, and Chicago.

A few Iranian Jews reached the United States before the overthrow of the shah in 1979, but they began to immigrate in large numbers only after that. They founded the Iranian Jews of America and are heavily concentrated in New York and Los Angeles, with other congregations in Burlingame, California, and Skokie, Illinois.

There was once an active and vocal Sephardic press in the United States, beginning with *La America*, inaugurated in 1910. The Judeo-Spanish press in America came to an end in 1948 when *La Vara*, which had become the community's major paper in the 1920s, ceased publication. All told, eleven Judeo-Spanish publications appeared at one time or another in America, at least three being Socialist in orientation. Beginning in the late 1930s, several efforts have been made to publish monthly or quarterly bulletins in English.

No account of the Sephardim in New York would be complete without reference to the coffeehouses of the immigrant generation. They were the true centers of Sephardic life, especially on the Lower East Side, replicating as closely as possible the coffeehouses of the Balkans.

The one institution that did unite the Sephardic Jewish community of New York from the 1940s on was the Home for the Aged. Needed by everyone and too expensive a prospect for each association to develop its own, it became the single communal endeavor of the Balkan Sephardim and for many years was the one arena in which all the Sephardic groups other than the Syrians met.

After World War II, the Sephardim along with other Jews moved out of these areas of first and second settlement into Queens and the suburbs. Today in the Bronx, only two congregations, the Sephardic Jewish Center of the Bronx and Congregation Shaare Rachamim, remain, both of Balkan origin. A far greater concentration of Sephardim has remained in Brooklyn, with eleven congregations reinforced by postwar immigration.

Brooklyn also has the greatest concentration of Syrian Jews in the United States, numbering some twenty-four thousand. The great majority of the community is from Aleppo, but there is also a group from Damascus. Most arrived between 1911 and 1920. Most American Sephardim of Syrian origin are concentrated in one Brooklyn neighborhood, although less so than in the past. The community is the most strictly Orthodox of all the Sephardic communities. Their strong commitment to Jewish education is of long standing. An estimated 90 percent of the children in the Syrian community study in the group's schools. Like other Orthodox communities, they are self-sufficient and tend to keep to themselves, limiting social and communal interaction with other Jewish groups. Their principal congregations have been served by rabbis of Ashkenazic origin for many decades. Shaare Zion on Ocean Parkway has about one thousand family members; Magen David is also a Halabi synagogue. Ahi Ezer was originally founded by Jews from Damascus.

Many members of the Syrian community maintain weekend and summer homes in New Jersey where they have created a subsidiary community at Bradley Beach and Deal (discussed in the appendix). Some of their children have permanently settled there.

Perhaps the greatest achievement of the Syrian Jewish community in the United States outside of its own communal edifice is Otzar HaTorah, a network of schools for the Sephardic communities in Asia, Africa, and France, founded by Isaac Shalom, one of the first wealthy members of the community—a noted philanthropist and devout Jew. These schools began as a counterbalance to the Alliance schools, emphasizing traditional Jewish religion in the Orthodox sense and English as the principal foreign language. In that way, they simultaneously counteracted the assimilationist orientation of the Alliance and provided young Sephardim with an education in the language that was replacing French as the world's "lingua franca."

Shalom's timing was excellent. Since even those parents who were not particularly religious wanted their children to learn English, they enrolled them in the Otzar HaTorah schools. After the Algerian Jews moved to France, Otzar HaTorah opened up schools and teacher-training institutions in that country. While the Alliance schools have faded since World War II, Otzar HaTorah schools are still going strong and represent the only indigenous Sephardic educational movement of their kind.

Emet Veshalom, the Sephardic synagogue in Cedarhurst, in Queens, now a modern Conservative congregation, was established by the transplanted Balkan community of Brooklyn, whose members moved from there in the 1950s. It is the leading congregation of the Balkan community and, after Shearith Israel, the most important Sephardic congregation in the New York City area. Its largest single group is composed of descendants of Jews from Monastir, now in Yugoslavia. Arnold Marans, its present rabbi, is a Jewish Theological Seminary graduate of Ashkenazic origin.

Although the Sephardic Jews of greater New York are not linked by any overall body, many are involved in common institutions, such as Yeshiva University's Division of Sephardic Studies. The division was founded in 1964 at the initiative of Rabbi Herbert Dobrinsky and under the leadership of the Hakham Solomon Gaon, then chief rabbi of the

British Sephardim, to train rabbis, *hazzanim*, and teachers for Sephardic communities throughout North America. It also has an Association of Sephardic Studies and an annual cultural festival. The major gatherings of Sephardim on the East Coast are generally under its auspices, or those of the American Sephardi Federation. Its journal, *The American Sephardi*, contains articles and information on past and contemporary Sephardic history and culture. The division has also become a major source of technical assistance for many Sephardic communities.

The general ethnic revival at the end of the 1960s reached into the Sephardic community as well, especially influencing many young Sephardic intellectuals and professionals who sought their roots in ways similar to other third- and fourth-generation Americans at the time. They were partially successful in their quest, but, like the rest of the ethnic revival movement, their energy diminished in less than a decade, having no place to go for reinforcement after reaffirming their sense of self-esteem. During that decade, however, they made a few attempts to institutionalize their efforts.

The World Institute for Sephardic Studies, started by Jose Faur, a Sephardic professor of Talmud at the Jewish Theological Seminary, for a short time in the 1970s was a significant factor in the effort to revive Sephardic identity and stimulate Sephardic cultural expression among young adults. Several other small institutes for the dissemination of Sephardic culture have also appeared from time to time; none has lasted.

In general, New York has been the major seat of Sephardic cultural and intellectual activity in the United States. It began with Professor Maier Joseph Bernadete, who taught courses in Sephardic history and culture at New York University after World War II, and has continued through the new Center for Sephardic Studies established at the City University of New York (CUNY) in 1985 by Professor Jane Gerber, a noted scholar of North African Jewry.

The serial publications of the Sephardic community all originate in New York City. They include those of the American Sephardi Federation; *The Sephardic News*, published monthly by the Sephardic Home for the Aged; the bulletin of the Sephardic program of Yeshiva University; and various congregational bulletins (that of Shearith Israel is circulated beyond the congregational membership).

New York is also the headquarters for all countrywide Sephardic organizations, including the American Sephardi Federation and the Union of Sephardic Jewish Congregations (see table 7.1).

TABLE 7.1
Organizations and Congregations Affiliated with the American Sephardi Federation in New York City

Manhattan
Association for Yugoslavian Jews
Committee for Secondary Education in Israel for Central Sephardic Committee
Congregation Anshe Shalom
Congregation Shearith Israel
Meshad Hebrew Society, Inc.
The Moroccan Jewish Organization
Sephardic New Americans
Sephardic Studies Program, Yeshiva University
Women's Division, American Friends of Alliance Israelite Universelle
Bronx
Congregation Shaare Rahamim
Sephardic Jewish Brotherhood
Sephardic Jewish Center of the Bronx
Brooklyn
Ahi Ezer Congregation
Congregation Beth Torah
Congregation B'nai Joseph
Magen David Congregation
Magen David Congregation of Ocean Parkway
Sephardic Center of Mapleton
Sephardic Home for the Aged
Sephardic Jewish Center of Canarsie
Shaare Zion Congregation
Temple Torah Israel
Yemenite Congregation Ohel Shalom
Queens
A.A. Society, Inc.
Deale Synagogue
Sephardic Jewish Center and Congregation of Queens
Long Island
Sephardic Temple
United Sephardim of Rockaway Beach

Los Angeles

Los Angeles has the second largest Sephardic community in the United States. An estimated twelve thousand to fourteen thousand Sephardim (excluding the most recent *yordim*) live in the metropolitan area: 80 percent in west Los Angeles, Beverly Hills, Westwood, and the southern sections of the city; and 20 percent in the San Fernando Valley. Many Los Angeles Sephardim are transplants from Seattle or the East

Coast. Others came directly from the Old Country. Five Sephardic synagogues and other local organizations serve this community, which is culturally diverse, representing the Sephardic traditions of Rhodes, the Balkans, Syria, Morocco, Iran, the Far East, India, and Burma.

The first Sephardim to arrive on the West Coast were Jews from Rhodes who settled in Seattle around the turn of the century. A number of those families later moved to Los Angeles. Turkish and Greek Jews also arrived in Los Angeles in the early 1900s.

There were only about sixty Sephardim in Los Angeles in 1912. A congregation was established named Ahvat Shalom, which disintegrated two years later because of conflict between natives of Rhodes and mainland Turkey. The latter formed the Sephardic Community of Los Angeles in 1914 and named its synagogue Ohel Abraham. It took the Rhodeslis (natives of Rhodes) three years before they were able to reorganize as the Peace and Progress Society, which came to be known as the Sephardic Hebrew Center. Its rabbi, Solomon Mizrahi, would serve the community for over sixty years. Today it has a membership of some 220 families, many Judesmo-speaking, and provides facilities for weekly services, youth activities, a Hebrew school, and an adult education program.

In 1926, Sephardic immigrants established the Sephardic Brotherhood, Hayim VaHessed. In the 1930s, the older two congregations joined together to establish a Jewish educational program for their children. Ultimately, each congregation established its own Talmud Torah. In 1937, these societies established the United Sephardic Organization of Los Angeles, which was later renamed the Council of Sephardic Organizations of Los Angeles. Except in fund raising for overseas relief in the 1940s, the council remained principally a paper organization. In 1973, the almost defunct council was replaced by the Los Angeles branch of the American Sephardi Federation.

After World War II, there was an influx of Sephardim into Los Angeles. In 1945, Syrians from Brooklyn and Aleppo formed Congregation Magen David. In 1959, immigrants from Iraq established Kehal Joseph. They were reinforced by Iraqi Jews from southern and eastern Asia who came to the United States after decolonization. The first Moroccan Jews settled after World War II and have been arriving in steady streams since then, many after having lived in Israel. Early in the 1970s, two Moroccan congregations were established, Em Habanim and Sephardic Adath Yeshurun. Cuban Jews arrived after Castro seized power in 1959. After the Khomeini revolution, thousands of Iranian Jews settled in the Beverly Hills area. By the end of the decade, they had established two congregations.

Also in 1959, the two oldest congregations merged to form the Sephardic Temple Tifereth Israel, now a Conservative synagogue and the largest Sephardic synagogue in Los Angeles. Its rabbi, Jacob Ott, although of Ashkenazic background, has fully adapted to the Sephardic *minhag*. The congregation has some five hundred member families, although not all are Sephardim. Activities include weekly worship, a men's club, sisterhood, a Hebrew school, adult education, Israel and local scholarship fund raising, and a summer camp. The Talmud Torah curriculum includes courses in Sephardic folklore and cooking and Judesmo.

Sephardi Magen David is a traditional Syrian congregation whose 125 families now include Greeks, Iraqis, and Cubans. It was founded by Syrian Jews from New York who continue to retain congregational leadership. The synagogue emphasizes religious and educational activities through its daily services and formal and informal educational programs. The Syrian community, primarily under the leadership of one family, has established a Sephardic day school, the Sephardic Hebrew Academy, which has recently been transformed into a communitywide enterprise.

Kehal Joseph is the spiritual and cultural center for Jews from India and Burma. Its approximately one hundred family members also include Iranians and Moroccans. The synagogue provides daily services, an intensive Talmud Torah, and a center for social activities.

The fifth congregation is the Sephardic Jewish Community and Brotherhood of Los Angeles. It claims a membership of about five hundred families, many Moroccan. The congregation currently provides weekly (with plans for daily) services, a religious school, a youth program, and adult education classes.

In addition to these synagogues, the Sephardic community of Los Angeles supports a number of other organizations. Los Hermanos is a cross-congregational Sephardic brotherhood active since 1935. Among organizations reflecting countries of origin, there are Em HaBanim, a nascent social group composed of Jews from Morocco; the Max Nordau Society, a Greek Jewish memorial foundation with approximately eighty members; and the Persian Sephardic Society of Southern California.

The California Friends of the Alliance Israelite Universelle and Otzar HaTorah raise funds for educational activities among Sephardim in Israel and in Muslim countries. Dr. Jose Nessim of Beverly Hills is the founder of and key figure in the Sephardic Educational Center, located in the reconstructed Sephardic Talmud Torah in Jerusalem's Old City, which fosters Jewish and Sephardic identity among Sephardic youth and young adults throughout the world. A separate wing for aged Sephardim has recently been established at the Home for Jewish Aged under the direct auspices of the Jewish Federation Council of Greater Los Angeles. The Beth Shalom Benevolent Society, with its five hundred members, is an independent organization that provides emergency medical care and burial services. There are also local Sephardic chapters for City of Hope, Cedars-Sinai Hospital, and Veterans of Foreign Wars. Within the last several years, a Sephardic division of the United Jewish Appeal Campaign has been created.

The Los Angeles chapters of the American Sephardi Federation and its youth division, the American Sephardi Youth Federation, are active. In 1977, Los Angeles hosted the ASYF National Youth Convention.

The Los Angeles Sephardic community is one of the most highly organized in the United States. Because it is beyond the sphere of influence of East Coast Jewry, its network of local institutions remains autonomous. In comparison to New York City, the Los Angeles Sephardic community exhibits considerable intergroup cooperation, a fact most likely related to size. However, even here there is evidence that institutions guard their own interests.

Seattle

Ranked as the third largest Sephardic community in the United States, Seattle's estimated four thousand Sephardim comprise about one-fifth of its total Jewish population, making Seattle's the only American Jewish community in which Sephardic Jews constitute a substantial and visible share of the whole community. For its size, the organizational network of Seattle's Sephardic community is quite dynamic, reflecting the strong historical consciousness of the Sephardim who settled there.

Responding to the opportunities for development in the Pacific Northwest shortly after the turn of the century, Judesmo-speaking Jews from Turkey and Rhodes arrived in Seattle. They found the climate to their liking and Greek non-Jews who made them feel at home, so they sent for their relatives and immigration began.

The Seattle community can almost be described as a deliberately planted colony. Its three founders set out for the city after hearing about it from a Greek friend, arriving in 1903. In the years that followed, Sephardim were sent there by the Industrial Removal Office, which had been founded to encourage Jews to move away from the crowded East Coast, and, more importantly, directly from their countries of origin into the interior of the United States. Thus, in 1907 the first three men were sent brides, escorted by the father of one of them. In the meantime, other immigrants arrived, and in that same year their first High Holy Day services were conducted.

The Turkish group founded Sephardic Bikur Holim Congregation in 1905 (not to be confused with Seattle's Ashkenazic synagogue of the same name). In 1965, the congregation moved to its present location and erected a new building. Today, Sephardic Bikur Holim is a modern Orthodox institution and the larger of Seattle's two Sephardic synagogues. Its membership stands at some 275 families. The present rabbi, the congregation's third, is of Moroccan birth, educated in England. The first two, father and son, were of Turkish origin. The *hazzan* has served the congregation since 1953, and the synagogue offers daily and Sabbath services and a modest adult education program.

The original Koupa Ezra Bessarot of Rhodes was incorporated in 1914. The first members actually arrived in Seattle as early as 1904, but the initial lack of numbers and later a community schism (1912) delayed its founding.

The present congregation is also modern Orthodox. Its approximately 240 families are almost exclusively Jews from Rhodes or their immediate descendants. Its rabbi, however, who has served since the early 1960s, is of Ashkenazic origin, a graduate of the Hebrew Theological College in Skokie, Illinois. Services are held daily and on the Sabbath. The synagogue has no youth program, relying instead on the local chapter of the American Sephardi Youth Federation. There is a men's club, and the women participate in an active auxiliary.

Since 1950, Bikur Holim and Ezra Bessarot have together operated a small Talmud Torah. The school meets twice a week and has an enrollment of about thirty students. Many of Seattle's Sephardic families send their children to the Seattle Hebrew Academy, an all-day Jewish school in the area. The two congregations also jointly sponsor a ten-day summer camp in cooperation with the local Jewish community center. There is a high-school youth program for about fifty students.

From time to time, a merger of the two congregations has been suggested. Although little divides them ideologically, customary differences do, and even generate a mild rivalry. Since the two institutions do cooperate on a functional basis, there is little incentive to force a merger in the face of very real congregational identities.

Other Sephardic organizations in Seattle include the Seattle Sephardic Brotherhood, established in 1935, which facilitates medical and burial services for its approximately 350 family members. Its youth interests are realized through local and national scholarships. In the past, both Sephardic congregations have attempted to restrict membership in the Brotherhood to their own members. Like its male counterpart, the Seattle Sephardic Sisterhood (two hundred members) links the membership of the two congregations to raise funds for charitable causes.

Ahavat Achim is a smaller society, currently with forty families, which was established in 1924 by Jews from Marmara (Turkey) as both a religious congregation and a conduit for participation in American society. As a congregation, it ceased to exist over thirty-five years ago, but the organization still sponsors a modest social program. Most of its members are affiliated with Sephardic Bikur Holim.

The Seattle Sephardi Federation mainly serves as a local address for the American Sephardi Federation. It does, however, organize a limited number of local cultural events.

The purpose of the Seattle Sephardic Youth Federation, first organized in 1973, is to help members maintain cultural tradition and thus deepen their commitment to the Sephardic community. It attempts to do this through activities and programs that both educate and create a sense of Sephardic camaraderie. In addition to local programming, the organization participates in national Sephardic youth conventions and summer seminars in Israel, which are subsidized by local and national bodies.

The Seattle Sephardic Culture Committee was founded in 1975, composed of representatives of the Sephardic Brotherhood, the boards of directors of both Sephardic synagogues, and the Sephardic Youth Federation. Through its coordinating capacity, this group has been successful in sponsoring a number of communitywide events.

In all, there are an estimated 575 families affiliated with Sephardic organizations in Seattle, and there is a limit as to how many communal obligations this same small leadership cadre can assume. As the differences between the two Sephardic traditions, Turkish and Rhodeslis, lose significance among younger generations, the community might benefit by consolidating some of its present institutions. Nevertheless, Seattle is thought to be the most successful Sephardic community in the United States; however, its future success can be measured only in terms of those capable and willing to sustain it materially and in spirit.

Seattle's Sephardic community tends to be insular. Most Sephardim remain uninvolved in the general Jewish community. To some extent, this reflects group self-segregation, a logical strategy for safeguarding Sephardic identity, cultural autonomy, and membership. In part, it points to the fact that the historical separation between Jews of one cultural tradition and those of another has not yet been overcome. Among those Sephardim who have taken on leadership roles within the general Jewish community, there is a pattern of affiliation with the more prestigious Baron de Hirsch Reform Temple (Ashkenazic).

The State of U.S. Sephardic Life Today

The original Sephardic benevolent societies have evolved over the years into modern suburban synagogues. The Sephardic coffeehouses of New York City, which once served as the retreats and havens for the immigrant generation, have disappeared. This is the price that Sephardic Jews have paid for success and acculturation. Today, most American Jews share common cultural and socioeconomic characteristics, and labels disappear. Unlike their parents, children of Greek Jews and Polish Jews have a common language.

Yet, all is not quite the same. Angel suggests that for Sephardim under thirty, the question of Sephardic identity is closely linked with the issue of Jewish identity in general. Those with a high attachment to Jewish identity have a strong attachment to Sephardic culture; others appear lost to both. Increasingly, what remains for individuals is a formal institutional framework. Like contemporary Jewish communities everywhere, associational ties have replaced the organic ties of the past, and organizational activity is now the landmark against which Jews measure their commitments. The Sephardim moved in this direction a generation or two after the Ashkenazim but, even more than among the Ashkenazim, the institutional ties of the Sephardim are focused on their synagogues and principally confined to matters of religious observance and education.

The Sephardim in America have suffered from two great problems: the inability to overcome their parochial divisions to develop active, unified communities, and lack of leadership capable of transmitting the Sephardic heritage. Although the community has had many dedicated volunteers from among its rank and file, it suffers from a chronic shortage of rabbis and educators.

Sephardic educators in the United States have generally found employment in the larger Jewish community serving basically Ashkenazic institutions following the national-cultural approach to Jewish education fostered by the Zionist movement. Thus, they have been among those advocating the teaching of the Hebrew language and Zionism, but they have not been available to the Sephardic community to teach Sephardic rituals and customs to the younger generation.

The situation with regard to rabbis has been no better. Only a handful of indigenous American Sephardim have entered the rabbinate, the largest single group from Seattle, which is the most secure and self-confident U.S. Sephardic community. Otherwise, Sephardic congregations have had to rely on immigrants, first from the Balkans and Syria and more recently from Morocco and Israel, or on Ashkenazim who have agreed to learn the Sephardic *minhag*. Today, rabbinical leadership is about 40 percent Sephardic immigrants, 40 percent Ashkenazic, and 10 percent American-born Sephardim.

The current position and image of Sephardim in the United States have emerged from the somewhat romantic view of them developed by many Ashkenazim. In recent years, this, along with the news from Israel, has helped place the Sephardic issue on the American Jewish agenda. It may be possible to capitalize on this interest to aid the Sephardim in their quest for the proper recognition of Sephardic culture within the overall framework of Jewish culture.

The emergence of the American Sephardi Federation as a force reflects today's trends among American Sephardim—unity among the various Sephardic subgroups, militancy in demanding a place in the Jewish sun, and involvement in the larger Jewish community. This writer had the honor to be elected the first president of the ASF in 1972, and along with Mati Ronen, its first executive director, to organize branches from coast to coast. The first national convention of the ASF that year was an outpouring of Sephardic sentiment from every quarter. The second president was Lilliane Winn Shalom who, with her husband Stephen Shalom, has made the Sephardic issue central in her public activities. Leon Levy, the third president of the ASF, has undertaken to institutionalize the organization in preparation for future work.

New Sephardic Communities in Canada

Canada has a serious concentration of Sephardim for the first time in its history as a result of recent immigrations, principally from North Africa and secondarily from western Asia. Beginning in the 1960s, Quebec drew French-speaking North African Jews because of its French-speaking character. Their number has been estimated as high as twenty-five thousand, but it is probably half that.

In Montreal there are also Sephardim from Tangier who still speak Spanish, from Algeria, from Iraq (about three hundred families), and from the Balkans. They have taken over the Spanish and Portuguese Synagogue of Montreal—the city's first synagogue, founded in the 1760s by Spanish and Portuguese Jews from London, who came with the British occupation of New France—and have given new life to one of the original colonial synagogues of North America. Several thousand Egyptian Jews have also settled in Montreal, as have smaller groups from Syria and Lebanon, but they have not organized separate institutions. There are also the omnipresent Israeli *yordim*. For a long time the *yordim* were overwhelmingly Ashkenazic, but in recent years a small number of Sephardim have also found their way to Montreal.

The first encounter between the Sephardic immigrants and the established Ashkenazic community was not successful because of language and cultural barriers. As a result, the Sephardim developed their own institutions as well as a certain hostility to the Ashkenazic majority. Perhaps also as a result, they assimilated more rapidly among the French Canadians than did the Ashkenazim. Even though they are a first-generation Jewry, the intermarriage rate between Sephardim and non-Jews in Quebec is higher than that of the already third-generation Ashkenazim. In the interim, however, the Sephardim have also realized the parochial nature of French-Canadian culture, and many have tried to build bridges to the English-speaking community of Canada, which also means building bridges to Ashkenazic Jewry, so the situation there is in flux.

The Sephardim who arrived in Canada encountered a Jewish community that was very close to its Eastern European Ashkenazic roots and that did not have any significant non–Eastern European Jewish population; hence, the gap between the two was great. In turn, the gap led to the kind of misunderstanding and lack of communication that had occurred in the United States two generations earlier. However, conditions have changed. Whereas the American Sephardim felt weak and remained passive, those who emigrated to Canada became militant and active. Because of their particular experiences, they often became the most militant of all the North American Sephardim. Moreover, they were assisted by a small minority of Ashkenazim who sympathized with them and gave them a platform.

A Sephardic community has also developed in Toronto and may be growing faster than the Quebec community at this point. Approximately four thousand North African Jews have settled there, with perhaps another four thousand Egyptian Jews as well. The Jews from Tangier have established a congregation, Petah Tikva, of approximately two hundred families.

Chapter 8

The Cultural Issue

IN THE FORGING of a new relationship between Sephardim and Ashkenazim, the cultural issue is likely to become greater and more difficult as the political issue is resolved. As the Sephardim become better established in Israel and in their diaspora communities, both economically and politically, they have more time to reflect on the adjustment process that, particularly in Israel, has stripped them of much of their heritage, and to demand remedial steps.

The strength of Jewish culture in the diaspora is relatively weak; so little has been preserved of the original Jewish cultures, Ashkenazic or Sephardic, that there is little feeling of deprivation among Sephardim. True, such phenomena as neopseudo-Hassidism and shtetl nostalgia leave the Sephardim out, but since in most cases Sephardim constitute such small minorities of the total Jewish population, there is little they can do in response except to try to encourage the revival of a measure of their own Old Country cultures in the same manner.

In Israel, however, the situation is more acute. The Sephardic majority feels culturally put upon. This is not merely a reaction to the Ashkenazic myth of the culturally inferior Sephardim. The roots are far deeper than that.

Zionist Triumphalism as Ashkenazification

When the first Ashkenazim arrived in Eretz Israel in the nineteenth century, they found a dominant Sephardic community already actively promoting the revival of Jewish life in its own way. The first Ashkenazim merely sought independence from that community. When the Zionists began arriving from Russia and Poland, however, they sought dominance on Zionist grounds. As long as the Ottoman Turks had ruled the country—until World War I—the old Sephardic elite remained in power, but with the coming of the British, the Zionist *halutzim* took over, excluding all others, Sephardim and Ashkenazim alike.

Between the world wars, the Third Aliyah and its leadership imposed a revolutionary Russian Zionist culture on Eretz Israel. When the mass immigrations of Sephardim occurred after 1948, newcomers were taught that this culture was, in fact, normative. Indeed, they were often forcibly assimilated to it—made to abandon religious traditions and practices, educated in secular Zionist institutions, and divided among the political parties according to relative strength of each party in the governing coalitions so that both the secular and Socialist parties gained control over the lives of most new immigrants and the education of their children.

Beginning with a strong belief in their own superiority as *halutzim* and bearers of Zionism, the Ashkenazic Zionist leadership sought to "civilize" the Sephardim by bringing them into Eastern European Jewish culture in the guise of teaching them Western ways. In the process, traditional Sephardic culture, including the Jewish dimension, was undermined. The Sephardic *olim* (immigrants to Israel) lost their self-respect and the respect of their children on the grounds that they had nothing of real value to contribute to the state or to the next generation.

This loss is brought home by Shulamith Hareven, a contemporary Israeli novelist, in a poignant passage in her novel *City of Many Days* that describes life in Jerusalem just before and after the establishment of the state. The son of the heroine comes home from school with a drastic proposal:

> He felt as if some part of him had been altered, and one morning, as though under duress, he asked Sara what she thought of changing their last name to Amir. It sounds more Hebrew, he said to her, embarrassed.

Sara agreed right away. Since her grandfather's death, the name Amarillo no longer meant much to her. She saw little of Gracia, who had meanwhile returned to Jerusalem, or of her pudgy mother-in-law, Allegra, who occasionally sent them jars of olives and olive oil from Tiberias, to say nothing of all her *tias* and *tios* scattered throughout Jerusalem. Hillel was enthusiastic about the change. By the standards of the Ashkenazi school he now attended, Amir was certainly a nicer name than Amarillo. His teacher Tzippora thought so too. Botanically derived names were in fashion that year, and Amir, which meant treetop, was right in keeping with style.

Amarillo, a classic Spanish name, was borne by a family that had bred eminent *halakhic* scholars and kabbalists, including three chief rabbis of the great Sephardic community in Salonika.

This assault on an entire segment of Jewish culture was conducted by members of every political camp, whether it involved the Hashomer Hatzair kibbutzim teaching children who fell into their hands a Zionist version of Russian Marxism to replace Jewish tradition; secular and Ashkenazic Youth Aliyah residential programs; or Orthodox *yeshivot* insisting that Sephardic boys learn Yiddish to study Talmud. The religious schools have always presented Eastern European Orthodoxy (sometimes in its Zionist version) to their students, a majority of whom are from Sephardic communities, as authentic Judaism.

When the Jewish identity program was introduced into the public nonreligious schools in the early 1960s to attempt to counteract de-Judaization of the children and grandchildren of the Zionist founders (which was as shocking to the founders as it was inevitable in light of the content of Socialist Zionist education), the image of the Sabbath that was placed before a school population with an emerging Sephardic majority was that gefilte fish and other Ashkenazic customs are universal requisites for Sabbath observance. There was no reference to anything from the Sephardic children's own highly developed traditions. The tragic irony was that the Sephardic children often came from homes that observed the Sabbath, whereas many of the Ashkenazic teachers had to read about Sabbath customs in books. Even later, when pressures forced the schools to pay at least minimum attention to Sephardic Jews, their culture was always presented as that of the minority, in the way that some American schools teach *Maoz Tzur* and *Hava Nagilah* at Christmastime to balance Christian carols. In other words, children are still taught that Ashkenazic culture from the shtetl as filtered through the Zionist movement is "Israeli" culture and that Sephardic culture belongs to an "ethnic" minority. The Ashkenazic establishment has always believed this, and they have convinced the Sephardim to accept their way of looking at the world.

As noted earlier, the Sephardim, not the Ashkenazim, are looked upon as divided into *edot*, or ethnic minority groups; while the Ashkenazim, now a minority in the country, continue to be presented as "Israelis"—that is to say, the normative majority. More than that, when they are categorized according to their origins, they are entitled to use the term *Ashkenazim*, even though Ashkenaz is specifically western Germany and northeastern France; but when Jews from Africa and Asia use the term *Sephardim*, the Ashkenazim quickly say they are Orientals and that only those whose ancestors came from Spain are Sephardim. This, of course, is a cultural putdown.

There are horror stories as well. Insiders have known for years what has recently come out in public: that in an effort to overcome the backwardness of Yemenite Jews, for a brief period immediately after they were airlifted to Israel, some presumably well-meaning people removed newborn and young children from their parents, claiming that they had died and sending them off to be raised among "proper Ashkenazim." It was only in 1985 that parents who had lost children were willing publicly to demand an investigation. Needless to say, the whole country was properly horrified and apologetic—thirty-five years too late.

Other insults have been less dreadful, but no less painful, as when Sephardic (but not Ashkenazic) children were persuaded to leave school after the seventh grade to work as farm laborers on the Zionist grounds that they would be redeemed through labor and did not need more education. Or when Jews from Iraq who had once lived in a most civilized manner in affluent surroundings were removed from permanent buildings in army camps (which were not much to begin with) and put in tents so that Jews from Rumania could take over the permanent buildings, on the grounds that Jews from Arab lands were used to living in tents while people from Europe were not. The list of such acts is long, and their recitation still infuriates.

Some of these prejudices have a tragicomic dimension. Ladybird Johnson, wife of the late U.S. president, writes in her memoirs of how the wife of the Israeli ambassador to the United States in the late 1960s paid her a courtesy call. The two women discussed America's racial problems, and the ambassador's wife said that Israel had a similar problem with regard to the assimilation of the "Oriental Jews" into Western civilization, who, Mrs. Johnson quotes her as saying, were people who did not know how to use toothbrushes or plumbing and had only their Jewish heritage in common with "Western" Jews. (Contemplate that statement for a moment—what kind of Jewishness is implied when toothbrushes and plumbing are valued so much more than a common Jewish heritage?) These kinds of statements were issued from virtually every UJA platform in the United States for two decades or more for the best of reasons—to raise money to integrate the newcomers.

It has now become known that when assembled by Israeli emissaries to leave their countries of origin, many Sephardic *olim* were forced to leave their sacred books behind on the grounds that they would have no need for such relics of the past in the new Israeli society. People who had joyously brought precious manuscripts bearing their Jewish heritage to carry with them to Eretz Israel were forced to bury them on the spot before they could leave.

The result of all this discrimination was not simply the creation of an economic gap between many Sephardim and Ashkenazim, but also a form of cultural disruption whose consequences may be even greater. The economic gap is real enough and has its own consequences. We have noted how many people whose families took them to the West instead of to Israel became professionals and prominent businessmen, while many of their classmates who went to Israel are now common laborers. In fact, many of the Sephardic immigrants did well enough, and some very well indeed; for them there is no economic gap, so the cultural disruption has a greater effect. The Moroccans who are vilified in Israel as the source of thieves and prostitutes in Israeli society maintained communities in Morocco for centuries under the most adverse conditions without any more thievery or prostitution than similar communities in, say, Lithuania. In Israel, however, with their culture broken down and their self-esteem diminished, with parental authority discredited, it is not surprising that many have become demoralized. The consequences of this breaking down of a culture harms not only the Sephardim but all of the Jewish world. Centuries of Jewish intellectual and cultural expression have been lost.

This harsh critique should not be left unqualified. It is clear that none of this was the result of deliberate malice. Misunderstanding—a familiar pattern in situations throughout the world where a strong dominant group sees itself as having *the* culture that is worth preserving and extending—is closer to the mark. It is also true that the Sephardim themselves did not exert the energies that they should have to hold their own. The reasons for this are complex but have to do with the fact that the natural leadership of the Sephardic *olim*, the Sephardic establishment of the old *yishuv*, was earlier weakened when the leadership of the *yishuv* was transferred to the Zionist movement. The Zionist leaders rapidly drove them out of their old positions of power. The Sephardim, in turn, retreated from public into private affairs. Having ignored the public dimensions of the evolving Israeli society, they have not been able to provide the leadership needed by their brethren.

The Sephardic Awakening

As long as Sephardim believed Ashkenazim to be right—that Zionist socialism *à la Russe* was indeed superior—they worked hard to adjust to it. But after the decline and fall of the Labor establishment, Sephardim began to question whether the Ashkenazim were right. They began to assert their own cultural interests and values.

The destruction of visible dimensions of a community's culture does not necessarily lead to the disappearance of the community itself. Communities persist in other forms, frequently reviving later on through hostility and bitterness toward those whom they see as having deprived them of their culture and status. Take, for example, the ethnic revival in the United States in the 1960s and 1970s. The ethnic groups that demanded their place in the sun had almost no obvious characteristics of the cultures from which they descended. They no longer shared those cultures' more sophisticated dimensions; at most, they preserved a few foods, perhaps some mannerisms and patterns of speech. Otherwise, they were culturally Americans, except that they lived principally within their respective ethnic communities.

The only difference in the case of Israel is that the assimilation process is less advanced. Individual country-of-origin communities still express themselves on social issues through various committees and organizations that they have established on the basis of their old home ties. Ashkenazic as well as Sephardic Jews have organized such groups. Most exist simply to record the life they left behind, to leave a remembrance of that life and their communities for posterity.

Sephardic Jews have developed organizations with a certain degree of political action as their goal, including the oldest Jewish organization in

Israel, the Va'ad HaEdah HaSepharadit B'Yerushalayim. Until the late nineteenth century, it was the governing body for all Jews in Jerusalem and the senior governing body for the Jews in the land. Today, it is a voluntary association that retains control of the community's properties and trust funds and publishes the leading Sephardic journal of opinion, *BaMa'arakhah*.

There are protest groups, too, that emerged from among the most underprivileged of the Sephardic community to attack the establishment, sometimes violently. The first violent public expression of Sephardic anger took place in the Haifa neighborhood of Wadi Salib in 1959. Once part of the Arab section of the city that had been resettled by *olim* from North Africa in 1948, it was a chronic slum with the usual poor housing, unemployment, and high crime. The reported cause of the riots was a café disturbance that got out of hand, but the real cause was the piling up of grievances dating back to the first settlement of *olim* in the neighborhood.

The riots shocked the Israeli public and government, leading to an unsuccessful first effort, in the form of school instruction, to recognize the Sephardic heritage. Those who were to teach the material had no background in the subject other than what was given them by the Ministry of Education. They knew almost nothing about this heritage, and the assumption that Sephardim have only folklore to contribute continued to prevail. Subsequent teaching efforts have been more systematic, but the situation remains the same—a smattering of folklore is taught as the Sephardic heritage, if it is taught at all.

In the late 1960s, Sephardic youth in the Jerusalem slums, particularly Musrara, imitating the American black radical movement, organized the Israeli Black Panthers, whose avowed purpose was to use near-violent means if necessary to attract attention to their plight. The key organizers were intelligent and talented young people who were soon coopted by the political establishment. Charlie Biton, a Black Panther leader, was elected to the Knesset on a Popular Front list, having been coopted by the Communist party. Other Black Panthers were hired by various government ministries to work in problem neighborhoods and on committees.

The Black Panther movement survived for several years and attracted considerable local and international attention. It presented more of a threat than actual violence and was eventually replaced by protest movements even less violent, such as the Ohalim movement, which grew up in Jerusalem's Katamonim neighborhood; a Sol Alinsky–type movement in Tel Aviv's Skhunat Hatikva, led by Haim and Vicki Shiran, which tried to combine progressive self-help with antiestablishment agitation; and HaMizrach El HaShalom, of Shlomo Elbaz, supported by the young poet Shelley Elkayam and others who came together to demonstrate that Sephardim were not all "superhawks" as they were being portrayed, and also to protest anti-Sephardic discrimination.

There were sporadic violent protests, sometimes abetted by an extreme group, which took place whenever Sephardim in the poorest neighborhoods were confronted by the authorities over some issue. This was particularly so in Tel Aviv when the city government tried to tear down the homes of poor Sephardim on the grounds that they were built or extended illegally. After a young man was killed defending his home, the authorities became more careful, and the amount of violence declined. Unfortunately, it took such violence to draw public attention to the problem. The more moderate and restrained groups had trouble doing so.

As the protest stage has passed, there has been a significant increase in the number and scope of cultural-educational groups. One of the most successful is the Association of Jews from North Africa, led by Sam Ben Shitrit. In less than a decade, it turned the Maimouna, a traditional Moroccan Jewish festival that takes place the day after Pesah, into what first became a publicly recognized ethnic festival and then a countrywide "happening" in which all major Israeli politicians and dignitaries, as well as increasing numbers of Israelis other than those of North African origin, participate.

Last but not least are the Sephardic-led political parties and factions. For years it was a truism of Israeli politics that no ethnic list could succeed unless it could present itself as a comprehensive programmatic party. Thus, the early successes of Sephardic and Yemenite lists in the first and second Knesset elections gave way to a long period during which no such list even came close. Of course, the mainstream parties themselves were dominated by coalitions of specific country-of-origin groups, but the only list that had a specific country-of-origin cast was the old Progressive party, made up of Jews from Germany or German-speaking areas of Central Europe and accepted as the symbol of liberal universalism in Israel.

Just prior to the 1984 elections, Aharon Abuhatzeira, leader of a mixed faction in the National Religious Party (NRP), broke away and established Tami, whose meteoric rise was paralleled by its equally rapid fall after Abuhatzeira ran afoul of the law. The younger Sephardim who did not break away from the NRP organized a new faction within it that was able to force the party Ashkenazim to accept parity on the party's Knesset list in the 1984 elections. Dr. Avner Sciaki, their Knesset candidate, immediately challenged the established party leadership, and in April 1988 won the first position on the party ticket. The most successful new party, however, was Shas, the Sephardic Torah Guardians, which not only attracted Sephardim who had previously supported Agudath Yisrael, but also picked up many former Tami voters and succeeded in winning three seats in its first election. Each of these parties or factions has emphasized the issue of Sephardic cultural and religious recognition.

Today, many Sephardim are searching for their roots, having discovered that their culture is at least equal to Ashkenazic culture. In matters of style and manners, music and cuisine, the Sephardim feel that they have as much to offer to emerging Israeli culture as the Ashkenazim. In religious matters, the Ashkenazic world is polarized between the Orthodox and the secularists; in contrast, the Sephardim remain open. Even ultraobservant Sephardim refuse to reject those who have drifted away from religious observance, and most of those who have drifted still maintain a positive attitude toward and frequently participate to some degree in traditional religious practices. More and more Sephardim are becoming convinced that in this they have something special to offer the religious life of the country and a vital role to play in shaping the Judaism of the state.

As a result, Sephardim are pressing for the revision of school curricula to give proper attention to the Sephardic cultural heritage. They are demanding that the *yeshivot* in which there are Sephardic majorities hold their prayers according to the Sephardic ritual. Sephardim are demanding that theatrical productions based on Sephardic themes and issues be given as much support as those based on other themes, and that attention be paid to rising Sephardic writers and playwrights. One of their major voices is *Aperion,* the literary journal dedicated to fostering Mediterranean culture, edited by poet Erez Biton, which has become the voice of many young Sephardic literary figures and which, in addition to publishing their works, holds periodic intellectual and artistic gatherings.

It should come as no surprise, then, that a new generation of Sephardic novelists and poets has emerged, writing in Hebrew, French, Arabic, Judesmo, English, and, in the case of Elias Canetti, the Nobel laureate who is a Bulgarian Sephardi, German. Ironically, there has been more recognition of these talents in the United States than in Israel, although most of them are Israeli or have strong Israeli connections. The first conference on contemporary Sephardic writing was held at the City University of New York (CUNY) in October 1984; figure 8.1 shows the program of that conference.

Popular culture, since it is less controllable by any given establishment, has come to be dominated by Sephardic expression, to the extent that it is not dominated by the universal pop culture of contemporary society, but there is far more criticism in Israel of the Sephardic dimension. Raucous, lewd rock music that emphasizes drugs and sex receives less criticism than the so-called cassette singers, who sing Sephardic popular ballads. The nickname reflects a sad reality. The cassette singers were so-called because legitimate studios would not record them. They had to make cassettes privately and sell them in the open-air markets, where they found a ready audience but no recognition. Ashkenazic prejudices kept the business leaders of the industry from treating these Sephardic singers seriously for a long time. Many cassette singers cannot get bookings as regular artists and make a living by singing at Sephardic weddings, yet their music is heard on the tape decks of almost every taxicab in the country. Only recently has the reality of the market overthrown these prejudices.

There are also "burekas" movies—named for a Sephardic pastry popular in Israel and incorrectly considered peasant food by most Ashkenazim—which were made by regular film studios, but in a most cynical manner, exploiting exaggerated anti-Sephardic stereotypes in subtle and not so subtle ways. Equally bad movies dealing with the themes of liberal universalism such as Jewish-Arab relations in which the Jews are shown badly receive rave reviews in the media, while little or no attention is given a "burekas" movie.

It is hard to overemphasize the discrimination, perhaps unwitting but no less real, against Sephardic culture in Israeli society. Ignorance may be an initial excuse, but continued ignorance shows an unwillingness to learn. The new Sephardic movement for cultural self-expression is a reflection of the fact that most Sephardim in Israel have "made it" and that the stereotype of the Sephardi as an underprivileged person living in a slum is grossly inaccurate.

Preserving the Sephardic Past

In the area of academic preservation of Sephardic culture much has been done, at first mostly by interested Ashkenazim who were attracted to the culture if not to Sephardim themselves. Indeed, outside of Israel even

FIGURE 8.1

The Center for Jewish Studies of the
CUNY Graduate Center
cordially invites you to a conference on

The Writer And the Sephardic Traditions

Monday October 29, 1984

4:00–6:00 PM

Welcome
Jane Gerber, Conference Director
Introductory Remarks
Irving Howe, Director, Center for Jewish Studies
The Quill's Embroidery: Untangling a Tradition
Ammiel Alcalay
Double Life
Sammy Michael

7:30–10:00 PM / Chair: Jane Gerber

Three Masks
Albert Memmi
From Baghdad to Montreal
Naim Kattan
A Literary Image: Jewish Life in Egypt
Ada Aharoni

Tuesday October 30, 1984

4:00–6:30 PM / Chair: Haham Dr. Solomon Gaon

Spain in the Balkans: The Ladino Tradition
Salvator Israel
A Jewish Writer in Yugoslavia
David Albahari
Sephardim in Modern Hebrew Literature
Lev Hakak

7:30–10:00 PM / Chair: Yael Zerubavel

Growing Up in Aleppo
Amnon Shamosh
My Itinerary
Edmond Jabès
Writing: Exile, Wandering, Return
Shmuel Trigano

non-Jews played a major role. Preservation efforts have gone through several stages and dimensions, beginning as part of the general preservation activity of the *Wissenschaft das Judentum* (Science of Judaism) movement in nineteenth-century Central Europe. Those scholars related particularly to the culture of Spanish Jewry as the expression of Jewish life at its most gracious and noble: in other words, an antidote to the stereotype of the backward, provincial, rather coarse Jew who emerged from the shtetls and ghettos of Eastern Europe in the nineteenth century to migrate westward. Occasionally, these scientists touched on the culture of other Sephardic communities besides the Spanish and of the post–1492 Sephardic diaspora, but not very deeply or very often.

A second stage came with the rediscovery of the Sephardim by Spanish scholars, non-Jews exploring Spanish culture at the turn of the century, who came across the Judesmo-speaking people of the eastern Mediterranean and were touched spiritually and gratified academically by what they found. They began by studying the Sephardic *romanceros* (ballads), a special musical genre that preserved much of the style and language of medieval Spain. Subsequently, they extended their work to other aspects of Spanish Sephardic culture. Ultimately, a special institute for Sephardic studies, the Instituto Arias Montanas, was established at the University of Madrid, approaching the subject as a branch of Spanish civilization. Subsequently, other non-Jews became interested, particularly in the United States and to some extent in Latin America, seeing the Sephardic experience as an interesting interface between Judaic and Hispanic culture.

A third stage began in the 1920s, when scholars of Sephardic background began to preserve elements of their culture that they saw disappearing as a result of the upheavals of the late nineteenth century and World War I. Much of this work was centered in Paris, which had become a refuge for Sephardic intellectuals from the Balkans and in some cases North Africa and the eastern Mediterranean. By and large, these efforts consisted of collecting musical and literary materials.

This work has continued and has produced a certain synthesis between preservation and adaptation of traditional materials. Musically, it reached its culmination in the late Isaac Levi's *Antologia de la Liturgia Sephardit*, a multivolume collection of Sephardic liturgical music from all communities and for all seasons—music that Levi used as the basis for contemporary choral and instrumental arrangements that kept Sephardic *hazzanut* a living art and extended it beyond the walls of the synagogue. His position at Kol Yisrael (Israel Radio) gave him the forum and resources to bring the results of his efforts to a larger public. Levi's premature death was a cultural tragedy for the Sephardim, since no one has succeeded him. His work, however, has influenced the artistry of many younger Sephardim in Israel today.

A fourth stage was the purely ethnographic work of anthropologists, principally but not exclusively Ashkenazim, who took advantage of the ingathering of the exiles in Israel to document their traditional cultures. This effort often began with the off-tune recordings of old women, but it continued with the systematic observation of life in Israel and, where possible, in the countries of origin. Most recently, these projects have stretched beyond traditional ethnography to include the rescue of important manuscripts of those communities. The publication of annotated versions of these manuscripts has made them available worldwide. Finally, since the late 1960s young Sephardim in both Israel and the diaspora searching for their roots have sought to rediscover that heritage through research. Ashkenazim and Sephardim alike have begun a substantial effort to publish neglected Sephardic *halakhic*, historical, and cultural materials and to place them in the mainstream of Jewish culture and scholarship. Funds from the Israeli Ministry of Education and Culture and other research institutes are still very limited, however.

It should be emphasized that the growing Sephardic search for roots will not lead to a restoration of the old Sephardic culture any more than the revival of *klezmer* (Eastern European Jewish popular music) and Hassidic folklore will lead to the restoration of the old Ashkenazic culture. Both cultures are gone forever. The new Israeli culture into which they have merged draws on three sources: Jewish culture as inherited from the various exiles, contemporary world culture, and Zionism—the basic faith of non-Orthodox Israelis. Traditional Sephardic culture has much to contribute to this new synthesis. Sensitive Israeli Jews, both Sephardim and Ashkenazim, have doubts about contemporary world culture, especially because of their Jewish and Zionist commitments; hence, they can find a common language in their mutual concern for Israel's Jewish culture.

The Special Character of Sephardic Zionism

In the last analysis, there are no real differences among Sephardim and Ashkenazim with regard to their commitment to the Zionist enterprise and to the State of Israel. This is true despite comments to the contrary over the past thirty years or more. Sephardim and Ashkenazim alike responded to the call of Zion during the century or more of resettlement before the establishment of the state. Since then, they have stood together to support Israel wherever they resided. Any analysis that fails to recognize this basic fact of Jewish unity misses the essence of the Jewish experience. It is one of unity with diversity, a shared sense of kinship uniting all the tribes of Israel, and a consensus with regard to the importance of a shared Jewish destiny as well as recognition of the common Jewish fate.

Within this framework, it is possible to identify a Sephardic role and set of attitudes that, although not radically different from the Ashkenazic, do add another dimension to the contemporary Jewish response to Zionism and renewed statehood. More a matter of emphasis than of kind, it is, nevertheless, an important emphasis, which we would be wise to consider at this stage in the history of the Zionist revolution and its political achievements.

What is special about Sephardic Zionism is its unquestioned merging of religious and political aspirations. Having never undergone secularization on one hand or embraced otherworldly pietism on the other—unlike the Ashkenazim in the modern epoch—the Sephardic world was earlier attuned to seeking political solutions to the Jewish condition, at the same time never divorcing such solutions from a deep religious commitment.

In a very real sense the Sephardic world was never outside of the political arena. Even in the aftermath of the Spanish exile, at the darkest period of their history, Sephardic leadership sought remedies for the Jewish condition in the political arena through alliance with the Ottoman Turks against their Christian persecutors, and in efforts to restore at least a measure of Jewish self-rule in Eretz Israel. These efforts failed, but the fact that they were made reflects the kind of practical messianism that is characteristic of the Jewish people and for a long time was given particular emphasis in the Sephardic world.

Another example of such political action was the effort initiated by Gracia Mendes and her son-in-law Joseph Nasi to organize the Jewish world in a boycott of the port of Ancona in Italy after the rulers of that city burned twenty-five Marranos at the stake in 1555 for secretly practicing Judaism. The boycott failed because other Jewish interests were harmed by it, but it represented a major step in Jewish efforts to improve their lot by political means.

In 1561, the same Joseph Nasi tried to establish Jewish political control over an area around the city of Tiberias in Eretz Israel, with the intention of resettling Jews there. For eighteen years he was titular lord of Tiberias. Nasi's successor as the leading Jew in the Turkish court, Solomon Abenaes, inherited that political control, which continued into the seventeenth century and led to the revival of Jewish life in the city, although without any special political standing. Both Nasi and Abenaes made the furthering of Jewish interests part of their involvement in Ottoman politics, including negotiation of an Anglo-Turkish alliance against Spain and support for the Dutch revolt against Spanish rule. These and similar Sephardic efforts represented the principal involvement of the Jews as a people in world politics until the Zionist movement; if they failed in these efforts, it was because the time was not yet ripe for them to succeed.

Sephardim consider this synthesis of religious and political impulses integral to their Jewishness. The Sephardic world has not produced a Neturei Karta (the most extreme of the ultra-Orthodox, anti-Zionist groups, which rejects the State of Israel as a sinful effort to interfere with God's plan for redemption), politically paralyzed while waiting for the Messiah, or a Shomer HaTzair, an antireligious, social revolutionary movement. With very few exceptions, no matter how far Sephardim have drifted from religious observance, their respect for Jewish tradition remains intact, and no matter how extreme they may become in observance, it has not been at the price of a commitment to political redemption. If there is any contrast between Ashkenazic and Sephardic Zionism, it is that the former was a Zionism that demanded internal revolution as much as a transformation of the Jewish condition, while the latter was a Zionism of redemption that sought continuity with tradition and did not require revolution.

It is said that organized Zionism was overwhelmingly Ashkenazic and that the Sephardim did not respond to the movement except in rare cases. A closer look at Zionist history reveals this to be untrue. Any assessment must start with the understanding that at the time of the rise of Zionism, Ashkenazic Jewry was at its numerical peak, including more than 90 percent of world Jewry. Thus, if both populations were equally involved in Zionist activity, one would still expect to find nine Ashkenazic Zionists for every one Sephardic Zionist. Evidence suggests that such a ratio did exist.

What this meant, of course, was that the concentration of numbers could lead to the generation of critical masses of Zionists in certain countries whose impact would be far greater. Curiously enough, the truth of this was first demonstrated in Bulgaria, whose Jewish community was overwhelmingly Sephardic and was the first to be captured by organized Zionism. Bulgarian Zionists were among the first to try to settle Eretz Israel. (Their failure may have had much to do with the fact that the predominantly Ashkenazic movement did not provide them with support in the way that it did for settlements established by Zionists from Russia.) Later, Bulgarian Jewry would be one of the four Jewish communities—all of them Sephardic—to migrate en masse to Eretz Israel.

In addition, Ashkenazic Zionism developed in the revolutionary environments of Central and Eastern Europe where collapsing and authoritarian regimes opened the door for revolutionary movements. Since the same conditions prevailed in the Balkans, the Sephardic Zionist organizations there also flourished. The Islamic countries of Africa and Asia, on the other hand, lacked similar revolutionary conditions until after independent states were established. Every Zionist effort in those countries had to be made under the watchful eyes of still relatively stable authoritarian regimes. Their hostility to Zionism was part of their general hostility to any movement that appeared to challenge the status quo, as well as to Jewish nationalism per se. There is a long and glorious history of Zionist underground movements in many of those countries, much of which has yet to be told, while the Ashkenazic Zionist movements (outside of the Soviet Union) were able to function openly, even under hostile conditions.

The Sephardim and Israel Today

Even today, Sephardic Zionism follows a pattern of being half inside and half outside. Sephardim are present but rarely prominent in Zionist bodies, which remain overwhelmingly Ashkenazic. This remains so even though the World Sephardi Federation was the first non-Zionist body to apply for and be granted membership in the World Zionist Organization after the Six Day War. The plight of being a part but separate is characteristic of the Sephardic relationship to the Zionist movement and, to a degree, to the State of Israel and to the Jewish people as well.

It should not be necessary to call for greater emphasis on the Sephardic role in the Zionist effort, for Jews should not have to make such distinctions in describing this most glorious chapter of recent Jewish history. But if the effort is not made, it is clear that the very real, substantial Sephardic role will simply disappear behind the myth of Zionism dominated by Russian and Polish Jewish revolutionaries.

Over and over again, it has been emphasized that the Sephardim who arrived in Israel after 1948 are now entering their second generation of resettlement, as are most of the Sephardic Jews who went to other parts of the world. During the first generation, like their Ashkenazic brethren, the Sephardim were basically occupied with settling in, with finding a place for themselves, with establishing themselves economically and otherwise. These are important facts to remember.

Whatever disadvantages the Sephardim have suffered in their new land, they are now sufficiently established to concern themselves with their status in Israel. Now the Sephardic star is rising, whether in the growing prominence of political leaders, the emergence of new leadership in the Defense Forces, or the increased activity of diaspora leaders in raising funds for Israel. Sephardic activity on these fronts is likely to continue and even intensify, not only because Sephardim are as determined as other Jews, but also because Sephardim have a special stake in Israel.

Earlier it was suggested that the difference between Ashkenazic and Sephardic Zionism is that the first saw Zionism as revolution and the second saw it as redemption. Ashkenazic Zionism triumphed in the founding of the state, so much so that nonreligious Israelis have raised at least two generations, and perhaps a third, that are detached from authentic Jewish roots. This matter has led to much handwringing and many expressions of concern from the heirs of the Zionist establishment who brought about this situation and are now seeking to remedy it.

But revolutionary Zionism has run its course. However great its successes in the past, and they were indeed great, it has little to do with the present and the future. Like all successful revolutions, its very success renders it obsolete. As a result, the Zionist movement is in crisis; yet, there is still room, indeed a definite need, for a Zionism of redemption, a vision of a renewed Jewish people, now that we have a Jewish state. The Sephardic version of Zionism is more in tune with the kind of Zionist expression that is needed today. Consequently, it should be explored, cultivated, and possibly used as a model for a new vision. Perhaps all Jews will yet benefit from the Sephardic revival if it produces a renewed Zionist vision.

Sephardic Responsibility

If the Sephardim have become the subject of deleterious myths and have undergone forced Ashkenazification, the blame is not only on the other side. The Sephardim, too, are responsible for their condition. Even when they were not at the mercy of the Ashkenazim, they allowed these things to happen to themselves. Those who have become wealthy and powerful by joining the larger Jewish world have not joined to use their resources and influence to make the Sephardic presence felt in Jewish life. Today's World Sephardi Federation (WSF) is a case in point. The leaders of the WSF, especially Nissim Gaon, deserve a great deal of credit for turning a shadow organization into one of some influence, at least to the point where there are efforts on the part of the Jewish establishment to accommodate its demands. In doing so, the WSF has successfully adopted many tactics of the establishment, but it has not used its resources wisely to build a solid base. Rather, it has dissipated them through political projects that may have suited the whims of the leaders but have not had lasting results.

Nor have these leaders been willing to match the public resources they have mobilized with their personal private resources. Many are reasonably generous and, indeed, one of the ways in which they have gained access for the Sephardim is through their own contributions to the general institutions of Israel and the Jewish people; but they have not made equivalent contributions to institutions that would give the Sephardim recognition as contributors to the Jewish state and the Jewish people from a position of strength.

In the Israeli religious sphere, there are now dozens of small Sephardic *yeshivot* but no great *metivta* (institute of higher Torah learning) in which the Sephardic way of Torah is expressed. Instead, each of these small *yeshivot* imitates one or another Ashkenazic model in ways that inevitably cause them to be inferior to the Ashkenazic *yeshivot*. Efforts to establish an institution of higher Torah learning that would reflect the broad Sephardic approach, combining the study of *halakhah* and classical texts with Jewish history and thought, rhetoric, and languages, have failed for lack of proper support—moral support from the Sephardic chief rabbis, monetary support from the Sephardic rich, or intellectual support from the Sephardic academic world.

On another level, scholarship funds to help young Sephardim in Israel are numerous, but few, if any, give more than a pittance to individual students, so that students must run from fund to fund for one hundred or two hundred dollars. After exhausting themselves in the running, they do not have much more than is needed to cover tuition—if that. Yet, every group wants to maintain its own fund, even if it deals in the smallest of sums.

Sephardic cultural institutions wither for lack of support; there are no wealthy Sephardim who will give them the money that they give to general (Ashkenazic-dominated) institutions where their names can appear on larger walls. Every Israeli university has an institute for the study of the Sephardic heritage, and the Hebrew University has at least two. In almost every case, though, they are run by Ashkenazim, and the money is siphoned off to serve general scholarly purposes or to support the general budget of the university.

The foremost of the institutes, Misgav Yerushalayim and the Ben Zvi Institute at the Hebrew University, have demonstrated what potential exists. The former has organized two world congresses of Sephardic studies, which have presented the wealth of contemporary Sephardic scholarship and samplings of Sephardic artistic and literary achievements, but has been unable to energize further and mobilize the talents revealed. The latter barely has the funds to publish standard scholarly works, much less such major efforts as the great Judesmo dictionary that has been under way for decades. Needless to say, there is minimum cooperation among these institutes.

A large synagogue in Jerusalem pretends to be the Great Synagogue of Israel, but, in fact, it is an Ashkenazic institution in which a small room has been set aside for the Sephardic chief rabbi to maintain a small service. Nominally, there is a Sephardic equivalent in the form of the Yisa Berakha synagogue, whose official name is the house of the *Rishon Le-Zion*, a few blocks away, but it is a modest building in a residential neighborhood. Moreover, no *Rishon Le-Zion* has identified with that synagogue since it was built over twenty years ago. Instead, each incumbent has organized his own small *minyan*, thereby diluting any influence he might have by presenting a visible model of the Sephardic *minhag* to Israel and the world. This frittering away of scarce resources comes while the Ashkenazic religious leadership has concentrated on developing just those kinds of models—role models—and major institutions.

Although the Great Synagogue has quasiofficial standing, it was a project developed on a voluntary basis by Ashkenazim committed to having such a presence in Jerusalem. No similar effort has been made by the Sephardim themselves. As a result, the most impressive Sephardic synagogue building in Israel is the Salonikan congregation in Tel Aviv, which is well out of sight of world Jewry. Probably the closest thing to a Sephardic synagogue that radiates universal symbolism is Shearith Israel in New York City.

Meanwhile, the Ashkenazification of Sephardim proceeds on all levels. Sephardim, even many who proclaim their Sephardic authenticity, have succumbed to this pressure to conform to Israeli—meaning Ashkenazified—ways. Why? Because it is the price of admission to Israeli society, particularly in its most elite manifestations. The more one strives to be part of the higher echelons of Israeli society, whether in the academic, business, political, religious, or social worlds, the more one is expected to accept what are in essence Ashkenazic norms. Indeed, a good rule of thumb is the more highbrow, the more prejudiced against Sephardic ways. And like most prejudices, it is irrational and therefore difficult to eradicate. It is as irrational among university professors as it is among clerks.

Not surprisingly, Ashkenazic condescension continues as well. It is especially prominent and painful in the schools, where Sephardic culture is still treated as folklore and considered peripheral. An example from a fourth-grade text in use in 1986 is indicative. In a story designed to teach a moral lesson about not embarrassing another in public, there are four characters: a woman, a man, and two boys. The woman falsely accuses one boy of taking her purse. The accused boy, the man who is a witness, and the woman are simply identified as *boy, man,* and *woman.* The second boy, who finds the purse and returns it, is identified as a *Yemenite* boy. Although it may seem as if the textbook's author wants to point out the honesty of *edot hamizrah,* the result is a kind of labeling that sets the Yemenite boy apart from the "real Israelis."

So the Ashkenazic majority continues to perpetuate the myths and stereotypes about two cultures in Israel. "Western" and "Eastern" remain code words for "modern" and "primitive." The Sephardim in Israel are still presented as less committed to democracy than the Ashkenazim, despite all evidence to the contrary. United Jewish Appeal propaganda still emphasizes the need to integrate the backward Jews from Arab lands. The Ashkenazim in Israel still hardly know the Sephardic community, and little if anything of Sephardic culture.

The Ashkenazic world and its leadership must put a stop to the negative aspects of the Sephardic-Ashkenazic relationship, to get to know the Sephardim and their culture, not only to repair the breach but also because the cultural heritage of the Sephardic world is for all Jews. Indeed, the Jews of the real West, namely, the English-speaking countries, are likely to appreciate Sephardic culture at least as much as their own original Ashkenazic culture, with its strong Eastern European character, precisely because the Sephardic strain is classical. Even the predominantly Ashkenazic North American community should find ways to encourage and foster Sephardic cultural expression of various kinds, including using Sephardic music in their concerts, on their radio and television programs, in religious services, and providing an audience and funds for the development of Sephardic literature and theater—in short, integrating such cultural contributions into their communal programs.

Closing One Era, Opening Another

Matters of culture are always more difficult to resolve than questions of political power, but we must address them in the best possible way. Doing so is not a question of one side making concessions to the other; rather, it is a question of reintegrating the romantic and classical strains of Jewish civilization so that each may make its contribution to the Jewish culture now emerging.

At the beginning of this book, it was suggested that the Jewish people are now in a period of transition, close to the end of the millennium in which they were divided into Ashkenazic and Sephardic spheres. Indeed, what we are witnessing is the last gasp of that division and the reintegration of the Jewish people around new dimensions of unity (and, one presumes, other divisions as well). The task of this generation is to bring about that reintegration in such a way that all parties can make their contributions as equals, so that all of Jewish life and culture will be enriched.

Appendix

Smaller U.S. Sephardic Communities

Alabama

Congregation Etz Ahayem in Montgomery, founded by Jews from the island of Rhodes, is the only Sephardic congregation in the state. Important dates include: 1906, the first Sephardim arrive; 1908, services begin; 1910, a benevolent society is established; 1912, a full congregation is organized; 1916, a cemetery is established; and 1927, the congregation establishes a Talmud Torah. Judesmo was used along with Hebrew until 1951. The congregation has been able to employ rabbis only periodically. Today, there are some two hundred Sephardic families in Montgomery.

Arizona

As the Sun Belt has become more attractive to many Americans, a growing number of Sephardim have settled in Phoenix. They have taken preliminary steps toward formalizing community organization.

California

San Francisco In the greater San Francisco Bay area there are reportedly five hundred Sephardic families. Although the origins of the community are believed to date back to the 1920s, the majority settled after 1945, when some thirty to forty families arrived from Greece. In the

1950s, about twenty families immigrated from Syria and thirty families arrived, via London, from Shanghai. During the 1960s, a relatively large influx came from North African and Middle Eastern countries, primarily Morocco, Algeria, Egypt, and Iraq, and some fifty to sixty families from Israel. There is also an enclave of some fifteen Jewish families from India. San Francisco's Sephardic community also receives a small but steady immigration from Sephardic communities in Seattle and Los Angeles.

The story of the San Francisco Sephardic community involves one Sephardic synagogue, Magen David, established in 1934. Although founded as a traditional institution, the present congregation has effected considerable compromise in Jewish custom and ritual. Magen David is an American Sephardi Federation affiliate. In the early 1970s, the synagogue was in the midst of an institutional crisis. A Sabbath *minyan* could not be guaranteed, nor was there a religious school. High Holy Day services were the only regular congregational activity. Within two years, however, after the appointment of a new rabbi, an Israeli of Ashkenazic origins, thirty to forty families, including many with young children, began worshipping together regularly on the Sabbath. These families were among the more recent arrivals, and although of lesser financial means, have succeeded the more established Spanish and Iraqi families in positions of responsibility and honor. Unfortunately for the community, the new spiritual leader left and the day school he established in 1977 as the Magen David Sephardic Academy also closed, but in 1984 a new young rabbi ordained in the Yeshiva University's Sephardic Studies program assumed leadership of the congregation, bringing to it new vigor.

Connecticut

There is a small Sephardic community in Hartford, founded as the Ermandad Orientale Sephardith, now the Sephardic Congregation of Greater Hartford.

District of Columbia

The Capitol Balkans is an organization consisting of second-wave Sephardic Jews, mostly successful businessmen and merchants, who meet for social and religious activities. On the High Holy Days, they use space in a local Conservative synagogue under the name of the Yom Tov Sephardic Society of Washington, D.C. Organized in the early 1900s, it has been conducting services and providing burial arrangements ever since. The Capitol Balkans also sponsor an annual Sephardic Festival, which is open to the general community.

The first Sephardim arrived from Morocco in 1924, with more settling after World War II. In 1970, they and the Syrian Sephardim left Yom Tov to form the Magen David Sephardic Congregation, which now has a membership of some three hundred families.

Florida

There are several Sephardic groups in Florida. Members of the Cuban Sephardi Hebrew Center and the Cuban Hebrew Congregation of Miami are refugees from Castro's Cuba. The Sephardic Jewish Center of Greater Miami is principally a congregation of transplanted New Yorkers, many elderly, organized in the late 1940s when Sephardim of retirement age moved to Florida from New York. It has about 150 member families, the same size as the Cuban Hebrew Congregation. Congregation Bnei Sephardim of North Miami is built around more recent immigrants from Morocco. The Sephardic Jewish Center of North Miami Beach, also known as Kehilah Sepharadith Magen David, is built around Syrians. The Union of Sephardic Congregations of Miami tries to promote cooperation among the various groups, and the B'nai B'rith Latin Lodge No. 2796 serves Cuban Jewish exiles. There is also a Sephardic group of senior citizens.

Georgia

The wave of eastern Mediterranean immigrants that arrived in the United States between 1910 and 1920 included a number of Greek and Turkish Jews who eventually settled in Atlanta. An early group consisted of some thirty bachelors who later sent to their countries of origin for wives. By 1912, this community was divided into two congregations. One group, Jews from Rhodes, founded Congregation Ahavat Shalom; the other, from Turkey, established Congregation Or HaHaim. In 1914, the groups merged into the Oriental Hebrew Association Or Shalom.

By 1924, the Atlanta Sephardic community had increased to sixty-five families, and in 1938, its synagogue became incorporated as Congregation Or VeShalom. Today it is a large and active Conservative synagogue that serves as the center of most formal and informal Sephardic community activities. The present membership is about four hundred families, one-third of whom are Ashkenazim who have either married into Sephardic families or have joined because they prefer the Sephardic *minhag*. The older members of the congregation are largely Judesmo-speaking, and it remains dominated by the Balkan Jewish cultural tradition. There is a congregational brotherhood, sisterhood, social club, monthly adult lecture program, three-day-a-week Hebrew school, and youth group, which is affiliated with the Conservative movement's United Synagogue Youth and the American Sephardi Youth Federation. Or VeShalom hosted the founding convention of the American Sephardi Youth Federation in 1973.

The Atlanta Sephardic community was also one of the first to become involved in the larger Jewish community. It has had rabbinical leadership almost throughout its history, including Rabbi Joseph Cohen, who served from 1934 to 1969 and continued to work in the community as rabbi emeritus until his death in 1981. He became a bridge between the Sephardic and Ashkenazic communities.

Illinois

There are an estimated one thousand Sephardic Jews in the Chicago metropolitan area. As in most other communities, the focal point of life is the synagogue, although the majority of the Sephardic community remains unaffiliated.

Chicago has two Sephardic synagogues. The Israel Portuguese Congregation (1906) was first located on the old West Side and for many years functioned primarily on High Holy Days. After its move north to accommodate the shifting Jewish population, the synagogue gained strength as an institution.

Originally a card-playing club founded by Portuguese and Turkish Jews, today, in its modern building, it provides evening and morning Sabbath services for a membership of approximately 165 families. The rabbi is a Sephardi, originally from Seattle. He, like many other Seattle-born Sephardic rabbis, was ordained at the Hebrew Theological College in Skokie. The synagogue, an American Sephardi Federation affiliate, is incorporated under the auspices of the Chicago Israelite Portuguese Fraternity. For a family to be a member of the fraternity, at least one spouse must be Sephardic; however, the majority of the synagogue's membership is Ashkenazic, as it is not necessary to be a member of the fraternity to affiliate with the congregation. After English, Judesmo is the language most often spoken. Although its adult education program is modest, the synagogue sponsors a youth group, which is affiliated with the American Sephardi Youth Federation and the National Conference of Synagogue Youth (NCSY).

The Iran Hebrew Congregation (1910) moved from the inner city in the early 1970s to Skokie, a near northwest suburb with a large Jewish population, expanding its activities in the process. The founding members of the Iran Hebrew Congregation were Kurdish Jews originally from Irmaya (Rezia) Persia, an area bordering both Turkey and Russia. Their native tongue was Aramaic. The Iran Hebrew Congregation is affiliated with the American Sephardi Federation. Out of a membership of about one hundred families, some sixty to seventy have at least one spouse who is Sephardic. Although the present rabbi, who has served the congregation part-time for the past ten years, is Ashkenazic, the synagogue follows the Sephardic *minhag*. There are no daily services, and Sabbath services, although regular, are usually sparsely attended. Most members attend principally on the High Holy Days. The rabbi is also the principal of the congregation's Talmud Torah, which meets three times a week for up to sixty pupils.

Although the congregation's overall membership appears stable, its percentage of Sephardic families is declining. Furthermore, their children are largely unsympathetic to the Sephardic tradition. Congregational leadership rests with a diminishing elite.

Until the 1960s, there was also a recognizable Syrian Jewish community in Chicago. Today, there is a loosely organized *landsmanshaft*-like group of some fifty Israeli-Moroccan families who meet socially and to celebrate Jewish holidays. The group calls itself the North African Jewish Organization and is affiliated with the American Sephardi Federation.

Indiana

The Etz Chaim Congregation of Indianapolis is the only Sephardic synagogue in Indiana. It was founded by immigrants from Monastir and parts of Turkey who arrived in 1912. They started a Talmud Torah at the beginning along with the *hevra kadisha* and *tzedakah* funds. Although they held classes within the citywide Talmud Torah of the Ashkenazim, the school remained separate until 1948 when their Hebrew teacher left.

Maryland

There are a number of Sephardic organizations in the Washington, D.C., area, including the Magen David Sephardic Congregation in Silver Spring and the Moroccan Society of Rockville, which is a cohesive group but has not yet established a synagogue. For the present, they hold activities at the Rockville Jewish Community Center.

Massachusetts

In Salem, there is a Sephardic synagogue, Congregation Tiphereth Israel, which has had a synagogue building since 1945. In Boston, there are some eighty Sephardic families who have made sporadic attempts at organization. They are now known as the Massachusetts Sephardic Community of Greater Boston and include members from throughout the Sephardic world. Their more recent success stems from the arrival of Syrians who maintain close connections with the Syrian communities in Brooklyn, New York, and Deal, New Jersey.

Michigan

Survivors of the Holocaust, principally refugees from the Balkans, settled in Detroit after World War II. They organized first as a social group and evolved into a congregation, building a synagogue largely through the efforts of the Chicorel family, with whom the community's leadership primarily rests. They are active in the American Sephardi Federation.

New Jersey

The Sephardic Kehilla of New Brunswick and Highland Park consists mainly of descendants of Jews from Salonika who arrived during the first part of the century. During World War I, they constituted close to one-third of the city's total Jewish population of twenty-five hundred, and for several years New Brunswick was the largest Sephardic community outside of New York City. Many of these immigrants had been members of the Socialist federation in Salonika and brought their socialism with them to New Brunswick, where they founded the Ahavah VeAhvah organization, which later merged with the Etz Ahaim society.

Within the framework of this Socialist club, the Liberos Pensadores (freethinkers) was organized. They attempted a publication, *El Imigrante*, and for a while performed plays written by their guiding spirit, Albert Covo. They worked in the Michelin Tire factories nearby, where, as French speakers educated in the Alliance Israelite Universelle schools, they had a relatively easy time adjusting.

Since World War I, the community has been in decline with substantial numbers moving to New York. The focus of Sephardic community life in this region is Congregation Etz Chaim, founded in 1912.

Deal, Bradley Beach, West Deal, and Elberon are centers of Syrian Jewry that were initially beach resorts for Syrian Jews from Brooklyn. The permanent community dates back to the early 1970s when some of the summer-vacationing families decided to settle in Deal on a year-round basis. By 1973, there were 60 permanent families, rising to about 450 today, with perhaps 1,350 in Deal during the summer. The permanent families built a synagogue and established a Talmud Torah. The Syrians took over the local Hillel day school, and more recently established a *yeshiva* high school.

Sephardim settled in Atlantic City after 1910 and established Congregation Shaare Zion. Over time, however, the congregation could not sustain itself as the members or their children either left or moved to better neighborhoods and joined Ashkenazic synagogues. In the early 1980s, however, the congregation was still holding Friday night and Sabbath morning services.

New York

New Rochelle and Scarsdale Approximately seventy Syrian families conduct regular Sabbath services at the Young Israel congregation and have established a Sephardic Studies program.

Rochester Congregation Or Israel (Light of Israel) was founded in 1909 by Jews from the Balkans. The first Sephardim arrived in the spring of 1906 from Monastir. In 1916, a social and cultural center, the Sephardic Alliance, was established, which subsequently became the Young Men's Sephardic Association with its own clubhouse and a ladies' auxiliary. In 1915, they opened a Hebrew school. By the 1940s, the community consisted of some 150 families. After World War II, they moved to better residential areas, and in 1957 the synagogue moved as well.

Syracuse The Sephardi Congregation of Syracuse was founded principally by second-generation Sephardim from North Africa, particularly

Libya, Morocco, and Tunisia. Its twenty families gather only for the High Holy Days and special occasions. The congregation offers no religious schooling, adult education, or youth program.

Ohio

Forty-two families from the Dardanelles area in Turkey and eight from Salonika settled in Cincinnati in the first decade of the twentieth century. They formed a mutual aid society, La Hermandad, in 1910 and began holding High Holy Day services in 1914, which evolved into Congregation Beth Shalom. The community was never large enough to organize its own Talmud Torah or to hold its members for other than the High Holy Days, Purim, and Hanukkah, especially after its members scattered among Cincinnati's other Jews in the suburbs.

Oregon

The Portland community was founded by Rhodeslis from Seattle around 1909, and still retains close ties with the mother community. Ahavat Achim, their congregation, was founded in 1916, and the first synagogue was built in 1927. Although there are some one hundred Sephardic families in Portland, only about forty are affiliated with the congregation, which has abandoned its Friday evening services for lack of a *minyan*. Services are generally conducted only on the High Holy Days and Purim. A new synagogue building was recently built. It maintains a Sunday school.

Pennsylvania

Mikveh Israel was founded in Philadelphia in 1740. Although the stimulus for the congregation and its initial leadership was Sephardic, it apparently had an Ashkenazic majority from the start. Nevertheless, the Sephardic *minhag* has consistently been maintained. During the American Revolution, as noted earlier, Gershom Mendes Seixas fled to Philadelphia from New York and there remodeled Mikveh Israel after Shearith Israel, instituting a *minhag* that has remained ever since. Mikveh Israel was the city's leading congregation into the midnineteenth century.

In the midnineteenth century, Isaac Leeser, the *hazzan* of Mikveh Israel, was undoubtedly the leading figure in American Jewry. His students continued to play very prominent roles in American Jewish life until World War I, giving the congregation a special place in American Jewish history. Locally, the leadership of Mikveh Israel was instrumental in establishing Gratz College (named after a member of the illustrious Gratz family of Philadelphia, which was associated with the congregation from its earliest days) and also Dropsie College, two important institutions of higher Jewish learning.

Subsequently, due to a shift in communal leadership and also to a declining neighborhood, the congregation lost members and its position in the community. Recently, however, it has relocated to Independence Mall, where, not far from its original location, it has established the Museum of American Jewish History, opened in 1976. The building also houses the synagogue.

Most of the original families in the congregation have long since disappeared or assimilated. The current membership has joined because they are attracted to the Sephardic *minhag*. A small group of Egyptian Jews who have settled in Philadelphia over the past twenty years attend High Holy Day services. Although Ashkenazim, including Leeser, have occupied the pulpit in the past, the current rabbi and his immediate predecessor are Sephardic.

Notes

What follows is a listing of materials that document this book and are available to English readers who wish to probe further the issues discussed in it. With the exception of chapters 2 and 8, where the use of Hebrew sources could not be avoided, most of the sources are in the English language. Obviously, there is an extensive literature in Hebrew on most of these subjects, and somewhat less extensive but still important literatures in Spanish, French, Judesmo, and Judeo-Arabic.

Scholars who wish to investigate the full range of sources used for this book should contact the Jerusalem Center for Public Affairs (JCPA), where a full bibliography is housed in its archives, including historical materials and studies of contemporary Israel and the diaspora communities. See also: for historical materials, publications from the JCPA's program on the Jewish political tradition, listed in its *Catalogue of Publications*, issued biennially; for studies of contemporary Israel, the bibliography to my book *Israel: Building a New Society* (Bloomington: Indiana University Press, 1986); and for diaspora communities, the extensive bibliography in my comprehensive study *People and Polity: The Organizational Dynamics of World Jewry* (Detroit: Wayne State University Press, 1988).

Chapter One

For an overview of Sephardic history and culture, see Richard Barnett, *The Sephardic Heritage* (New York: Ktav, 1971); M. J. Bernardete, *Hispanic Culture and the Character of the Sephardic Jews* (New York: Hispanic Institute in the United States, 1953); and Moshe Lazar, *The Sephardic Tradition* (Washington, D.C.: B'nai B'rith Books, 1972).

S. D. Goitein describes the Sephardic world of the eastern Mediterranean in its early days in *A Mediterranean Society: The Jewish Communities of the Arab World as Portrayed in the Documents of the Cairo Geniza* (Berkeley: University of California Press, 1967–83); see also his *Letters of Medieval Jewish Traders* (Princeton: Princeton University Press, 1973). The best available histories of the Jews in Spain are: Eliyahu Ashtor, *The Jews of Moslem Spain*, 2 vols. (Philadelphia: Jewish Publication Society of America, 1973); and Yitzhak Baer, *History of the Jews in Christian Spain*, 2 vols. (Philadelphia: Jewish Publication Society of America, 1966). For the Jews of North Africa, see Andre Chouraqui, *Between East and West: A History of the Jews of North Africa* (Philadelphia: Jewish Publication Society of America, 1968). Cecil Roth's *A History of the Marranos*, 4th ed. (New York: Schocken, 1974) describes Marrano life in the Sephardic world. His biography of Manasseh Ben Israel presents the curriculum of the Sephardic school in seventeenth-century Amsterdam. Yosef Haim Yerushalmi, a major historian of the post–1492 Sephardic diaspora, gives an overview of Ladino culture in "In Praise of Ladino: Sephardic Tradition, Ladino and Spanish Jewish Literature, A Review Essay," *Conservative Judaism* 27 (Winter 1973): 56–66.

Abraham J. Heschel's classic work, *The Earth Is the Lord's* (New York/Philadelphia: Harper & Row/Jewish Publication Society of America, 1950), claims to present a full description of Ashkenazic society. It should be noted that it essentially describes the Jews in Eastern Europe of Hassidic and Polish backgrounds, not the Litvaks of Lithuanian background. The *Encyclopedia Judaica* offers capsule descriptions of Ashkenazim and Sephardim. Hirsch Jakob Zimmel's *Ashkenazim and Sephardim, 1958: Their Relations, Differences and Problems as Reflected in the Rabbinical Responsa* (Farnborough, England: Greeg International Publishers, 1958) also contrasts Ashkenazim and Sephardim.

The list of Sephardic classics is too long to note here. Moreover, most of the classics, such as the writings of Maimonides, the poetry of Judah HaLevi, and the commentaries of Don Isaac Abarbanel, have been incorporated into the general corpus of Jewish knowledge, so much so that many Ashkenazim do not even know that the authors were Sephardim. Most are available in English translation. The popular Bible commentary *Me-Am Lo'ez*, one of the classic works of the Sephardic diaspora in the Balkans, is now available in English translation as well. The record of late-nineteenth-century Ladino literature can be found in H. V. Besso, *Ladino Books in the Library of Congress* (Washington, D.C.: U.S. Government Printing Office, 1963).

On the flourishing of Judeo-Spanish (Ladino) culture in the late nineteenth century, see David F. Altave, "Konsezo a Tomar: A Haskalah Work in Judeo-Spanish," *Tradition* 15 (Spring 1976): 91–100; and Marc D. Angel, "Judeo-Spanish Drama: A Study of Sephardic Culture," *Tradition* 19 (Summer 1981): 182–85.

Jose Faur is one of the major contemporary voices presenting the Sephardic way as normative tradition in Jewish life. One of his early pieces in English is "Sephardic Culture," which appeared in *The Jewish Spectator* 41 (Spring 1976): 33–35. Marc D. Angel's article "A Sephardic Approach to *Halakhah*," *Midstream* 21 (August/September 1975): 66–69, is written from the perspective of one of the leading Sephardic rabbis in the United States today. See also Marc D. Angel, "Sephardic Approaches to Teaching Siddur," *Pedagogic Reporter* 33 (December 1981): 19.

Chapter Two

For this chapter, the reader is provided with some Hebrew sources, mainly to document the claims advanced. Wherever possible, however, the sources are in English.

On genetics, see Harry I. Shapiro, *The Jewish People: A Biological History* (Paris: UNESCO, 1960); and James Green-Hamilton, "The Use of Genetic Markers in Oriental Jewish Studies," *Jewish Quarterly Review* 62 (April 1972): 288–313.

There is very little in English about the Sephardic role in Eretz Israel prior to the rise of Zionism, although a number of recent studies have appeared in Hebrew. The record is summarized briefly in Daniel J. Elazar, *Israel: Building a New Society* (Bloomington: Indiana University Press, 1986); and, as is usually the case, the basic facts are available in the *Encyclopedia Judaica*, in the article on Israeli history. See also Moshe Maoz, *Ottoman Reform in Syria and Palestine, 1840–1861: The Impact of the Tanzimat on Politics and Society* (Oxford: Oxford University Press, 1968).

For a picture of life in Sephardic Jerusalem in the nineteenth century, see Yaakov Elazar, *Harova Hayehudit B'Yerushalayim Ha'atika* (Jerusalem: privately printed by the author, 1975); *Hatzerot B'ir Ha'atika* (Jerusalem: Yad Larishonim, n.d.); and *Diyur V'klita B'yishuv*

Hayashan (Jerusalem: Yad Larishonim, n.d.). See also Yaakov Yehoshua, *Yaldut B'Yerushalayim HaYashana,* 6 vols. (Jerusalem: Reuven Maas, 1965–79); and *Ben Masoret L'havai,* 2 vols. (Jerusalem: Vaad Adat HaSephardim, 1979–82).

Eliahou Eliachar chronicles the transition from Sephardic to Ashkenazic control of Eretz Israel in *Living with Jews* (London: Weidenfeld and Nicholson, 1983); and Avraham Haim studies the same topic in depth in his dissertation "Sephardi Leadership in Jerusalem and its Relations with the Central Institutions of the Yishuv under the British Rule 1917–1948," Tel Aviv University, 1983. The best source for materials on the Sephardim in Eretz Israel from the thirteenth century to the present is *BaMarakhah,* the principal monthly editorial journal of the Sephardic community, published in Jerusalem.

The historical demographics are based on the figures in the *Encyclopedia Judaica* and in Raphael Patai's *Tents of Jacob: The Diaspora Yesterday and Today* (Englewood Cliffs, N.J.: Prentice-Hall, 1971), which are in turn based on the works of Arthur Ruppin and Jacob Letschinsky. For contemporary demographic data on world Jewry, see the studies of the Institute for Contemporary Jewry, particularly the work of U. O. Schmelz and Sergio DellaPergola. Current statistics on Israel are from Israel's Central Bureau of Statistics.

On the Sephardic reaction to the Beirut massacre, the Israeli public opinion polls of that time demonstrate the point made here. My own extensive contacts and conversations correspond. See Daniel J. Elazar, "Challenging Begin from Within: The Response of the Religious Parties and the Sephardim to the Beirut Massacre," *Jerusalem Letter* 52 (October 7, 1982); and David Clayman, "Israel in the Wake of the Beirut Massacre: Ten Days in Search of Answers," *Jerusalem Letter* 53 (October 15, 1982).

The matter of Sephardic tolerance as compared to Ashkenazic extremism has recently become a common topic in Israel. Nevertheless, there is still relatively little published research on the subject beyond a few articles that have appeared in Israeli and other journals. Recent studies on Sephardic and Ashkenazic attitudes and voting patterns include Maurice M. Roumani, "Ethnic Voting and Social Change in Israel," in *Some Perspectives on Ashkenazi-Sephardi Relations in Israel* (New York: Institute on American Jewish-Israeli Relations, The American Jewish Committee, 1985); Efraim Ben-Zadok and Giora Goldberg, "Voting Patterns of Oriental Jews in Development Towns," *Jerusalem Quarterly* 32 (Summer 1984): 16–27; Asher Arian and Michal Shamir, "The Ethnic Vote in Israel's 1981 Elections," *Electoral Studies* 1 (December 1982): 315–31; Asher Arian, "National Security and Public Opinion" (in press); Hanoch Smith, *Israeli Elections in a Time of Crisis: An Analysis of Issues, Parties, and Personalities* (New York: American Jewish Committee, 1984); Sammy Smooha, "Ethnic Stratification and Allegiance in Israel: Where Do Oriental Jews Belong?" *Il Politico* 41 (December 1975): 635–51; Yochanan Peres, *Ethnic Relations in Israel* (in Hebrew) (Tel Aviv: Sifriat Hapoalim, 1976); and Hanoch Smith, *Highlights of Israel's Election Results: Polarization, Fragmentation, and Ethnicity* (New York: American Jewish Committee, 1984). Consistent reading of the Israeli press has also influenced my opinions.

Periodical sources for material on the Sephardim in Israel are *The Jewish Digest, The Jewish Observer,* and *The Jerusalem Quarterly. The Jewish Digest,* published in New York City, provides extensive coverage of Sephardic communities and the Ashkenazi-Sephardi issue in Israel, usually treating the Sephardim as exotic, but doing so sympathetically. *The Jewish Observer,* published in London, which offers important analyses of the Israeli scene, deals periodically with questions of Sephardic culture and is generally also quite sympathetic to the Sephardim. *The Jerusalem Quarterly,* published in Israel, is dominated by the same group of Ashkenazim who have been most prominently associated with spreading the myth of Sephardic backwardness. Although its articles are somewhat more scholarly than newspaper accounts, the bias is apparent.

In the Israeli press, *The Jerusalem Post* accepts the establishment view but presents it with moderation, much like *Ma'ariv. Ha'aretz* is blatantly anti-Sephardic; *Yediot Aharonot,* whose readership is heavily Sephardic, is more neutral. *BaMarakhah,* published by Vaad

Adat HaSephardim, is actively, even stridently, aggressive in its treatment of the issue, defending Sephardic rights and interests. *Megamot*, the leading Hebrew social science journal in Israel, is generally fair, but its bias is that of the Ashkenazic academic establishment, like *The Jerusalem Quarterly*. Even people who consider themselves friends of the Sephardim generally have a patronizing attitude toward them.

On the history of intergroup relations in Israel, see Steven Zipperstein and Eliezer D. Jaffe, "In B.A.S. Relief: Antecedents of Jewish Ethnic Relations in Israel," *Forum* 42/43 (Winter 1981): 14–32.

For a general overview of issues discussed in this chapter, see Shmuel Trigano's article "The Guilt of the Israeli Left," *Jerusalem Letter/Viewpoints* 30 (November 6, 1983). For two of the earliest discussions on the myth of Israel's two cultures, see Daniel J. Elazar, "Israel's Sephardim: The Myth of the Two Cultures," *The American Sephardi* (June 1967), which was updated in a second article, "A New Look at the Two Israels," *Midstream* 24 (April 1978): 3–10.

The most useful general works are: Sammy Smooha, *Israel: Pluralism and Conflict* (Berkeley: University of California Press, 1978), written by a very angry young Sephardic political scientist of Iraqi origin who strongly attacks the Ashkenazim for discriminatory behavior; and Nissim Rejwan's "The Two Israels: A Study in Europocentrism," *Judaism* 16 (Winter 1967): 97–108.

Typical of Ashkenazic bias are the articles by M. Bar Natan, "Israel's East-West Problem," *Jewish Frontier* 30 (October 1963): 4–7; and Nehemiah Meyers, "Israel's Demographic Dilemma," *Jewish Frontier* 31 (May 1964): 24–26. *Jewish Frontier* is the American voice of what was once Mapai and is now the Israeli Labor party. On the other hand, during the same period, *The Jewish Observer* was publishing such articles as "Look Back with Dignity: A Warning to Israel's Europeans" (August 2, 1963): 12–13. For a more recent statement of Israeli Ashkenazic and Sephardic views, see *Some Perspectives on Ashkenazic-Sephardic Relations in Israel* (New York: American Jewish Committee, 1985). For an American Sephardic view of Israel's demographic and political transformation, see Marc D. Angel, "Israel's Majority," *Moment* 6 (July/August 1981): 4.

There is substantial anthropological literature on the Sephardim in Israel, most suffering the usual biases. One of the foremost offenders is Yohanan Peres, professor of sociology at Tel Aviv University, who is widely considered in Israel to be an expert on the subject. His approach typifies the essence of the problem. The works of Shlomo A. Deshen, who considers himself very close to the Sephardim, are far more sympathetic, as is Alex Weingrod's *Studies in Israeli Ethnicity: After the Ingathering* (New York: Gordon and Breach Science Publications, 1981).

Other ethnographic studies of integration include: Judith Bernstein and Aaron Antonovski, "The Integration of Ethnic Groups in Israel," *Jewish Journal of Sociology* 13 (June 1981): 15–23; Erik Cohen, "Ethnicity and Legitimation in Contemporary Israel," *Jerusalem Quarterly* 28 (Summer 1983): 111–24; Percy S. Cohen, "Ethnicity, Class, and Political Alignment in Israel," *Jewish Journal of Sociology* 15 (December 1983): 119–30; Moshe Lissak, "Ideological and Social Conflicts in Israel," *Jerusalem Quarterly* 29 (Fall 1983): 20–37; and Tamar Ruth Horowitz, "Integration and the Social Gap," *Jerusalem Quarterly* 15 (Spring 1980): 134–44. For the other side of the coin, see Todd Jick, "The Israeli Development Town: Coming of Age in Sderot," *Response* 5 (Winter 1971–72): 64–73. Jick, an American and now a professor of labor relations at the University of Toronto, was a volunteer in Sderot who came without the preconceptions of either side. Another American with a sympathetic approach is Arnold Lewis, "Educational Policy and Social Inequality in Israel," *Jerusalem Quarterly* 12 (September 1979): 10–11.

General works on the absorption of new immigrants include: Judith T. Shuval, *Immigrants on the Threshold* (Englewood Cliffs, N.J.: Prentice-Hall, 1963); Dov Weintraub et al., *Immigration and Social Change* (Jerusalem: Israel University Press, 1971); S. N. Eisenstadt,

Rivka Bar-Yosef, and Haim Adler, eds., *Integration and Development in Israel* (Jerusalem: Israel University Press, 1970); and Judah Matras, *Social Change in Israel* (Chicago: Aldine, 1965).

For the official view of the absorption of the Jews from Africa and Asia, see Joseph B. Schechtman, *On Wings of Eagles: The Plight, Exodus and Homecoming of Oriental Jewry* (New York: Thomas Yoseloff, 1961); Jacob Schatz and Jehoash Beiber, eds., *Metzukatam shel HaYehudim B'Artzot Arav* (in Hebrew) (Jerusalem: Information Center Publications Service of the Ministry of Education, 1971); and Government of Israel, *The Jewish Exodus from Arab Countries and the Arab Refugees* (Jerusalem: Ministry of Foreign Affairs, 1973).

The Jerusalem Center for Public Affairs (JCPA) has studied the encounter between Israeli and diaspora Jews in Project Renewal and has discovered that those involved quickly found a common language, growing out of common Jewish attitudes, beliefs, and sensibilities. See, in particular, Daniel J. Elazar, Paul E. King, and Orly HaCohen, *The Extent, Focus, and Impact of Diaspora Involvement* (Jerusalem: Jerusalem Center for Public Affairs, 1983).

Haim Adler and Michael Inbar treat the differences in progress among Sephardim from the same family who emigrated separately to Israel and to other parts of the Western world in *Ethnic Integration in Israel* (New Brunswick, N.J.: Transaction Books, 1977). For a discussion of discrimination against Sephardim in educational matters, see Arnold Lewis, *Power, Poverty, and Education* (Ramat Gan, Israel: Turtledove, 1979).

For further background on the Jewish political tradition, see Daniel J. Elazar and Stuart A. Cohen, *The Jewish Polity* (Bloomington: Indiana University Press, 1985); and Daniel J. Elazar, ed., *Kinship and Consent* (Lanham, Md./Jerusalem: University Press of America/ Jerusalem Center for Public Affairs, 1983).

On the Sephardim and Israel's political and electoral processes, see Howard Penniman, *Israel at the Polls: The Knesset Elections of 1977* (Washington, D.C.: American Enterprise Institute, 1979), especially the introduction by Daniel J. Elazar; Howard Penniman and Daniel J. Elazar, eds., *Israel at the Polls, 1981* (Bloomington: Indiana University Press, 1986), especially the sections by Daniel J. Elazar; and Daniel J. Elazar, Howard Penniman, and Shmuel Sandler, eds., *Israel's Odd Couple: The 1984 Elections and the National Unity Government* (Detroit: Wayne State University Press, 1988). On local government as the channel for Sephardic entry into Israeli politics, see Daniel J. Elazar, "Local Government as an Integrating Factor in Israeli Society," in Michael Curtis and Mordecai S. Chertoff, eds., *Israel: Social Structure and Change* (New Brunswick, N.J.: Transaction Books, 1973); Mark Iris and Avraham Shama, "Political Participation and Ethnic Conflict in Israel," in Gregory S. Mahler, ed., *Readings on the Israeli Political System: Structures and Processes* (Washington, D.C.: University Press of America, 1982); and Shevah Weiss, "Local Government in Israel: A Study of Its Leadership," Ph.D. dissertation, Hebrew University, 1968. An update on the positions of Sephardim in Israeli politics can be found in Harry M. Rosen, *Growing Political Leadership Roles of Sephardi Jews in Israel* (New York: American Jewish Committee, 1985).

For the relationship between Begin's victories and the Sephardic vote, see Louis Guttman, "The Vote, Yesterday and Today," *The Jerusalem Post* (August 26, 1977); Dan Caspi, Avraham Diskin, and Emanuel Guttman, eds., *The Roots of Begin's Success: The 1981 Elections* (London: Croom Helm, 1983); Hanna Herzog, "The Ethnic Lists in Election 1981: An Ethnic Political Identity?" in Asher Arian, ed., *The Election in Israel, 1981* (Tel Aviv: Ramot, 1983); and Michal Shamir and Asher Arian, "The Ethnic Vote in Israel's 1981 Elections," *Electoral Studies* 1 (December 1982): 315–31.

BaMarakhah chronicles the anger of the Sephardim at the Labor party; see also Daniel J. Elazar, "Israel's New Majority," *Commentary* 75 (March 1984).

On the Sephardim and religious parties, see Daniel J. Elazar, "The End of the Chief Rabbinate," *Jerusalem Letter* 42 (October 31, 1985), "Challenging Begin from Within: The Response of the Religious Parties and the Sephardim to the Beirut Massacre," *Jerusalem*

Letter 52 (October 7, 1982), "The Future of Israeli Politics," *Jerusalem Letter* 56 (January 19, 1983), and "The 1981 Elections: Some Observations," *Viewpoints* 19 (August 15, 1981).

On Sephardic religious practice, see Shlomo Deshen, "The Judaism of Middle Eastern Immigrants," *Jerusalem Quarterly* 13 (Fall 1979): 98–110; and Marc D. Angel, "Sephardic Culture," *The Jewish Spectator* 37 (December 1972): 23–24.

With regard to the Sephardim and the Arabs, see, among others, Sharon Cohen, "Report from Tel Aviv: The Sephardim and the Arabs," *Present Tense* 7 (Summer 1980): 17–18; Maurice Roumani, "Ethnic Voting and Social Change in Israel," in *Some Perspectives on Ashkenazi-Sephardi Relations in Israel* (New York: American Jewish Committee, 1985); and Yochanan Peres, *Ethnic Relations in Israel* (in Hebrew) (Tel Aviv: Sifriat Hapoalim, 1976). Again, there is much material in Hebrew on this subject. All that is written by the Sephardim follows the thrust of my argument here, whereas much of that written by the Ashkenazim suggests that the Sephardim and Arabs have a special antipathy.

Chapter Three

One place to begin is the *Encyclopedia Judaica*, in which there are articles on every country where Jews reside, most at least mentioning the Sephardic presence if there is one. Where there is a substantial presence, it is discussed at least in outline. For some communities, the *Encyclopedia Judaica* articles are almost the only source of reputable scientific quality. Unfortunately, since it was completed in the late 1960s, those articles are becoming increasingly dated. More current information often may be found in articles of the *American Jewish Year Book*, which is published annually by the American Jewish Committee and the Jewish Publication Society of America. Unfortunately, only a few countries are covered each year—apparently depending on the availability of authors—of which even fewer countries have significant Sephardic communities, and in many entries those communities are not discussed separately.

The most complete overview is found in David Sitton, *Sephardi Communities Today* (Jerusalem: Council of the Sephardi and Oriental Communities, 1985). He offers a country-by-country survey based on his own travels. See also Edouard Roditi, "From All Their Habitations: Voices from the Sephardic Diaspora," *Judaism* 16 (Spring 1967): 214–21; "Sephard: Diaspora and Aliya," *European Judaism* 1 (Summer 1969): 15–22; and Raphael Patai, *Tents of Jacob: The Diaspora Yesterday and Today* (Englewood Cliffs, N.J.: Prentice-Hall, 1971).

For a general view of diaspora Jewry today that emphasizes the Sephardic presence, see *European Jewry: A Handbook* (Paris: European Council of Jewish Community Services, 1982). On the demography of European Jewry, see U. O. Schmelz, *World Jewish Population: Regional Estimate and Projections*, Jewish Population Study Series (Jerusalem: Hebrew University, 1981); U. O. Schmelz and Sergio DellaPergola, "World Jewish Population," *American Jewish Year Book 1982*, 285–87; and Sergio DellaPergola, "Megamot Demografiot BeKrav Yehudi Ma'arav Europa," *Tefutsot Yisrael* 28 (Winter 1980): 67–94 (in Hebrew).

On the role of Sephardim in contemporary Europe, see Ignaz Maybaum, "Sephardim and Ashkenazim," *European Judaism* 4 (Summer 1967): 29–33; Ernest Stock, "The Emerging European Jewish Community Structure," *Jerusalem Letter* 46 (March 14, 1982); *European Jewry: A Handbook* (Paris: European Council of Jewish Community Services, 1982); and Daniel J. Elazar, "The New Agenda of European Jewry," *Jerusalem Letter/Viewpoints* 35 (October 17, 1984).

On Balkan Jewry, see Daniel J. Elazar, Harriet Friedenreich, Baruch Hazzan, and Adina Weiss Liberles, *The Balkan Jewish Communities: Yugoslavia, Bulgaria, Greece, and Turkey*

(Lanham, Md./Jerusalem: University Press of America/Jerusalem Center for Public Affairs, 1984).

On Turkey, see Alan C. Harris, "Report from Turkey," *The Reconstructionist* 33 (May 3, 1966): 7–15, and *The Reconstructionist* 33 (May 17, 1966): 17–24.

On Greek Jewry, see Jacob Beller, "On Greek Shores," *Jewish Life* 34 (November-December 1966): 43–50; "The 5,000 Jews in Greece," *Israel Horizons* 21 (May-June 1973): 18, 29; S. Victor Papacosma, "The Sephardic Jews of Salonika," *Midstream* 24 (December 1978): 10–14; and Marc D. Angel, *The Jews of Rhodes: The History of a Sephardic Community* (New York: Sepher-Hermon Press/the Union of Sephardic Congregations, 1978).

On the Jews in Yugoslavia, see Harriet Pass Friedenreich, *The Jews of Yugoslavia: A Quest for Community* (Philadelphia: Jewish Publication Society of America, n.d.); Savo Lagomdziya, "The Jews of Sarajevo," *World Jewry* 9 (November-December 1966): 25; and Yakir Eventov, *Toldot Yehudai Yugoslavia* (in Hebrew) (Tel Aviv: Hitahdut Olai Yugoslavia, 1971).

On Italian Jewry, see Cecil Roth, *The History of the Jews of Italy* (Philadelphia: Jewish Publication Society of America, 1946); Moses A. Shulvass, *The Jews in the World of the Renaissance* (Leiden, the Netherlands: E. J. Brill, 1973); Marcel Grilli, "The Role of the Jews in Modern Italy," *Menorah* (Autumn 1939): 260–80, (Winter 1940): 60–81, and (Summer 1940): 172–97; Massimo Adolfo Vitale, "The Destruction and Resistance of the Jews in Italy," in Yuri Sahl, ed., *They Fought Back: The Story of Jewish Resistance in Nazi Europe* (New York: Crown, 1967), 298–303; L. Poliakov, "Mussolini and the Extermination of the Jews," *Jewish Social Studies* (July 1949): 249–58; Meir Michaelis, "The Attitude of the Fascist Regime to the Jews in Italy," *Yad Vashem Studies on the European Catastrophe and Resistance* 4 (1960): 7–41; Chaim Bermant, "Rome Report: 'He No Like to Interfere,' " *Present Tense* 5 (Winter 1978): 16–18; Luciano Tass, *Yehudei Italiyah* (in Hebrew) (Tel Aviv: *Ma'ariv*/World Jewish Congress, 1978); Eitan Franco Sabatello, "Youth in Italy," *European Jewry* 5 (Winter 1970–71): 27–31; and "The Jewish Community in Italy," *Israel and World Jewry* (1971): 72–83.

On the new Jewish community in Spain, see Lavy M. Becker, "Jews in Spain," *The Reconstructionist* (September 1973): 24–28; Jorge Tallet, "Spain: The Jew Within," *National Jewish Monthly* 14 (July-August 1973): 10–14; and Stephen Klaidman, "Jewish Renaissance—A Spanish Phenomenon," *The New York Post* (January 16, 1973), 71.

On the Jewish community of Gibraltar, see L. A. Sawchuck and D. A. Herring, *The Sephardim of Gibraltar, 1704 to 1939* (Scarborough, Ont.: University of Toronto, 1984); L. A. Sawchuck, "Reproductive Success Among the Sephardic Jews of Gibraltar," *Human Biology* 52 (1980): 731–52; R. A. Preston, "Gibraltar: Colony and Fortress," *Canadian History Review* 27 (1946): 402–23; A. B. M. Serfaty, *The Jews of Gibraltar Under British Rule*, 2d ed. (Gibraltar: Garrison Library Printing Press, 1958); W. Stein, "Gibraltar," in *The Universal Jewish Encyclopedia*, vol. 4 (1939), 605–6; and Meir Persoff, "Rock Solid: Gibraltar's Jewish Community," *Jewish Chronicle* (June 1983).

On the Jews of Portugal, see Ignacio Steinhardt, "Portugal's Secret Jews," *Jewish Chronicle* (November 29, 1974): 15; Jacob Beller, "Jews in Portugal, Past and Present," *Pioneer Woman* (October-November 1973): 10–12; R. D. Barnett, *The Sephardi Heritage* (1971); Charles Arnhold, "The Isolated Jews of Portugal," *Jewish Digest* (September 1969): 77–78; and Sidney DuBroff, "Jews in Portugal," *Hadassah Magazine* (October 1970): 18–19.

On the Sephardim in the Netherlands, see Mozes Heiman Gans, *Memorbook: History of Dutch Jewry from the Renaissance to 1940* (Baarn, the Netherlands: Bosch and Keuning, 1971); Werner Keller, "The Dutch Jerusalem," in *Diaspora* (London: Pitman Publishing, 1971), 317–29; and Joel S. Fishman, "The Jewish Community in Post-War Netherlands, 1944–1975," *Midstream* 22 (January 1976): 42–54.

On Sephardim in France, see Jordan Elgrably, "French Jewry Today: The Sephardic Community of Paris," *Present Tense* 10 (Summer 1983): 52–56; W. Rabi, "The New Face of French Jewry," *World Jewry* 6 (May/June 1963): 56; Dominique Schnapper, "French Jewry Today: A Remarkable Revival," *Present Tense* 10 (Summer 1983): 50–52; Ilan Greilsammer, *The Democratization of a Community: The Case of French Jewry* (Jerusalem: Center for Jewish Community Studies, 1979), and "Jews of France: From Neutrality to Involvement," *Forum* 28–29 (Winter 1978): 130–46; Simon Schwarzfuchs, *Les Juifs de France* (Paris: Albin Michel, 1975); Marc Salzberg, *French Jewry and American Jewry* (Jerusalem: Center for Jewish Community Studies, 1971); Dominique Schnapper, *Jewish Identities in France: An Analysis of Contemporary French Jewry* (Chicago: University of Chicago Press, 1983); Doris Bensimon-Donath, *L'integration des Juifs Nord-Africains en France* (Paris: Mouton, 1971); C. Klineberg, G. Levitte, and G. Benguigui, *Aspects of French Jewry* (London: Vallentine Mitchell, 1969); David Landes, "The State of French Jewry," *Moment* (March-April 1981): 12–18; and Albert Memmi, "On Jewishness and the Social Contexts of Jews in France," *The Jewish Journal of Sociology* 1 (January 1970).

For historical background, see Diogene Tama, ed., *Transactions of the Parisian Sanhedrin or Acts of the Assembly of Israelitish Deputies of France and Italy* (London, 1807); "French Sanhedrin," in *Encyclopedia Judaica*; Jacob Katz, *Out of the Ghetto: The Social Background of Jewish Emancipation, 1770–1870* (Cambridge, Mass.: Harvard University Press, 1973), 139–41; Phyllis Cohen Albert, *The Modernization of French Jewry: Consistory and Community in the Nineteenth Century* (Hanover, N.H.: Brandeis University Press, 1977); and Paula Hyman, *From Dreyfus to Vichy: The Remaking of French Jewry, 1906–1939* (New York: Columbia University Press, 1979).

On the history of the Sephardim of Great Britain, see Cecil Roth, *History of the Jews in England* (Oxford: Clarendon Press, 1949); V. D. Lipman, ed., *Three Centuries of Anglo-Jewish History* (London: The Jewish Historical Society of England, 1961), and *Social History of the Jews of England* (London: Watts, 1954); A. M. Hyamson, *The Sephardim of England: A History of the Spanish-Portuguese Community, 1492–1959* (London: Methuen, 1951); Todd M. Endelman, *The Jews of Georgian England, 1714–1830* (Philadelphia: Jewish Publication Society of America, 1979); Stephen Aris, *But There Are No Jews in England* (New York: Stein and Day, 1971); and Chaim Bermant, *Troubled Eden: An Anatomy of British Jewry* (London: Vallentine Mitchell, 1969), and *The Cousinhood: The Anglo-Jewish Gentry* (London: Eyre and Spottiswoode, 1971).

On the Sephardim and the Board of Deputies, see Charles H. L. Emmanuel, *A Century and a Half of Jewish History: Extracts from the Minute Books of the London Committee of Deputies of the British Jews* (London: Board of Deputies of British Jews, 1910).

Chapter Four

For background information on the Sephardim in North Africa and western Asia, see Norman A. Stillman, *The Jews of Arab Lands* (Philadelphia: Jewish Publication Society of America, 1979); Maurice M. Roumani, *The Case of the Jews from Arab Countries: A Neglected Issue* (Tel Aviv: World Organization of Jews from Arab Countries, 1983); Mark Robert Cohen, "The Jews Under Islam: From the Rise of Islam to Sabbetai Zevi," in *The Study of Judaism II* (New York: Anti-Defamation League of B'nai B'rith, 1976); S. D. Goitein, "Jewish Society and Institutions Under Islam," in H. H. Ben Sasson and S. Ettinger, eds., *Jewish Society Through the Ages* (New York: Schocken, 1971), and *Jews and Arabs: Their Contacts Through the Ages*, 3d ed. (New York: Schocken, 1974); Shimon Shamir, "Muslim-Arab Attitudes Toward Jews: The Ottoman and Modern Periods," in Salo W. Baron and George S. Wise, eds., *Violence and Defense in the Jewish Experience* (Philadelphia: Jewish Publication Society of America, 1977); Government of Israel, "Jews in Arab Lands," in *Information Briefing* (Jerusalem: Ministry of Foreign Affairs, 1973); Devora and Menachem Hacohen,

One People: The Story of Eastern Jews (New York: Funk and Wagnalls, 1969); and Jacob M. Landau, *Jews in Nineteenth-Century Egypt* (New York: New York University Press, 1969).

For a description of the situation at the time of the establishment of the State of Israel, see S. Landshut, *Jewish Communities in the Muslim Countries in the Middle East* (London: The Jewish Chronicle, 1950); *The Treatment of Jews in Egypt and Iraq* (New York: World Jewish Congress, 1948); and Nehemiah Robinson, *The Arab Countries of the Near East and Their Jewish Communities* (New York: Institute of Jewish Affairs, 1951).

Works on the Jews of specific countries include: Abraham L. Udovitch and Lucette Valensi, *The Last Arab Jews: The Communities of Jerba, Tunisia* (London: Harwood Academic Publications, 1984); "Yemen," in *Encyclopedia Judaica;* S. D. Goitein, *The Land of Sheba and Tales of the Jews of Yemen* (New York: Schocken, 1947); Ernest Stock, "Jews in Egypt, 1983," *Jerusalem Letter* 60 (June 15, 1983); "Morocco," in *Encyclopedia Judaica;* Mark A. Tessler and Linda L. Hawkins, "The Political Culture of Jews in Tunisia and Morocco and Arabs in Israel," *Comparative Studies in Society and History* 20 (1978): 359–73; and Norman A. Stillman, "Muslims and Jews in Morocco," *The Jerusalem Quarterly* 5 (1977): 76–83.

On the Sephardim in black Africa, see B. A. Kosmin, *Majuta: A History of the Jewish Community in Zimbabwe* (Gwelo, Zimbabwe: Mambo Press, 1981); and Geoffrey Wigoder, "The Jews of Rhodesia," *The Jerusalem Post* (March 23, 1976).

Chapter Five

For historical background, see Jacob Neusner, *A History of the Jews in Babylonia,* 5 vols. (Leiden, the Netherlands: E. J. Brill, 1965–70); David Solomon Sassoon, *History of the Jews in Baghdad* (Letchworth: Solomon D. Sassoon, 1949); Maurice M. Roumani, *The Case of the Jews from Arab Countries: A Neglected Issue* (Tel Aviv: World Organization of Jews from Arab Countries, 1983); and Norman A. Stillman, *The Jews of Arab Lands* (Philadelphia: Jewish Publication Society of America, 1979).

For the recent history of individual communities, see Max Sawdayee, *All Waiting to Be Hanged: Iraq Post-Six Day War Diary* (Tel Aviv: Levanda, 1974); Menachem Persoff, ed., *The Jews in Syria* (Jerusalem: Ahva, 1975), 41–43; and "Lebanon," in *Encyclopedia Judaica.*

The section on Iran is drawn primarily from the author's study of the Iranian Jewish community conducted in Teheran in August 1970 and published as Daniel J. Elazar, *The Jewish Community of Iran* (Jerusalem/Philadelphia: Center for Jewish Community Studies, 1975). See also Ezra Spicehandler's fine essay *"Yahadut Iran, Kiyyumah v'Ve'Bayoteha"* ("Iranian Jewry"), published in Hebrew by the Study Circle on Diaspora Jewry under the auspices of the President of Israel; and Joseph Glanz's comprehensive study of Jewish education, *"HaHinukh Hayehudi b'Iran"* ("Jewish Education in Iran"), prepared in Hebrew for the Jewish Agency. These essays can be found in *"Yehudei Paras Bezman Hazeh"* ("The Jews of Iran Today"), *Tefutsot Yisrael* 19 (January–March 1975). Secondary sources in English are very inadequate. Furthermore, documentary material on contemporary Jewish life in Iran, outside of the closed files of the Joint Distribution Committee and the Israeli Foreign Ministry, consists primarily of reports from Israeli emissaries who have visited the country and a few studies of Jewish education commissioned by the Jewish Agency and COJO (Conference of Jewish Organizations).

For the history of Iranian Jewry, see I. Ben Zvi, *The Exiled and the Redeemed* (Philadelphia: Jewish Publication Society of America, 1957), 112–19 (on the crypto-Jews of Meshed) and 255–70; Walter J. Fischel, "Israel in Iran," in Louis Finkelstein, ed., *The Jews: Their History, Culture and Religion,* vol. 2 (Westport, Conn.: Greenwood Press, 1960), 1149–90; "Secret Jews of Persia: A Century-Old Marrano Community in Asia," *Commentary* 7 (January 1949): 28–33; "The Jews Under the Persian Kajar Dynasty (1795–1925)," *Jewish*

Social Studies (1950); Walter Fishel, "Isfahan: The Story of a Jewish Community in Persia," in *Joshua Starr Memorial Volume* (New York: Conference on Jewish Relations, 1953), 11–128; "Persia" and "Iran," in *Encyclopedia Judaica.*

On Afghanistan, see Raphael Patai, *Tents of Jacob: The Diaspora Yesterday and Today* (Englewood Cliffs, N.J.: Prentice-Hall, 1971), 253–55; Reuven Kashani, *Yehudei Afghanistan* (Jerusalem: BaMarakhah, 1973); I. Ben Zvi, *The Exiled and the Redeemed* (Philadelphia: Jewish Publication Society of America, 1957); "Afghanistan," in *Encyclopedia Judaica;* Nimat Allah, *History of the Afghans* (London: S. Gupta, 1829); Louis Finkelstein, ed., *The Jews: Their History, Culture and Religion*, vol. 2 (Westport, Conn.: Greenwood Press, 1960), 1149–90. The most correct information is from the author's unpublished field notes, Kabul, February 1976.

For material on Pakistan, see "Pakistan," in *Encyclopedia Judaica;* Institute of Jewish Affairs, *Jewish Communities of the World* (London: World Jewish Congress, Institute of Jewish Affairs, 1971), 72; Louis Finkelstein, ed., "Pakistan," in *The Jews: Their History, Culture and Religion*, vol. 2 (Westport, Conn.: Greenwood Press, 1960), 1689.

For the history of the Jews in India, see Flower Elias and Judith Elias Cooper, *The Jews of Calcutta* (Calcutta: The Jewish Association of Calcutta, 1974); Daniel J. Elazar, *The Jewish Community of India*, unpublished report prepared for the Study of Jewish Community Organization under the auspices of the Center for Jewish Community Studies, 1976; *India Jewish Year Book 1969* (Bombay: B. J. Israel, 1963); M. D. Japheth, *The Jews of India: A Brief Survey* (Bombay: M. D. Japheth, 1969); Schifra Strizower, *The Bene Israel of Bombay* (New York: Schocken, 1971); Ezekiel N. Musleah, *On the Banks of the Ganga: The Sojourn of Jews in Calcutta* (North Quincy, Mass.: Christopher Publishing House, 1975); Eliya Ben Eliahu, *Indian Jewry '84* (Haifa: Ben Eliahu, 1984).

On Singapore, see "Singapore," in *Encyclopedia Judaica;* I. Cohen, *Journal of a Jewish Traveller* (London: J. Lane, 1925); and Daniel J. Elazar, unpublished field notes, 1985.

On Hong Kong, see "Hong Kong," in *Encyclopedia Judaica;* I. Cohen, *Journal of a Jewish Traveller* (London: J. Lane, 1925), 115–21; Dennis A. Leventhal, "The Call of History," *Bulletin* (Association of Former Residents of China), no. 279 (May 1985), 9.

On the Philippines, see "Philippines," in *Encyclopedia Judaica;* G. A. Kohut, "Jewish Heretics in the Philippines in the Sixteenth and Seventeenth Century," *American Jewish Historical Society Publications*, no. 12 (1904), 145–56; and Daniel J. Elazar, unpublished field notes, 1985.

On Australian Jewry, see Daniel J. Elazar with Peter Y. Medding, *Jewish Communities in Frontier Societies* (New York: Holmes and Meier, 1984); Peter Y. Medding, ed., *Jews in Australian Society* (Melbourne: Macmillan/Monash, 1973); Walter Lippman, *Demography of Australian Jewry: Analysis of 1971 Census* (Melbourne: Federation of Australian Jewish Welfare Societies, 1975); and C. A. Price, *Jewish Settlers in Australia* (Canberra: Australia National University, 1964).

Chapter Six

The Sephardim of Latin America are treated, albeit unevenly, in the various studies and travelers' reports dealing with Jewish life as a whole south of the Rio Grande. There are few works that single them out and most deal only with the early colonial period or the Caribbean islands. The best overall book is Judith Laikin Elkin, *Jews of the Latin American Republics* (Chapel Hill: University of North Carolina Press, 1980) More in the line of a traveler's report is Jacob Beller, *Jews in Latin America* (New York: Jonathan David, 1969). A historical overview is provided by Martin A. Cohen in *The Jewish Experience in Latin America*, 2 vols. (Waltham, Mass.: American Jewish Historical Society, 1972); and in Cecil Roth, *A History of the Marranos* (New York: Schocken, 1974).

On Caribbean Sephardim, see Frances P. Karner, *The Sephardics of Curaçao: A Study of*

Sociocultural Patterns in Flux (Assen, the Netherlands: Van Gorcum, 1969); Celia S. Rosenthal, "The Jews of Barranquilla," *Jewish Journal of Sociology* 2 (1956): 262–74; E. Alvin Fidenque, "Early Sephardic Jewish Settlers in North America and the Caribbean," *Journal of Reform Judaism* (Fall 1978); S. J. Maslin, "Sephardim of Curaçao: Can These Bones Live," *CCAR Journal* (October 1963); Zvi Loker, "Jewish Presence, Enterprise and Migration Trends in the Caribbean," in Jeffrey K. Wilkerson, ed., *Cultural Traditions and Caribbean Identity: The Question of Patrimony* (Gainesville: Center for Latin American Studies, University of Florida, 1980); Jacob Rader Marcus, "The West Indies and South American Expedition of the American Jewish Archives," *American Jewish Archives* 5 (January 1953): 5–21; Isaac S. Emmanuel and Suzanne A. Emmanuel, *History of the Jews of the Netherlands Antilles*, 2 vols. (Assen/Cincinnati: Royal Van Gorcum/American Jewish Archives, 1970), and *Precious Stones of the Jews of Curaçao*, 2 vols. (Assen: Van Gorcum, 1957); and B. W. Korn, "Barbadian Jewish Wills," in *Bicentennial Festschrift for Jacob Rader Marcus* (Waltham, Mass.: American Jewish Historical Society, 1976).

On the Jewish community of Surinam, see P. A. Hilfman, "Notes on the History of the Jews in Surinam," *Publications of the American Jewish Historical Society* 18 (1909): 179–208; and Manfred Lehmann, "Our Own Banana Republic," *The Jerusalem Post Magazine* (April 7, 1978), 6–7.

On the Sephardim of Argentina, see Daniel J. Elazar with Peter Y. Medding, *Jewish Communities in Frontier Societies* (New York: Holmes and Meier, 1983); Haim Avni, "Argentine Jewry: Its Socio-Political Status and Organizational Patterns," *Dispersion and Unity* 12 (1971): 128–62, 13/14 (1971–72): 161–208, and 15/16 (1972): 158–215; Seymour B. Liebman, "Argentine Jewry: Its History, Ethnicity and Problems," *Midstream* 20 (November 1974); Robert Weisbrot, *The Jews of Argentina from the Inquisition to Peron* (Philadelphia: Jewish Publication Society of America, 1979); Irving Louis Horowitz, "The Jewish Community of Buenos Aires," *Jewish Social Studies* 24 (October 1962): 195–222; and Victor A. Mirelman, "The Jews in Argentina (1890–1930): Assimilation and Particularism," Ph.D. dissertation, Columbia University, 1973.

On the Sephardim in Brazil, see Arnold Wiznitzer, *Jews in Colonial Brazil* (New York: Columbia University Press, 1960), and *The Records of the Earliest Jewish Community in the New World* (New York: American Jewish Historical Society, 1954); and Henrique Lemle, "Jews in Northern Brazil," *The Reconstructionist* 3 (March 1967).

On the Sephardim in Mexico, see Seymour B. Liebman, *The Jewish Community of Mexico* (Jerusalem: Center for Jewish Community Studies, 1978); Isaiah Austri-Dan, "The Jewish Community of Mexico," *Dispersion and Unity* 2 (1963): 51–73; Corinne Azen Krause, "The Jews in Mexico: A History with Special Emphasis on the Period from 1857 to 1930," Ph.D. dissertation, University of Pittsburgh, 1970; Seymour B. Liebman, ed., *Jews and the Inquisition in Mexico: The Great Auto da Fé of 1569* (Lawrence, Kansas: Coronado Press, 1974); Harriet Lesser, "A History of the Jewish Community of Mexico City, 1912," Ph.D. dissertation, New York University, 1972; Marlin Zielonda, "The Jews of Mexico," *Year Book of the Central Conference of American Rabbis* 33 (1923): 425–43; and Shirley Kolack, "The Ambiguous Status of Jews in Mexico," *Conservative Judaism* 33 (Fall/Winter 1976–77): 79–85.

On Uruguay, see Asher Sapolinsky, "The Jewry of Uruguay," *Dispersion and Unity* 2 (1963): 74–88.

On Chile, see Mauricio Pitchon, "The Sephardic Jewish Community of Chile," unpublished manuscript, Archives of the Jerusalem Center for Public Affairs.

On the Sephardim of Cuba, see Boris Sapir, *The Jewish Community of Cuba*, trans. Simon Wolin (New York: Jewish Teachers' Seminary Press, 1948), and "Jews in Cuba," *Jewish Review* 5 (July-September 1946): 109–44; Seymour B. Liebman, "Cuba," *American Jewish Year Book 1969*, 238–46; and Larry Luxner, "Los Hebreos Cubanos," *The Jerusalem Post* (December 17, 1985), 5.

On the Sephardim in Ecuador, see Benno Weiser, "Ecuador: Eight Years on Ararat," *Commentary* 3 (June 1947): 531–36.

On the Jews of Panama, see Geoffrey Wigoder, "Jews of Panama," *The Jerusalem Post* (March 2, 1978); and Dennis C. Sasso, "One Century of Jewish Life in Panama," *The Reconstructionist* (September 1976). Victor Perera provides a view of life in a Central American Sephardic family in "A Death in the Family," *Present Tense* 2 (Autumn 1974): 17–24.

Chapter Seven

The principal work on Sephardim in the United States is Marc D. Angel, "The Sephardim of the United States: An Exploratory Study," *American Jewish Year Book 1973*. He gives a summary overview in "The Sephardim in America," *Present Tense* 4 (Autumn 1976): 12–14, and in "Sephardic Culture in America," *Jewish Life* 38 (March/April 1971): 7, 11. Edouard Roditi's review essay, "The Grandees: America's Sephardic Elite," *Commentary* 52 (October 1971): 93–96, is "must" reading to understand the true place of the first American Sephardim in Sephardic history. The most recent book and perhaps the most comprehensive on the Sephardic Jews in the United States is Joseph M. Papo, *Sephardim in Twentieth Century America: In Search of Unity* (San Jose/Berkeley: Pele Yoetz Books/Judah L. Magnes Museum, 1987). Papo has done an excellent job of tracing the history of the Sephardim in the United States.

For information on the recent Sephardic immigration to the United States, see David Maladinov, "Iranian Jewish Organization: The Integration of an Emigré Group into the American Jewish Community," *Journal of Jewish Communal Service* 47 (Spring 1981): 245–49; and Edith Weiner, "The Iranian Jews in Chicago: Service Through a Communal Team," *Journal of Jewish Communal Service* 47 (Spring 1981): 250–56. On relations between Sephardim and Ashkenazim in the United States, see Victor D. Sanua, "A Study of the Adjustment of Sephardic Jews in the New York Metropolitan Area," *Jewish Journal of Sociology* 9 (January 1967): 25–33; and Sherry Rosen, "Jewish Intermarriage," *Midstream* 28 (March 1982): 30–34.

On the problems of Sephardic Jewish identity in the United States, see Marc D. Angel's "Communications About Sephardic Identity," *Midstream* 18 (March 1971): 64–67. On the history of the Sephardim in the United States up to World War II, see David de Sola Pool, *An Old Faith in the New World* (New York: Columbia University Press, 1955).

More specialized studies include Marc D. Angel, "The Sephardic Theater of Seattle," *American Jewish Archives* (November 1973); and Hayyim Cohen, "Sephardi Jews in the U.S.: Marriage with Ashkenazim and Non-Jews," *Dispersion and Unity* 13–14 (1971–72): 152–53.

On the Sephardim in Canada, see Esther I. Blaustein, Rachel A. Esar, and Evelyn Miller, "Spanish and Portuguese Synagogue (Shearith Israel), Montreal, 1768–1968," *The Jewish Historical Society of England Transactions* 23 (1971): 111–42; Evelyn Bloomfield-Schachter and Jean Claude Lasry, "Jewish Intermarriage in Montreal," *Jewish Social Studies* 37 (Summer-Fall 1975); and Evelyn Miller, "The Learned Hazan of Montreal: Reverend Abraham de Sola, L.L.D., 1825–1882," *American Sephardi* 7–8 (1979): 23–24.

Chapter Eight

Perhaps the angriest book yet written about the place of the Sephardim in Israel is Michael Selzer's *The Outcasts of Israel: Communal Tensions in the Jewish State* (Jerusalem: Council of the Sephardic Community, 1965). For a summary of his views, see his article

"The 'Other' Israel: Zionism's Biggest Problem—A Personal Investigation," *Jewish Observer* 12 (December 13, 1963): 26–27. Selzer also edited an English version of *BaMarakhah* for a few years in the 1960s, which presented the angriest possible Sephardic face to the English-speaking world. A decade later, S. Ben Moshe's article "Israel's Communal Tension: Two Sephardi Leaders Speak Up," *The National Jewish Monthly* 86 (January 1972): 14–18, reflected the next stage of protest, that of the Black Panthers. Alysa Levenberg made an interim summation of the situation in "Israel—The Sephardim," *Present Tense* 2 (Spring 1975): 8.

Some descriptions of recent Sephardic cultural assertiveness and its results can be found in current publications. See, for example, Jacquelyn Kahanoff, "The Maimouna Festival," *Israel Magazine* 12 (March 1972): 20–28, one of the earliest descriptions of the festival, when it was still a private ethnic celebration.

Concerning Ashkenazic reaction to Sephardic efforts to develop their own popular culture, see Nekki Stiller, "The Sephardic Image in Israeli Film," *Midstream* 57 (May 1975): 62. Isaac Levi published eight volumes of his *Antologia HaHazanut HaSepharadit* (Jerusalem: BaMarakhah, 1960) before his death.

On Zionism and the Sephardim, see Daniel J. Elazar, *The Place of the Zionist Vision and the State of Israel in the Sephardic World* (Jerusalem: Study Circle on Diaspora Jewry under the auspices of the President of Israel, 1983); and Jose Faur, "Early Zionist Ideals Among Sephardim in the Nineteenth Century," *Judaism* 25 (Winter 1976): 54–64. Most of the writing on the history of Sephardic Zionism has appeared in Hebrew, including such works as Michel Abitol, "Zionist Activity in North Africa Up to the End of the Second World War," *Pe'amim* 2 (1979): 65–91; David Benveniste, *From Salonica to Jerusalem: My Life* (Jerusalem: Sephardic and Oriental Community Publications, 1981); and Israel Mishael, *Between Afghanistan and Eretz Israel* (Jerusalem: Sephardic Community Committee, 1981).

With regard to discussions of the Sephardic approach to Zionism, there is relatively little available, but one very good book is Dan V. Segre, *A Crisis of Identity: Israel and Zionism* (Oxford: Oxford University Press, 1980). Segre, from one of the great Italian Sephardic families, is a veteran member of the Israeli foreign service who left to take up a professorship in political science at Haifa University. He is also a Fellow of the Jerusalem Center for Public Affairs.

On the new place of the Sephardim in the Jewish world, see Daniel J. Elazar, *Sephardic Jewry in a New World Role* (New York: Council of Jewish Federations, 1982).

Index

INDEX

INDEX

ABBOT PUBLIC LIBRARY
3 3011 00163 6610